good
Money

Six Steps
to Building
a Financial Life
with Purpose

good
Money

JOHN COLEMAN

HARVARD BUSINESS REVIEW PRESS
BOSTON, MASSACHUSETTS

Copyright 2026 Harvard Business School Publishing Corporation

Printed in the United States of America

10 9 8 7 6 5 4 3 2 1

The web addresses referenced in this book were live and correct at the time of the book's publication but may be subject to change.

Library of Congress Cataloging-in-Publication data is forthcoming.

ISBN: 979-8-89279-050-5
eISBN: 979-8-89279-051-2

The paper used in this publication meets the requirements of the American National Standard for Permanence of Paper for Publications and Documents in Libraries and Archives Z39.48-1992.

To my wife and four children, who have allowed me to flourish in ways I never imagined.

Contents

good
Money

Building a Financial Life for Flourishing

What is Good Money?

At one level, that's a silly question. Isn't money always good? You and I and everyone we know use it to survive and thrive. Money affords us shelter, food, clothing, and all of life's necessities. It allows us to take part in fun activities, like vacationing with family and friends. It purchased the computer on which I'm writing this book and is one of the rewards I'll get for publishing it. Money can be used to acquire an education, physical safety, quality health care, and a family pet. And its absence can be devastating.

When I was born, my mom and dad lived in a single-wide mobile home in Florida. When bad storms would come, they would purchase tickets to the local movie theater to wait them out in relative safety. I remember times when I was hungry or my clothes didn't fit. And even though my family's financial prospects improved as I got older, I never forgot the fear financial insecurity can bring.

Among the world's poor, I was quite lucky. As an American, I was well-off by global standards. Many suffer deeply in poverty. Whole nations experience famine, natural disaster, violence, or disease without the financial resources to adequately combat those horrors. Individuals still die of hunger, thirst, or a lack of basic medical needs. In those contexts, any money seems good.

But the evidence indicates the money can, indeed, be bad. Financial abundance without the proper mindsets, habits, and values to guide it can ruin your life. Lottery winners, for example, often commit suicide at higher rates than those who haven't experienced a financial windfall. The very wealthy are often unhappier than the poor or (especially) the middle class and frequently worry about the impact of wealth on their children and intimate relationships.

We see this in studies of happiness at the level of nations. To be sure, poor, war-torn countries—places like Haiti or Afghanistan—are subject to the highest rates of stress and unhappiness in global surveys. But there is ample evidence that wealthy countries are often no better off, or are even worse off, than middle-income countries or peaceful low-income countries when it comes to happiness, rates of depression or loneliness, and other signs of flourishing.

How can we make sense of this tension between money's necessity and its power to be a destructive force in our lives? We need money, and its absence can be wrenching. But money doesn't solve our deepest problems, and an overreliance on it or a poor approach to its use can be personally and societally devastating. Money is a necessity. It is a reality. But money can be both good and bad in a person's life.

The Origins of Good Money

So what makes money good? What are the habits, mindsets, and values we can adopt about money that can turn this omnipresent and necessary thing into a tool for human flourishing? How can we develop a relationship with money that leads to the good life?

The world's major religions and philosophical traditions have long wrestled with these questions. They have focused extensively on money—knowing how central it is to human experience and how dangerous it is in the wrong circumstances but simultaneously and consistently offering a path by which money can serve us and the things we care about the most.

Buddhism, for example, encourages enjoyment without attachment. Money is necessary. It can even be used for good. But an overreliance on it can lead to a disordered soul and unhappiness. Many of the most revered figures in both Jewish and Christian scriptures were blessed with immense wealth—Abraham and David, for example—but those scriptures also regularly warn of money's misuse and the pitfalls of making money central to one's goals or identity. The New Testament's 1 Timothy, for example, admonishes, "The love of money is the root of all kinds of evil." Hinduism clearly indicates that money can be good or evil depending on how it is used. And even anti-materialist philosophers like Karl Marx held, on the one hand, that capitalism and money could free us from desperation and need and, on the other hand, that the materialism that arises from a love of money is dangerous and destructive.

In my work, I see this tension every day. I'm an investor, and my clients have ranged from high-net-worth individuals to sovereign wealth funds. My whole professional world revolves around money. My job is to take money from clients, invest it with the intent of growing it, and give them back more than they gave me. I am a professional success or failure, depending on how much I'm able to grow the wealth of others. And I'm regularly entrusted to steward vast sums of wealth that dwarf my own resources. I've lived a life more immersed in the challenges and opportunities of money than most. I also spend a great deal of time with families who are grappling with material success and worried about its impact on their lives and the lives of their loved ones: Will money help or hurt my kids? Will the wealth I've created make it harder for my family to be happy? Do the people around me really care about me, or do they merely want something from me? Do I have any value as a person apart from the money I've made?

To complement this, I frequently write on the subjects of purpose and human flourishing. My first book with Harvard Business Review Press, *Passion & Purpose*, explored the central role of purpose and meaning in the lives of young leaders. My next book, *The HBR Guide to Crafting Your Purpose*, sought to help individuals understand how they could create lives of meaning and purpose—how in the midst of demanding professional careers they could flourish and not falter. My writing and thinking often revolves around how we as individuals can experience joy and meaning in our own lives and how we, as leaders, can encourage it in our organizations and the lives of others.

I believe that the right habits, mindsets, and values about money are essential to that equation—particularly in a modern world as obsessed with financial wealth as any other time in history. It's at the intersection of my life's work as an investor and my long obsession with purpose and meaning that the concept of Good Money takes shape. Many of the messages we receive about money in popular culture can be ruinous for our ability to use it well. From TikTok videos advocating for overpriced clothes and skin-care products to reality television stars who flaunt wealth in the most crass and superficial ways, we are bombarded with messages telling us that money will buy happiness and, worse, that money is a sign of our value as human beings.

This is a lie. Every human has inherent dignity and worth. We are all capable and deserving of love, hope, and purpose. And money has little to do with the things that make us most deeply human. Viewed properly, it can be an enormous force for good in our lives and the lives of others. But it is a means to the good life, not an end in itself.

The Good Money Mentality

This book aims to share the habits, mindsets, and values of those who have mastered money and used it to create flourishing in their own lives and the lives of others. My goal here is not to offer tactical tips on financial success (though I will offer a few). There are many personal finance books that can teach you about budgeting, managing expenses, originating a mortgage, or paying down debt. And those topics—along with many more—are incredibly important. But that's not my focus nor, I believe, the root of our problems.

Rather, I hope to offer you a blueprint for building a relationship with money that leads to comprehensive human flourishing. I want to introduce you to people who seem to have mastered the art of making money work for them as they craft lives of meaning, and I lay out a simple framework that can allow anyone to earn, spend, give, and invest money well. We'll also explore how once we have embraced that framework, we can best apprentice it with our children.

This is a book for those who now have or hope to one day have more money than they need—those who achieve savings and investment, who hope to send kids to college or retire, and who have the luxury of thinking about the proper use of money over and above their basic needs. That's a wide array of people, including the college student just starting out, the middle-income person in the skilled trades, and the billionaire reflecting on a family legacy. But I genuinely believe there are many commonalities among those otherwise-disparate groups. And because this book is not focused on tactics (e.g., how to get a mortgage) but on habits, mindsets, and values, its lessons apply to the middle manager and third-generation heir alike.

Most of these readers will be mid-to-late career, thinking about the money they are accumulating and the way to steward it well. But my hope is that younger readers will engage just as deeply, thinking about the habits that they can develop right now and that can create a framework for flourishing for the entirety of their financial lives. It's a beautiful thing to adopt a proper relationship to money once you have it, but it's even more prudent and powerful to do so before you have a chance to form bad habits in the first place. In many ways, a recent graduate is just as well positioned to begin this journey as a new parent or an empty nester.

Good Money is not, however, designed to help someone living paycheck to paycheck escape the vicious cycle of poverty and debt. That situation is all too common around the world, even in wealthy countries like the United States. And it's the most urgent crisis both for the individuals experiencing it and for the societies in which they live. Advice on how to avoid or address deep financial challenges like poverty lie outside the scope of this book. Although such advice is important, there are other, better books, articles, and podcasts to help those living in more dire circumstances. Trying to address both the issues of financial scarcity and abundance (or future abundance) in one single work would be too complex to manage responsibly and well.

For those struggling, I hope you find support in creating a freer and easier life. And for those for whom this book applies, I hope you find its lessons timely, practical, and relevant for the financial journey ahead.

The old adage is right: Money won't make you happy. But it doesn't have to be bad. Viewed and used properly, Good Money can improve your life and the lives of others. Let's find out how.

Chapter 1

Money and the Good Life

For more than a decade, I've been speaking about purpose with audiences around the world—colleges, corporations, nonprofits, government entities, and collections of friends. And I often like to begin my talks by asking the audience a simple question: Who is someone in your life who is flourishing?

The answers are beautiful, heartfelt, and encouraging. One by one, audience members raise their hands and tell stories of the people they admire in their lives. One woman told me of a grandmother who had lost her husband but who remained an encouragement to all around her. She maintained a garden at her home, going outside each day to cultivate beauty and grow plants she could eat and serve to those she loved. No longer working full-time, after a career as a teacher, the grandmother volunteered at a youth center in the community each day. She had a close-knit group of friends who played bridge together and shared life's sorrows and joys. And she spent lots of time with her children and grandchildren, fully experiencing the people she loved the most.

A young man told me of a professional mentor who had counseled him. Working in the high-powered, fast-paced world of management consulting, this mentor invested heavily in the young people on his team, held firm lines on work-life balance, and openly prioritized his family over work, encouraging others to do the same. He was extraordinary at his craft, caring deeply for his clients and the work he did for them, but balanced that with a love of his team and those closest to him in a profession that could too often become all consuming. He was serious about his work but committed to caring for the people in his life.

And an older gentleman spoke of a younger colleague sitting near him. This colleague had been an encouragement in his life. When he had been sick, she had helped take care of him. She had joyfully picked up the slack for him at work and been available to talk or to help when he was receiving treatment. As he got to know her, he learned that she volunteered frequently in the community, had young kids whom she loved, and was active in a faith and church that offered her meaning and community.

Flourishing is a complicated concept. It can be elusive. The ancient Greeks referred to it as *eudaemonia*, the highest human good and the practice of living well in a way uniquely aligned with the nature of a human being. It means more than happiness. After all, happiness without purpose can be shallow and short-lived. The ancient Greeks' focus, and ours, is instead the *good life*—a life aligned with the deepest hungers, desires, and needs of a human being and in service of a higher calling. Flourishing is hard to define, but as the previous examples prove, we know it when we see it. In fact, when I ask people to tell stories about the flourishing people in their lives, each story is unique, but they all gravitate toward some common traits: those who love others, live in community, engage in meaningful work, help those in need, care for their craft, and embrace a higher calling. Importantly, given the subject of this book, not a single person of the hundreds or perhaps thousands I've asked has ever mentioned wealth or possessions. Often, the people they describe live humbly. But they live well. They live fully human.

This isn't a book about the good life generally. It's about financial flourishing—adopting the habits, mindsets, and values that make money a force for good in our lives. And to lay the foundation for what might constitute a flourishing financial life, we need to understand what human flourishing entails. To do that, I'll review two of the best guides to human flourishing that modern social science has to offer. These evidence-supported frameworks can anchor us in a common understanding of what human flourishing looks like and give us the vocabulary to discuss what makes Good Money.

Flourishing in Positive Psychology

Martin Seligman is known as the father of positive psychology. Born in Albany, New York, in 1942, Seligman was a natural academic. He earned his PhD at the University of Pennsylvania in 1967 and has built a career there after a brief stint at Cornell University. Seligman became troubled by the way psychologists viewed depression, and he became intensely interested in the idea of learned helplessness, a state in which a person (or an animal) begins to feel and act helplessly after experiencing an unavoidable adverse event. Once they have learned that behavior, they continue to act helpless even when they recover the agency to make a change.[1]

Positive psychology was founded as a result of Seligman's concern that so much of his discipline was focused on what could go wrong with a person's mental state (i.e., mental illness), whereas he wanted to focus on what could go right—our strengths.[2] He began studying subjects like happiness and learned optimism. This husband and father of six has published hugely influential papers and books throughout his career, and I've had the privilege of meeting and speaking with him about them. One of my favorites is his book *Flourish*, in which he lays out his framework for human flourishing.[3] To live a good life, a person needs five characteristics, which are summarized by the acronym PERMA:

- *Positive emotions:* an enhanced version of happiness, inclusive of deeper emotional states like joy and gratitude.

- *Engagement:* a condition similar to psychologist Mihaly Csikszentmihalyi's concept of flow, which describes the state of becoming so enamored with what we are doing that we lose track of time and space. Engagement, Seligman explains in *Flourish*, "occurs when the perfect combination of challenge and skill/strength is found."

- *Positive relationships:* those leading us to "feeling supported, loved, and valued by others." We are communal creatures and can't live in isolation. Relationships are central to our ability to achieve well-being.

- *Meaning:* the feeling of having purpose in life—at work, at home, in the community, in creative endeavors, and everywhere in between. A sense of meaning is the conviction that what we do matters.

- *Accomplishment:* the state of achieving goals, most powerfully when those goals are intrinsic and not extrinsic, pursued ends for their own sake, not as a means to something else.

To Seligman and his research team, these five characteristics collectively lead to human flourishing, which he defines as "to find fulfillment in our lives, accomplishing meaningful and worthwhile tasks, and connecting with others at a deeper level—in essence, living the 'good life.'"[4] Importantly, none of these activities to achieve flourishing are instrumental; they are not used just to reach some other higher state. Instead, they are pursued independently for their own sake.

Notably absent is money. Money is, of course, not intrinsically good. It may certainly be an outcome of an accomplishment, but it is not what creates true flourishing. And in important ways, it can even be a hurdle. As we will see, money has the ability to help or hurt relationships. It can help or hurt our sense of meaning. It can lead to positive or negative emotions. So, its value rests not in itself but solely in whether it can be used in a way to support rather than distract from those inherently good traits in the PERMA framework.

Of course, Seligman's is only one framework for flourishing. It lines up pretty well with observations in religion, philosophy, and ancient tradition. But before moving on—given how central an understanding of flourishing and well-being are to our ability to use money well—it's worth examining a second, independently developed framework by Tyler VanderWeele.

The Financial Aspect of Flourishing

Born in Chicago, Tyler VanderWeele spent his childhood traveling the world. His father first took the family abroad as a financial executive and then switched careers to work for Opportunity International, a global faith-based nonprofit organization dedicated to helping those living in extreme poverty. VanderWeele lived in Austria, Bulgaria, Costa Rica, and a host of other places, along the way encountering people who made him ask questions about what it meant to lead a good life.

Always intellectually curious, VanderWeele earned degrees from the University of Oxford, the University of Pennsylvania, and Harvard University, ultimately working in epidemiology and public health. He found this work rewarding but incomplete. He explained a revelation when I spoke with him on the subject:

> I saw all this extraordinary research on physical health and on income and we've learned a great deal about these matters. And health and financial security are important in life, but people care about more than that. They care about being happy, and about having a sense of meaning and purpose in life. They care about trying to be a good person. They care about their relationships. So I was sitting there thinking, well, why aren't we studying these other aspects of well-being with the same level of rigor that we devote to physical health and income? Why do we know so much more about the determinants of cardiovascular disease than what brings about a sense of meaning and purpose in life in spite of that being a desired end of everyone?[5]

VanderWeele's experiences and his faith led him to the study of human flourishing and to found the Human Flourishing Program at Harvard. According to the program's mission, it "studies and promotes human flourishing, and develops systematic approaches to the synthesis of knowledge across disciplines." VanderWeele has a simple definition of flourishing as a whole: "a state in which all aspects of a person's life are good."[6] And in 2017, he proposed five essential measures for a flourishing life: happiness and life satisfaction, physical and mental health, meaning and purpose, character and virtue, and close social relationships. These are accomplished through four "pathways" by which these measures are achieved: family, work, education, and religious community.

Effectively, the pathways are the important contexts through which we experience the measures of flourishing and are, like the characteristics in Seligman's PERMA framework, ends worth pursuing in themselves. Like Seligman's positive emotions, happiness and life satisfaction are about the positive feelings we experience from our lives. Meaning and purpose are also common features of the two frameworks, as is the central importance of positive relationships. VanderWeele doesn't have an exact approximation for engagement or accomplishment in his framework (as Seligman does), but neither of those qualities seems at odds with character and virtue (good, ethical living according to one's values) or physical and mental health. Indeed, these concepts may intersect in important ways.

What's missing from VanderWeele's framework? Once again, money. For VanderWeele, as for Seligman and so many of the older philosophical traditions, money is not an end in itself—like happiness, health, purpose, and character—but is simply a means by which we are recognized for our contributions or achieve other things.

With that in mind, the Human Flourishing Program does measure one additional characteristic of flourishing: financial and material stability. But unlike the other measures, this one is not intrinsically good. It's simply important because without it, the other measures of flourishing are hard to attain.

This makes sense. If you are poor and can't afford food or shelter, you'll find it quite challenging to achieve health or cultivate strong social relationships. If you're hungry or constantly worried about your physical safety, you'll struggle to achieve happiness or focus on meaning and purpose. And when we see people suffering in poverty, we know that flourishing is scarcely possible, because baseline human needs aren't met.

But as countries and individuals get wealthier, the relationship between their material prosperity and measures like character, close social relationships, and meaning and purpose breaks down. VanderWeele explained:

> And what we see with regard to flourishing is that individuals in the richer developed world do tend to report higher levels of life evaluation, do often have better health, and do have better financial security. But we find that for other aspects of flourishing, actually middle-income countries are doing better. If you look at levels of meaning and purpose, if you look at social connectedness, if you look at self-assessments of their own character, many middle-income countries— Indonesia, the Philippines, Mexico—are doing better than the richer developed world—better than the United States, Europe, or Japan.[7]

What's important here, again, is that financial security is a means to an end. It's a baseline. Once we reach a threshold of material and financial prosperity, additional wealth doesn't seem to make us happy. The absence of financial means and material stability can make flourishing incredibly hard. But once our basic needs are met, the things that truly lead to flourishing are largely nonfinancial. They have to do with character, love, meaning, happiness, community, family, and work—things valuable to almost anyone whose basic needs are met.

This is a liberating premise. Like the Seligman framework, it offers a foundation on which to consider what a financial life for flourishing might mean. With money and with each financial decision we can ask several questions:

- Will this purchase, gift, or investment make me happier and more satisfied?

- Does it enable greater mental or physical health?

- Does it offer more meaning and purpose in my life?

- Does it cultivate, in me, character and virtue, and is it aligned with my most deeply held values?

- Does it build or break close social relationships?

We will spend a great deal of time working through these concepts throughout the remainder of this book, but it's important to understand up front that a good life is not a wealthy, materially prosperous life. It is one that is supported by financial and material stability, but once those needs are met, flourishing in life is defined by positive relationships, feelings of well-being and happiness, health, character, engagement, accomplishment, and a deep sense of meaning. Those characteristics are the building blocks of human flourishing. They are ends—valuable in and of themselves. Money, on the other hand, is a means. It's a tool meant solely to help us achieve the more important things in life. There is some evidence that having more money, or being more focused on money, actually makes us less focused on the inherently meaningful characteristics that make a good life.

The real questions with money, then, are these: What are the habits, mindsets, and values that allow a person to use money to achieve this sense of flourishing? And, on the contrary, what habits, mindsets, and values might stand in the way of a more deeply human life? How can we use money to enable rather than obstruct flourishing in our lives?

A Simple Framework for Good Money

To begin to answer these questions, we have to understand the basic ways in which our lives intersect with money and a subsequent framework to make it a tool for building a better life.

We regularly interact with money in four ways: we earn it, spend it, give it, and invest it. One of those activities brings money in (earning). Two send money out (spending and giving). And one both sends money out and, if successful, brings more back in (investing).

The vast majority of the money we receive is the money we *earn* through our work. There are exceptions. Some people win the lottery, and others inherit. But for most people, most of the time, earning money is the primary way to bring it in. And we do this most of our lives! I remember first cutting grass and raking leaves for my parents and my neighbors when I was only eight or nine years old. I got my first official job, working as a busboy at Applebee's, when I was sixteen and worked all through college in the student cafeteria and the writing center. Finally, I went full-time into the workforce within weeks of college graduation. For most of my life, I've worked in one way or another and earned money for that effort. There's pride in this, because we are paid for our work when it has value to others. And whether it's cutting lawns, busing tables, or building financial models, there's meaning in the idea that our craft—whatever that may be—is so valuable to someone that they are willing to reward us for it.

Once we have money, there are only three things we can do with it. The first is to *spend* it, and that's what most people do with most of their money most of the time. Americans, for example, spend approximately 88 percent of what they earn each year.[8] Globally, few countries have household savings rates of more than 10 percent. This means that other than earning, spending is the highest interface we have with money. Thinking about how to spend well—in a way that makes life truly better—is a critical way in which we can adjust our financial mindsets, habits, and values.

Some of what we don't spend, we *give*. Around 61 percent of Americans donate to charity, for example.[9] Eight countries globally have even higher giving rates than the United States, with Indonesia having the highest giving rate in the world—84 percent of its population.[10] Looked at differently, the United States is the most charitable nation in the world, with Americans giving away approximately $260 billion per year, or 1.4 percent of its gross domestic product (GDP).[11] That figure probably understates, at least somewhat, the amount of money that we all use to help others every year, as it only counts formal "charitable giving." In reality, most of us are generous in other ways, helping someone down on their luck we pass in the street, buying dinner for a friend, loaning money to a relative who has fallen on difficult times, or giving gifts to someone in need. Overall, we probably give too little considering the remarkably positive impact that giving has on our sense of meaning and well-being. And deep reflection on our giving is an easy way to develop a flourishing relationship with the resources we have.

Finally, most of us *invest* in some way. This activity is often referred to as savings, but I think of it differently. Savings implies something passive—like cash stored under a mattress. That's a complacent approach and a negative financial mindset in itself. Every dollar we save has the ability to simultaneously earn, whether the earnings come from the basic interest rate on a money market account or investments in the stock market. Viewing those dollars for their earning potential—thinking of them as an active part of our financial lives—is critically important. The median net worth of an American household, for example, is nearly $200,000, while the average net worth is more than $1 million—this average figure influenced by the large balances of the wealthiest among us (or older people who have had more time to accumulate).[12] Around two-thirds of that net worth is housing (itself an investment) for the typical American, though that percentage declines as wealth increases. Some 96 percent of Americans have financial accounts, while 60 percent have retirement accounts (the most common savings vehicle). Obviously, these investment figures differ dramatically across countries, with many in poorer nations living with no meaningful savings or investment options. But investments are important because they are one of our biggest outlays each year (the median American has twice as much in net worth as they spend each year) and because investments are the only way to deploy money to earn money.

With that in mind, I suggest a simple rubric for crafting financial lives with impact—for cultivating financial habits, mindsets, and values for a flourishing life. This framework isn't necessarily exhaustive. It doesn't seek to address mortgage rates or household budgets. But it does touch on each of the areas I've described in an attempt to make sure that for each major way that we encounter money, we have an intellectual and emotional framework to make that touchpoint a positive force rather than a negative one in our lives.

I'll detail the basics a bit more in this chapter and then spend most of the remainder of this book deconstructing each point, offering practical advice to implement each tenet, and seeking to adopt a fresh perspective on how money can be a source of flourishing and engagement in every area of our lives. Simply put, Good Money looks like the six-part framework in figure 1-1.

Develop Good Money mindsets

Building the right habits starts with cultivating the right mindsets. Money is as old as civilization. It's essential. Its absence can create great hardship. But its presence doesn't always create a good life. Making money good in our lives requires first establishing a fundamental framework for flourishing—the things that are intrinsically good in our lives, like positive relationships, meaningful work, service to others, strong character,

FIGURE 1-1

Good Money: A six-part framework for financial flourishing

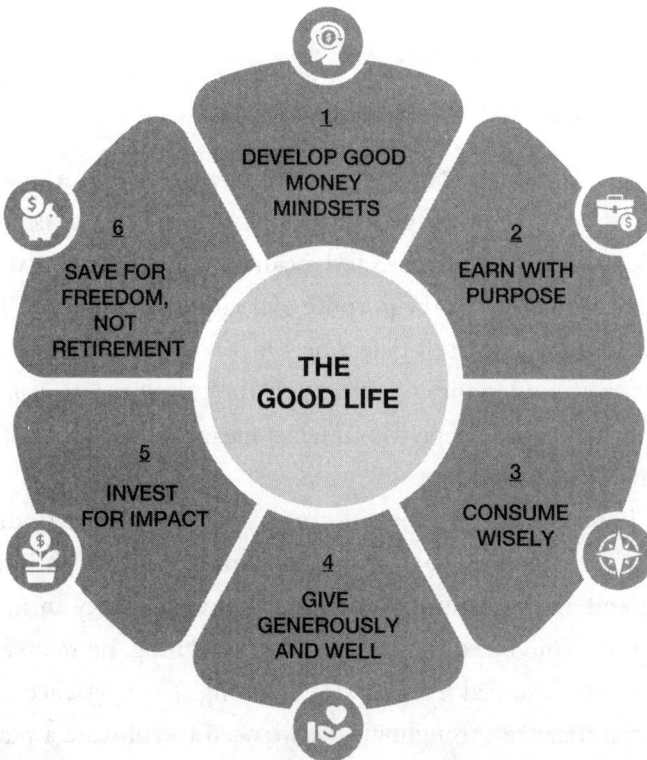

1 DEVELOP GOOD MONEY MINDSETS

2 EARN WITH PURPOSE

3 CONSUME WISELY

4 GIVE GENEROUSLY AND WELL

5 INVEST FOR IMPACT

6 SAVE FOR FREEDOM, NOT RETIREMENT

THE GOOD LIFE

and a healthy body and mind. With that in place, we can thoughtfully consider how money can enable those elements rather than distract from them.

To flourish, we must relegate money to its proper place—grounding our understanding of money in the right mindsets and values, understanding that all people (including us) are worth far more than our financial assets. We must understand that money itself cannot buy happiness. Instead, it enables people to achieve the more meaningful things in life. Ironically, the more we focus on money, the harder it might be to attain the things that will make our lives and families better.

We must also understand ideas like hedonic adaptation and how these human tendencies can lead us to the endless and fruitless pursuit of more wealth and "stuff" even when it's counterproductive to flourishing. And we should address questions like "How much is enough?" in our lives to set a financial finish line and reorient ourselves to the proper ways to live well.

Earn with purpose

Deploying money well is of little value if we live our lives working without purpose and joy. One of the great errors most people make is neglecting their work as a source of purpose and meaning in life—viewing their work as a job executed solely for the purpose of accumulating wealth. This attitude is demoralizing and self-defeating. Once we've adopted the right initial mindsets around money—particularly the concept of *enough*—we are free to consider more deeply the intense meaning we can get from the professions we pursue.

When I coauthored *Passion & Purpose*, one of our core findings was that two of the top three reasons people chose jobs were an intellectual challenge and an opportunity to impact the world. Early in my career, however, I had convinced myself I could do anything, no matter how tedious, to create financial freedom. I was wrong. To experience both success and significance throughout life, we need to cultivate a purposeful career. And while that career needs to pay enough to meet our needs outside of work, once those needs are met and we're able to save a bit for the future, the smartest thing we can do is work with purpose.

It would be naive to ignore financial necessities entirely when choosing a job. If you need to take a job for the money, by all means do—and work hard to craft meaning in the job you have. But if you have the ability, opt for a job with great people, with a mission worth achieving, with autonomy and responsibility, and with the ability to weave purpose into all you do. Those things will matter more than the incremental money you've sacrificed, and chances are you'll end up better at a career that brings you joy. Beyond that, we each have the opportunity to design our work in ways that liberate us from bad habits and that open up new opportunities for flourishing in our day-to-day lives.

The option of earning with purpose never ends. If someone can craft a meaningful career from the start, that's ideal. But anyone at any stage in life, whether early or late in a career, can decide to shape their work into something more purposeful. And the best time to start for anyone—from the college student to the recent retiree—is today.

Consume wisely

Consumption isn't always bad. But overconsumption or consuming the wrong things makes us worse off spiritually, mentally, emotionally, and sometimes materially. We live in a culture obsessed with status and showy displays of material wealth. But those things don't make us happier or more fulfilled. Because of this, we need to consume more wisely, spending less than we make; focusing on experiences, time, wellness, and relationships; directly addressing our issues head-on when we go off-track; and embracing an attitude of minimalism and spending less along the way.

There is ample research supporting this precept. Material possessions have been associated with decreased well-being when they result in comparison (e.g., trying to buy a nicer watch or car than your neighbor). But experiences (trips, outings, and other activities) are associated with increased well-being, particularly experiences that open us to new things and are shared with others. Rather than spending money on a more expensive car, consider investing in a vacation with friends to a new and exotic place. Rather than purchasing a pricey piece of jewelry, do a service trip with a significant other or your family—one that can expose you to new things while allowing you to serve others.

Broadening our view, we will see that spending on experiences can be a conduit for deeper relationships, an investment in education, a way to care for those closest to us, and an exercise in enjoyment without attachment. A framework oriented toward investment and experience can also help us avoid the mindsets that so often trap people in insecurity, jealousy, and greed. That mindset, and the value system it spawns, is one of the most toxic into which people, rich and poor alike, fall. It's one of the biggest barriers to flourishing in the lives of everyday people.

Relatedly, we can direct our dollars spent to time, health, and relationships. Countless studies show that shortening commutes, eliminating unpleasant activities, and using our resources to capture more time with the people we love and on activities we enjoy can indeed buy happiness. Where we have to choose between material possessions and spending our time more wisely, the latter is always the right choice. Health and wellness—spiritual, mental, and physical—are central to flourishing, and wise uses of money can enhance all three. Further, any expenditure that allows us to build deeper, broader relationships will improve our lives and the lives of others.

Finally, I'll talk about spending less overall and dramatically confronting the areas of consumption that become the most problematic for us. Central to the idea of enjoyment without attachment is not spending to accumulate status. When a material thing becomes an obsession, we should actively force it from our lives.

Give generously and well

Whether you have a lot of expendable income or a little, the most fulfilling thing you can do with your wealth is give generously and serve others. In 2013, nine psychologists published a paper with a landmark finding: "Human beings around the world derive emotional benefits from using their financial resources to help others."[13] Evaluating data from 136 countries, they found that "prosocial spending is associated with greater happiness around the world, in poor and rich countries alike." This paper has since been complemented by several others emphasizing the increased well-being associated with generosity—even apart from its obvious social good.

Nothing impacts flourishing as much as the depth and breadth of positive relationships in our lives. Few activities in life lead to greater social and psychological benefits than helping others. Greed, avarice, and jealousy—the mindsets of accumulation and selfishness—too often accompany the acquisition of wealth. But openhandedness and a willingness to share what we've earned with others can make our own lives better and dramatically improve the lives of everyone around us.

Cultivating the right values and habits around helping others—giving to charity, volunteering, and being casually generous with all those we encounter—can free us from our most toxic attachments and provide us with the foundation for a life well lived.

We must, however, give *well*, ensuring that the causes or people to which we give will benefit from that giving and that we do so in a way that preserves our intent. Helping can actually hurt if done poorly. But giving well can ensure that our generosity achieves its intended ends.

Invest for impact

Investing early, consistently, and well is one of the greatest ways to enable financial stability. A dollar invested at a 10 percent return doubles roughly every seven years. And carefully investing for thirty or forty years can assure even those with a moderate-income financial wealth thanks to the miracle of compounding returns. Countless books address this technical feature of investing. Many fortunes have been made through disciplined and consistent investing. But our investment dollars can unlock more than personal financial prosperity. They can be an extension of our values and create enormous positive (or negative) impact on the world around us.

The idea that we should align all our resources with our values is ancient, resilient, and true. The Torah, the Christian Bible, the Quran, and Hindu scriptures all talk about how we should align our stewardship of wealth with our values. Billions of people are now aware that their savings can be invested for good, with 86 percent of millennials interested in impact investing, and 72 percent of Gen Zers hopeful that investing can improve sustainability.[14]

There are now a wide variety of ways to influence the world through our investments. Whether through screening (positive and negative), proxy voting, corporate engagement, or conventional impact investing, we have thousands of choices to align our investments (at least to a degree) with our values. And we can often do so with little to no impact on our financial returns. Investing in this way can be a source of joy and purpose and can contribute meaningfully to positive change in the world.

The first step is to stop thinking of savings and instead to think of every dollar we have at our disposal as a tool for investment—in our own lives, the future of our families, the market, and the people around us. With this in mind, I'll lay out a detailed process that can help almost anyone steward their money well—investing for return and positive impact in parallel with and in alignment with their most deeply held convictions.

Save for freedom, not retirement

For decades, one of the primary aims of people throughout the Western world has been retirement. But conventional retirement is the wrong goal. There is limited evidence that retirement improves life and mounting evidence that the wrong kind of retirement can have adverse social and psychological effects, such as increased mortality and cognitive decline.

As noted previously, we are designed to need purpose and meaning in our lives—much of which comes from our work and our communities. As we age, we certainly may need to have savings for failing health or to cut back on the intensity and time we spend at work. But for most people, full retirement isn't the right choice. Instead, the goal of savings should be freedom to work the way we want until the age we want, without the constraint of financial need. When we view retirement this way, we may still contribute to our retirement plans, but we do so to buy freedom and purpose, not just leisure. And if we experience some life-changing liquidity event in our thirties or forties, we'll have the insight to know that money should mean more than life on the golf course or the beach. Instead, it's the license to lean harder into meaningful work for those around us.

As you read this book, you'll find advice and exercises that will allow for deeper exploration of the topics at hand. But at its simplest, the chart in table 1-1 will help guide your journey as you explore each element of the Good Money framework. It aims to help you identify how you're currently thinking about these topics and then make the necessary changes to improve. Keeping tabs and making notes as you read may make the exercise easier and more fulfilling.

Finally, while most of this book discusses how we can make money a tool for flourishing in our own lives, most readers will at some point think about passing on these lessons to future generations, namely, their kids. Few subjects are as fraught as that of kids and money. Most parents want their children's lives to be better than their own, and in our pursuit of that

TABLE 1-1

Good Money values and strategy worksheet

	What are 3 to 5 values that drive my "why" in this area?	What 3 to 5 steps can I take this year to align my life with those values?
Develop Good Money mindsets		
Earn with purpose		
Consume wisely		
Give generously and well		
Invest for impact		
Save for freedom, not retirement		

goal, we sometimes develop habits that hinder their ability to flourish. Those problems can grow as wealth does—and almost all of us know families who have been fractured and kids who have been ruined by the downfalls of unearned wealth with ill-considered values. While not everyone will struggle with these challenges, enough of my clients have asked me for advice on the topic that I've dedicated an additional chapter on applying this framework to developing Good Money habits in our children.

Leaning In to Good Money

Building a financial life for flourishing is about putting money in its proper place, crafting lives of meaningful work, giving generously to others, indulging in life-changing experiences with friends and family, and stewarding our wealth to impact the world positively. It's about sharing this perspective with those around us and living in community. It's about earning, spending, giving, and investing in ways concordant with our most deeply held values and creating alignment in our lives in such a way that enables human flourishing—for us and others.

Not all money is good, but you can make the right changes now to ensure that yours is. Adopting the right mindsets and values about money can be foundational to living with greater purpose and meaning. Now that we have this framework in mind, let's dig in and spend the remainder of this book reimagining how we view and live out our financial lives.

Chapter 2

Develop Good Money Mindsets

Mindsets are the beliefs we have about the world. These are formed by our experiences, our innate tendencies, and what we learn from others. Research increasingly indicates what we intuitively grasp: our beliefs about ourselves and the world around us influence the way we act, feel, and process new information.

Carol Dweck, a Stanford University psychologist and pioneer on mindset research, in an article with David Yeager articulates the core power of mindsets: "People . . . as they navigate and learn about their environments, must inevitably develop beliefs about how the world works. How can these beliefs not have important implications for what they do and how they do it?"[1] What we believe about ourselves and the world around us shapes the way we behave and the outcomes we achieve through those behaviors.

Positive mindsets and belief systems are enormously beneficial. Positive thinking, for example, can reduce stress and improve health.[2] Martin Seligman's work on learned optimism has shown how developing the skill of optimism (as opposed to pessimism) can improve physical and mental health as well as achievement.[3] Dweck has developed a whole field of research around a *growth mindset*, defined as "the belief that intelligence, abilities, and talents are not fixed traits but can be developed through dedication, effort, and a willingness to learn."[4] She has shown that this frame of mind leads to greater adaptability, resilience, and success. The right mindsets improve learning and subjective well-being in academic environments.[5] And a growing array of research shows that the right attitudes around health can help with achieving a proper weight, living an active lifestyle, and even improving your metabolism.[6] Positive psychological habits create a virtuous cycle, and they translate into better mental and physical health, professional and academic success, and relationships with others.

But negative outlooks and beliefs can have the opposite effect. If we believe we can't get healthy, for example, we are less likely to. If we believe we can't learn, we will shy away from the process and our beliefs become self-fulfilling. If we believe others are out to hurt us, we will be guarded toward them in ways that alienate them and make it difficult to form relationships. Memorably, one 2012 study showed that increased stress can increase the likelihood of death—but only if we believe that stress is bad. People who don't see stress as harmful are no more likely to die.[7]

Unfortunately, many of the mindsets we develop around money are harmful. A *scarcity mindset*, for example, which believes resources are finite and are hard to come by, often focuses people so much on the resource they believe to be scarce that they develop high anxiety around it, and their ability to make good decisions to escape that scarcity declines. Researchers like Harvard economist Sendhil Mullainathan have begun to study this phenomenon extensively, noting that those who are trapped or who have grown up in poverty often have difficulty making better, longer-term financial decisions—a reason many disadvantaged people end up entering into damaging financial arrangements like payday loans. Conversely, wealth can just as easily create bad beliefs. Wealthy people can come to believe that they are uniquely gifted in every way simply because they are rich, leading them to treat others poorly or to make bad decisions in areas in which they are confident but not competent. Think of the powerful CEO who thinks he is funny because people laugh at his jokes, not understanding they laugh because he is powerful, not funny.

Some of our mindsets seem to be innate tendencies. But many are influenced by our personal histories and culture. What are some of the dominant messages about money in culture? I recently came across a social media video of a prominent influencer who is a champion of quite negative and destructive behaviors. In this video, he had an array of expensive watches laid out on a table. He panned around a beautiful home and showed off a multimillion-dollar array of cars in his driveway. Very explicitly, he claimed that these ostentatious displays of wealth made him a more attractive and better man, shaming those without such showy (but ultimately meaningless) possessions. You've probably seen these videos as well—influencers waving cash, driving impractical sports cars, dressing in tailored (though ill-fitting) clothes, and connecting the idea that being rich or at least acting rich makes them superior. Movies and TV, even when they are nominally criticizing the wealthy, similarly show the power and luxury money can buy. The explicit and implicit messages are hard to ignore: your self-worth is connected to how much money you have, the rich are better people, money is the true path to happiness, and acquiring lots of money is the end goal of a successful life and career. Or, conversely, if you are poor, you will always be poor, it's because you are a failure in life, and you will never find a path to happiness and meaning.

These messages are lies—destructive lies. You and I and everyone else in the world have based our mindsets about money on our personal histories; the lessons from our families; the messages we absorb from the media, our coworkers, our formal education; and a host of other sources. These attitudes often lead to poor values around money and destructive practices that hinder our ability to flourish. But we rarely intentionally reflect on them. Unpacking our mindsets and developing new and healthier ones is the cornerstone of making money good in our lives. So, building a financial life for flourishing begins with Good Money mindsets.

Relegate Money to Its Proper Place

Ebenezer Scrooge is one of British novelist Charles Dickens's classic creations. Scrooge is the protagonist of Dickens's masterwork *A Christmas*

Carol. "A squeezing, wrenching, grasping, scraping, clutching, covetous, old sinner," Scrooge is a wealthy businessman who seems to live without pleasure and solely for the purpose of accumulating money.[8] He cheats those who work for him, notably the unfortunate Bob Cratchit, father of the sick child Tiny Tim. He harasses his debtors.

On Christmas Eve, Scrooge is visited by three spirits. The Ghost of Christmas Past shows Scrooge's difficult childhood. This spirit shows his relationship with the love of his life, Belle, who leaves him when she realizes Scrooge loves money more than her. As Scrooge looks on his past, he brims with regret. Next, the Ghost of Christmas Present shows Scrooge the pain his greed causes in the present day, including the suffering of the Cratchit family, who can't care for Tiny Tim on the wages Scrooge pays. Finally, the Ghost of Christmas Future shows Scrooge a bleak look-forward, in which he dies alone and unmourned. Even worse, Tiny Tim passes away, to the dismay of those who love him. Treated to this vision, Scrooge wakes up on Christmas morning a changed man, dedicated anew to generosity, kindness, and love of others.

Of course, Scrooge did everything wrong. While Seligman or Vander-Weele could have told him that the most valuable things in life are those that are good in their own right—virtue, love, community, engagement—Scrooge became obsessed with something that would never give him joy and meaning. And in so doing, he lost his humanity and hurt those around him.

No one watches a production of *A Christmas Carol* and yearns to be Ebenezer Scrooge. And yet, every day, some of us live as he did. We prioritize the accumulation of wealth over the accumulation of friendship. We decline to be generous with others. We are greedy. We think the next dollar will make us happy, and we end up in the throes of a fruitless pursuit, never asking ourselves why we should pursue wealth to begin with.

The first step to developing the habits, mindset, and values for financial flourishing is learning to situate money in its proper place—as a means, not an end. Money is not inherently bad or good. The way we think about it and treat it makes it bad or good. When money takes too great a role in our lives, when it becomes as important as it was for Scrooge, then it is dangerous and misleading. But viewed properly and valued well, money can be an essential avenue to achieving the truly meaningful things in life.

So, what are the right mindsets for money? We'll explore four.

Realize That Money Can't Buy Happiness

Born in 1952, David Robinson experienced the US civil rights movement from a unique perspective. He was, after all, the son of Jackie Robinson, who in 1947 became the first Black player to play in Major League Baseball.[9] Jackie is a sports legend, an outstanding athlete who endured horrific racism as he pioneered the integration of US sports. His athletic prowess and otherworldly resilience provided financial security for his family, but from the beginning, he taught David that money wasn't a path to meaning or happiness.

"I learned early on that too much attention is given to accruing wealth and material things when meaning is to be found in sacrificing your life to the service of others," David once recounted.[10] Diverging from the path of so many children of the rich or powerful, David dedicated his own life to the service and impact his father had so beautifully endorsed.

David worked in self-help housing and community development in the United States in the 1970s before relocating to Tanzania in 1983 and starting Sweet Unity Farms, a coffee company, in 1989.[11] Sweet Unity's mission is to "enhance the economic position and quality of life for rural coffee farmers and their communities."[12] David lives and works with the coffee farmers there, investing his life and work in bringing that community to life.

"My father's legacy has always been about uplifting others, building communities, furthering humanity. I am very proud to have dedicated my life to this, and to have been graced with opportunities to expand this legacy," David says.[13] The Robinson family, which experienced so much hard-fought material success, was always anchored in the idea that money alone can't make life meaningful.

Research supports these claims. Angus Deaton and Daniel Kahneman are two of the most respected economists in history (Kahneman sadly passed away in 2024). As a child, Kahneman, who was Jewish, had to flee the Nazis while living in Paris in 1940, and he lived on the run for the entire war. He ended up in Israel, where he studied in Jerusalem before moving to the United States in the 1960s. Kahneman studied cognitive psychology and developed a deep interest in behavioral economics, happiness, and life satisfaction, earning a Nobel Prize in economics in 2002—despite never having taken a course in the subject.[14] Deaton, meanwhile, was born in Scotland in 1945 and studied economics from an early age, earning his PhD in the subject at the University of Cambridge and similarly but separately earning a Nobel Prize in 2015 for his work on consumption, poverty, and welfare.[15]

In 2010, these two titans of psychology and economics released a groundbreaking paper on money and well-being.[16] Building on a study of more than 450,000 people, they found that "life-evaluation"—their proxy for well-being—rose steadily from poverty to around $75,000 per year (or approximately $105,000 in 2024 terms) but effectively stopped at that point. In short, money was essential to happiness and life satisfaction when providing for basic needs and helping a person to escape material instability, akin to VanderWeele's own measure. But after those needs are provided for, money has no correlation to further improvements in well-being.

The study sent shockwaves through the academic and popular imaginations, though it echoed what many religious and philosophical traditions had historically preached. Some people disputed its claims—notably University of Pennsylvania professor Matthew Killingsworth—but even the latest research shows that while money can indeed keep making some people happy after that $75,000 (or $105,000) threshold, its marginal benefit is less. After a certain point, the incremental dollar begins to make us less incrementally happy. As Kahneman showed in a separate paper in 2003, although additional wealth can make us happy to a point, seeking money or caring about it too much actually hampers happiness and life satisfaction.[17]

In a recent conversation with me, Tyler VanderWeele described the diminishing returns: "I think pretty much everyone would agree that there's diminishing marginal returns after you reach a certain level. Maybe happiness continues to slightly increase with higher and higher income and wealth, but the contribution becomes smaller and smaller, and there's a threshold beyond which it really doesn't contribute all that much to your happiness."[18]

New evidence indicates that this is even true at lower income levels. In 2016, while at Y Combinator, OpenAI founder Sam Altman pioneered a plan for a broad-based test of the impacts of universal basic income (UBI). The premise of UBI is that instead of a complex social safety net, societies should provide their citizens with a base level of income regardless of work to ensure that their needs are met. Altman and his collaborators at OpenResearch eventually initiated the study in 2019, monitoring three thousand participants over three years.[19] The average household selected earned about $30,000 per year, and they were spread out among ten counties in Illinois and Texas. One-third of the participants were given an additional $1,000 per month, a roughly 40 percent increase in their income. Two-thirds of the participants—the control group—were given $50 per month.[20]

What happened? Very little. Those who received the extra $1,000 per month saw no long-term improvement in their mental, physical, or financial health. The recipients perceived an improvement in their mental health for one year, but the improvement then faded. They dreamed of entrepreneurship but didn't start businesses. The net worth of the recipients remained unchanged, and their incomes actually fell by $1,500 per year relative to the control group.[21] Payments increased leisure, but the leisure didn't result in personal improvement or happiness.

Finally, new evidence from the Global Flourishing Study (a collaboration between Harvard University, Baylor University, Gallup, and the Center for Open Science) indicates that at the country level, there is an inverse relationship between GDP per capita (how rich a country is) and composite measures of human flourishing. The richer a country is, on average, the lower its flourishing score. The study finds that "economically developed countries have high average scores for self-rated financial well-being, access to education, and life evaluation. Poorer countries, by contrast, have higher scores for positive emotions, meaning and purpose, character and virtue, and social connection and relationships."[22] In short, some of the most meaningful measures of flourishing, as articulated previously by VanderWeele, one of the study's authors, actually decline as nations grow richer. And while the current iteration of the study stops short of causation, this negative relationship at least indicates that national prosperity does not lead to national flourishing.

There is, however, some evidence that money (particularly earned money) can help us achieve happiness by providing the material stability. But money without the right mindsets rarely leads to lasting positive impacts on our well-being. Caring too much for money or focusing too much on earning it can make it harder for us to flourish.

The right approach seems to be what academic Arthur Brooks termed "abundance without attachment."[23] Money itself is not bad, and it can provide us the stability to pursue the better things in life. But it is a means, never an end. And confusing its role can lead us down a destructive and darker path.

My business partner Henry Kaestner is one of the kindest, most generous, and most authentic people I've ever known. When I was considering joining Sovereign's Capital, the firm he cofounded, to take his place as co-CEO, Henry—who is wealthy enough to afford private air travel and nice hotels—flew out from California in an economy seat on a commercial airline. He stayed in my basement, jumped on the trampoline with my kids, and ate takeout with my wife at our dining room table. A serial entrepreneur, Henry's big financial break was when a company he had founded, Bandwidth, went public on the Nasdaq and he could suddenly afford everything he had ever dreamed of. But he once told me that he was almost immediately disillusioned. "I could suddenly purchase almost any nice thing, but I found it didn't really make me happy. Or maybe it made me a little bit happy at first, but probably 5 percent as much as I thought it would." The lesson he learned was what the research describes. Having money is not bad. In fact, we need some amount of financial stability to flourish and engage in the more noble pursuits described by VanderWeele and Seligman. But money is a false love. And the hope that it will make us truly happy, fulfilled, and flourishing is similarly misplaced.

VanderWeele had an interesting comment on this topic when we spoke:

> One of our studies looked not just at levels of flourishing across these domains, but what people value.
>
> When people valued relationships or valued meaning, they tended to improve over time in those things and also in the other domains of flourishing as well. When they valued relationships, they would also increase in happiness and they would improve in health over time. It was less so with money. When they valued money, they would improve in financial security. But the effects on other domains were a lot less clear and a lot smaller. . . . If we orient our lives and our pursuits around money, then we'll get the money and that will contribute a bit to our life satisfaction and to our health. But it doesn't contribute typically to meaning or to relationships, or to our character. So, I do think some of the challenge is valuing the right things.[24]

Developing the right mindset about money begins with realizing that money alone won't make life more meaningful. We can and should seek some material stability for ourselves and our families. But if we are ever privileged enough to have more than we need, we should practice *abundance without attachment*. We should never confuse money with the more important ends of human flourishing. We should never value money above the more intrinsic goods in life.

What does this look like for you? If you make an honest assessment, are you living as if acquiring a little more wealth will make you happy and your life more meaningful? Is money at the center of your goals, or is it merely an outcome of more purposeful pursuits? It's so easy to slip into the habit of making money a goal in itself and assuming that the material comforts money can acquire will make us happy. But after our needs are met, money is only as good as our ability to use it for those intrinsically good things that matter more.

Set a Financial Finish Line

What flows from that realization—that money won't make us happy and that it is a means and not an end—is the idea that we should learn to develop better mindsets and habits around money. Part of that process is picking a *financial finish line*. In the absence of one, you'll always want a little more.

In 1886, Russian writer Leo Tolstoy wrote a remarkable short story titled "How Much Land Does a Man Need?" A peasant named Pahom dreams of acquiring enough land to be happy, and the Devil overhears him. Pahom's fortunes gradually improve. He becomes wealthy, moving among the communes of his native land, growing and selling more crops. He begins to buy and sell more land as his fortunes continue to improve. Finally, he encounters a group, the Bashkirs, who make him an unusual and irresistible offer. For a sum of money, they will let him walk around an area of land all day from sunrise to sunset. As long as he can be back before sunset, he can keep everything he has walked around.

Avaricious in the extreme, Pahom pushes himself mightily throughout the day, at one point realizing how far he is from his starting point and rushing to make it back in time to consummate the offer by dusk. He does so, crossing the finish line at the last possible moment—then immediately falls dead from exhaustion.

How much land did Pahom need? A little less, and he could have kept his life. But the desire for material wealth can be so entrancing, and the hope for more so compelling, that it can be hard to know when the accumulation should stop.

John D. Rockefeller, by some estimates the wealthiest man in history, echoed this paradox in his own life. At the height of his power, he controlled business interests equivalent to 1.5 percent of US GDP. Yet once (perhaps apocryphally) asked by a reporter, "How much money is enough?" Rockefeller replied, "Just a little more."

It sounds silly, but it's how most of us think. One recent study found that Americans define rich as an income band (or two) above them—regardless of whether they earn $30,000 or $300,000 per year.[25] A second survey found that only 8 percent of American investors with $1 million consider themselves wealthy, with a staggering 31 percent of millionaires considering themselves middle class.[26] Of course, only around 9 percent of Americans are millionaires, and the median net worth of the middle class in America is just over $100,000.[27] Globally, only 1 percent of people are millionaires, and worldwide GDP per capita is just shy of $12,000.[28]

Financial services company Empower has done a series of studies on this front. The most revealing of the studies asked participants, "How much does your annual salary need to be for you to feel happy/less stressed?" It found that not only is the number just out of reach at any income but, as incomes rise, the number grows ever more distant. The poorest among us need only a little more, in their minds at least, while the richest need the most (figure 2-1).

No amount of money will make us happy. The truth, as Tolstoy realized, is that in the absence of any real conception of how much is enough

FIGURE 2-1

"Enough" money is always out of reach

How much does your annual salary need to be for you to feel happy/less stressed?

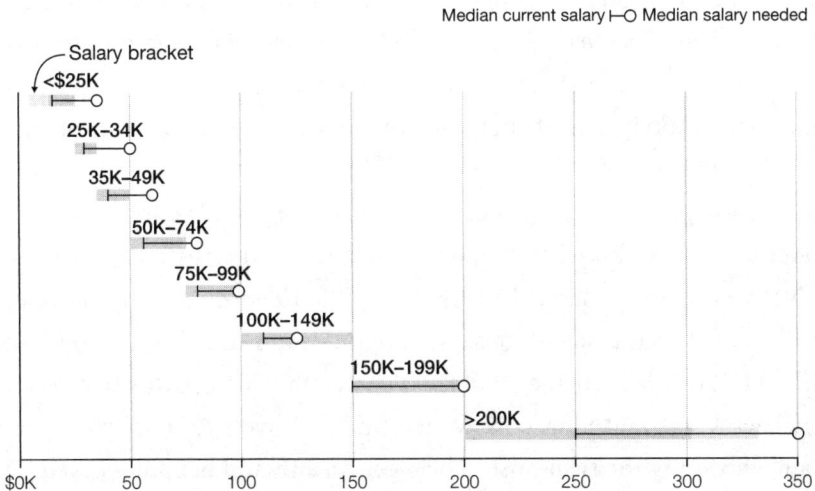

Median current salary � Median salary needed

Note: Data from a Harris Poll of 2,034 Americans aged eighteen and older, conducted August 7–14, 2023. Margin of error ±2.9 percentage points.
Source: Joe Pinkser, "The Pay Raise People Say They Need to Be Happy," *Wall Street Journal*, November 19, 2023. Used with permission.

in our lives, we always want more. Avarice and greed are rarely as transparent as Scrooge's exhibition of those traits; rather, they are more often the slow creep of lifestyle and comparison in our lives.

I saw this tendency at a firm where I once worked. Watches are a common status symbol in finance. When I was a kid, I remember dreaming of a particular watch I thought was the paragon of style (it was perhaps $300 or so, well out of my reach at the time). When I finally started working, I bought one, but I soon began to notice that others had much nicer watches than mine. As people rose through the ranks at my firm, the watches became nicer—TAG Heuers became Omegas; Omegas became Rolexes; Rolexes became Patek Philippes. And at every rung on the ladder, the person who had just upgraded their timepiece—often worth tens of thousands of dollars!—began to feel self-conscious about the nicer watches others had and what that might say about their professional success. At one point, I swore off expensive watches entirely, just to make sure I wasn't tempted to mount the status treadmill they represented.

That's not to criticize watches or make anyone feel bad. Some people love the history, engineering, and beauty of a finely made watch, and that authentic appreciation may have purpose. But like so many things—designer bags, designer cars, designer clothes, or even the latest iPhone—watches are more often a status symbol than a meaningful pastime, one that as likely as not increases the anxiety and obsession of those who buy them.

Psychologists refer to this as the *comparison trap*. We too often don't judge our own well-being in an objective way. We do it by comparing ourselves to others—a natural instinct amplified enormously by the social media era.[29] As the old adage says, "Comparison is the death of joy." And this applies with particular acuteness to wealth. Yale University professor Michael Kraus and Singapore Management University professor Jacinth Tan, who study the relationship between wealth and happiness, weigh in on the sway of comparison: "Our findings also suggest that improving from past levels of material resources alone is insufficient for increasing happiness. Even if people today are earning higher wages or attaining higher educational levels than their parents or compared to 10 years ago, there is going to be limited impact on their happiness if they are not doing at least as well as, if not better than, others at the present."[30]

What's the way out? Step off the treadmill. Define, in advance, how much is enough, and thoughtfully craft your lifestyle around it. The best time to define the level of material wealth we need to make us happy is not when we begin to achieve wealth but before we have it, when we can see more clearly the baseline we need to be secure.

My friend Casey Crawford grew up in a little Maryland neighborhood outside of Washington, DC. His dad ran a hardware store in Southeast DC, and while his family never had much, he was deeply loved and cared for. He was also blessed with remarkable athletic ability. He would grow to be six feet six and well over 250 pounds, and he excelled at football and baseball. He was so good that he was drafted by the Atlanta Braves out of high school before going on to play tight end for the University of Virginia football team and ultimately for the Tampa Bay Buccaneers (where he won a Super Bowl) and the Carolina Panthers. In the National Football League (NFL), he was faced with a new challenge. Even as a rookie, he made more than his family ever had, and he wasn't sure exactly what to do with it! He began to get wise counsel from an adviser at Ronald Blue Trust (a firm he would buy in 2021 and rename Blue Trust) on managing his wealth in accordance with his religious faith.

On leaving football, Crawford was even more successful, founding a mortgage company—Movement Mortgage—at the height of the financial crisis in 2008 with a vision for building a more redemptive financial ecosystem than the one he saw melting down around him. As Movement became successful, Crawford faced a dilemma. Money was coming in even faster than it had when he played football, and he knew that absent real constraints, his competitive personality could become addicted to accumulating wealth. Money, after all, is a scoreboard in business not so dissimilar from the scoreboards he had measured himself by his entire athletic career.

So, Crawford set what many term a financial finish line—a net-worth goal for his life, after which he wouldn't keep any more money for himself. For a wealthy person, Crawford set a modest goal that he achieved in a matter of years. And true to that initial commitment, he is now investing deeply in the employees of his companies and dedicating all the additional wealth from his myriad business interests to his charitable work over time—particularly the public charter schools he builds through Movement Schools. Crawford described his ambitions for Movement: "The vision is that everything beyond our capital requirements would be reinvested back into communities across the U.S. People will come to us, because we give them great service and great rates. But how cool would it be for people to know that because they patronize our organization, they're helping reinvest in the community, doing good, and loving others. That's the story I want to tell."[31]

All that reinvestment is only possible because Crawford decided he had already made enough for himself. He pre-answered the question "How much is enough?" And he stuck to that answer even when his wealth grew more than he'd ever dreamed.

In a world of excess—where a tech mogul recently built a custom yacht in Europe that wouldn't even fit through their canals and where the wealthy are often buying islands and sports teams, building almost impenetrable fortresses of abundance—this idea of a more modest financial finish line may seem a little more than odd. Why would someone who is good at making money ever set a limit? How does someone even go about deciding how much is enough?

A finish line can take the form of establishing either a goal for total net worth or a goal for annual living expenses and lifestyle. Cody Hobelman and Kealan Hobelman, for example, established the Finish Line Pledge, which encourages people to establish a target for annual expenses.[32] They have calculators that help people understand what the median annual (or bottom or top quartile) expenses for a household like theirs looks like and commit to that level of spending. A net-worth target might be one that allows for the permanent maintenance of that standard, for example, or perhaps even throws in a bit extra for the dream purchases a person might have—a second home, a boat, private school tuition, or something similar. Some people set these numbers relatively low. The Hobelmans shoot for median income, for example.

Similarly, the FIRE community (financial independence, retire early) cultivated on Reddit and other sites often advocates for very modest lifestyles and high savings rates that allow people to leave their jobs early and enjoy the good life (retirement or an alternative—something we will examine in a later chapter).[33] Some advocate more aggressive lifestyles, often referred to as Fat FIRE, but even there, the goals are generally achievable in a world in which 44 percent of Americans think they have the tools to become billionaires.[34]

The point of the finish line is less about the specific number. The finish line figure may be more or less, depending on your family structure, your needs, and your aspirations. It's about choosing a point at which you will freeze your lifestyle, step off the wealth accumulation and comparison treadmill, and be content with the money you have, focusing instead on the intrinsic goods that are so essential to flourishing.

Once your goal is defined, you must then establish a lifestyle above which you won't creep. As people get more money, they spend more money. The desire for a Movado watch becomes the desire for a Rolex. The desire for a Miata morphs into the "need" for a Porsche. The house gets bigger. The vacations get nicer. We see what our neighbors or professional peers are doing, and we meet or exceed it. Not only do many people end up on the wealth treadmill, but they also end up hurting their financial stability.

Thirty-eight percent of high earners—those making more than $100,000 per year—carry credit card debt, and high earners are actually more likely than middle- and lower-income people to hold their debt for five years or more.[35] Think about that! From personal experience, I can tell you a shocking number of seemingly wealthy people are driving exotic sports cars on leases and carrying mortgages they can't afford. They see the lifestyles of those around them and handicap their financial futures to achieve these ways of life.

A wiser path, of course, is to understand how much you can afford and to spend less than you make. And then once you've set your financial finish line, you'll avoid lifestyle creep that might tempt you to reset it (which will inevitably put you back on the accumulation treadmill). I find that this path is best taken with the assistance of a financial adviser—someone experienced at understanding the long-term costs of life and committed to helping you stick to your goals and limits. But if you're doing this on your own, you might think through the real necessary expenses you have in life: your bills, car payments, mortgage, kids' schools or colleges, savings for unexpected medical situations or other problems, a reasonable standard of vacation, and anything else you think is appropriate to a comfortable life for you and your family. Figure out what that costs per year (including savings), and set a finish line that would allow you to sustain those expenses through investment returns of, say, 4 percent per year. Again, the real planning behind this is something to engage a trusted partner and financial professional on. But the basics are simple.

Setting a financial finish line and avoiding lifestyle creep can help you put money in its proper place—as I've said, a means to flourishing, not an end. But that doesn't mean you have to stop earning. When Crawford stepped off the treadmill of wealth accumulation, he committed to putting the proceeds of his businesses over time into his nonprofit work. And he has now dedicated millions of dollars to schools, hope centers, and other worthy causes. In a later chapter, we'll explore the remarkable joy of using wealth to help others. Think what life could look like for you if you could turn your attention from personal accumulation to earning to make life better for others. The character, engagement, and relationships that could result are exactly the types of flourishing that finances can help enable.

Don't Let Money Distract You from Your Callings

My friend Frank Hanna is a successful businessman in Atlanta and the author of *What Your Money Means: And How to Use It Well*. In that book, he recounts the story of when he and his wife decided to build a cottage on a lake near his home. The intent was to have a place to rest and relax with family. They didn't want it to be ostentatious. But Hanna, who likes to do everything with excellence, soon became wrapped up in the process of building the cottage—the thousands of decisions that can go into a home like that. Over time, he realized that this cottage—a nice but unnecessary expense and project—was eating up valuable time he'd otherwise use building his business, engaging in his community, spending time with his friends and family, and giving to the causes he cares for.

There was nothing wrong with the cottage per se, but building it was becoming so all-encompassing that it was pulling him away from the things that made his life more meaningful.

I've experienced this dilemma often in my own life—on expenditures both trivial and important. When I need to buy a new T-shirt, I will sometimes spend far too much time online researching which shirts are best and trying to balance cost and performance among the thousands of options available to a modern shopper. When my wife and I were house hunting, I became a Zillow obsessive, spending evenings in bed surfing houses in the areas we liked, building models for the purchase, and researching neighborhoods and the materials the homes were constructed with. I sometimes got so into this habit my wife would have to call a Zillow Sabbath and get me off the app and away from the minutia that were distracting me.

There's nothing wrong with being thoughtful about our purchases. Buying a good, reliable T-shirt is better than buying a flimsy one that will deteriorate too quickly. Purchasing a house in a neighborhood that was safe for our kids and constructed in a way that would suit our needs was important—the biggest purchase decision we had ever made. But when the uses of money become obsessions—when they take time we might otherwise dedicate to our families, meaningful work, or community involvement—they become counterproductive. Much like the dangers of social media, where we can find ourselves consumed by activities that provide a brief dopamine hit but drain our capacity for more worthwhile endeavors, the dangers of thinking about money and its uses too frequently can hamper our ability to pursue life's more worthwhile things.

Again, this observation is a bit overly simplistic. When my parents and I lived in a single-wide trailer, our problems really would have been helped (and eventually were helped) by more money for health care, food, education, transportation, and other necessities. The constant insecurity excised its own mental toll. But when we come into too much money, we often spend so much time trying to defend it or spend it that we lose time for the things that make life worth living, the callings in life that are genuinely worth our time. Like Frank Hanna, we may become so caught up in using our money perfectly that we neglect the calling that allowed us to create that financial well-being in the first place. I've seen it happen time and again, often distracting some of the most talented people I know from their real work and the positive impact they could otherwise have on the world.

So how do you know if a material concern is distracting you from the more important things in life? Note a few warning signs:

- Are you missing time with family and friends or failing to work purposefully or serve others because you're spending too much time worrying over a house, a car, or another potential purchase?

- Do you find yourself deprioritizing something you know to be important because you're spending too much time thinking about or researching something you want to buy?

- Is any nice but unnecessary material good in your life (a second home, a car, etc.) eating into time you wish you could spend on something more purposeful?

All of those might be reason to take note and reevaluate the thing you have bought or want to buy. Discuss it with your spouse, your partner, or a trusted friend. And try to objectively see if obsessing over something material is leading to unneeded anxiety and distracting you from your meaningful relationships or the good work you feel called to do.

Stop Equating Your Worth with Your Net Worth

Agnes Gonxha Bojaxhiu was born on August 26, 1910, in North Macedonia under the rule of the Ottoman Empire.[36] An ethnic Albanian, Agnes was poor. Her parents were deeply religious, and at twelve years old, she strongly felt God's call on her life. She wanted to be a missionary and, at eighteen, left to join an Irish order of nuns, the Sisters of Loreto.

This young woman from Skopje was almost immediately sent to a school run by the Sisters of Loreto in Kolkata, India, and for seventeen years she taught high school in then one of the poorest cities in the world.[37]

By 1948, India was already a country of 358 million people, having exploded from 280 million just twenty years earlier.[38] The United States, by contrast, was home to 146 million people. With well over 10 percent of the world's population, India held a paltry 3 percent of global GDP.[39] Childhood mortality nationwide was more than 25 percent, and its literacy levels were around 12 percent.[40] Around that time, Kolkata's population was nearly 4.5 million people—more than the entire population of Ireland, from whence Agnes's order of nuns had originated.[41] The poverty of the area was suffocating. Having been devastated during World War II, Kolkata was one of the poorest cities in India and certainly one of the poorest in the world, racked by hunger, disease, poor sanitation, and desperate poverty.

Looking out over this suffering, Agnes—who chose her religious name to honor Saint Thérèse of Lisieux and became known as Mother Teresa—decided that she could no longer stay behind the walls of the convent or its school. In 1948, with the support of her order, she ventured out into the most desperate slums in India to serve the poor, disenfranchised, and broken.[42] Two years later, she founded the order of the Missionaries of Charity, which by the time she won the Nobel Peace Prize in 1979 included more than 1,800 nuns, 120,000 lay workers, eighty centers in India, and a presence in a hundred other countries around the world. The order focused on the poorest of the poor, opening schools, orphanages, homes for people with Hansen's disease (leprosy), and hospices for terminally ill people. Agnes didn't retire until 1997, the same year she died at eighty-seven, still living in the city of Kolkata, to which she had dedicated her life.[43]

Mother Teresa went into the slums of Kolkata because her faith and her intuition told her that every human being is born equal in worth and dignity, that a baby suffering from disease in a slum is every bit as worthy of love as the wealthiest person in the world. She knew that despite the way so many of us measure worth—through success or the accumulation of material wealth, fame, or power—the real worth of a human being is embedded in their simple humanity.

That lesson was echoed in her own life. This tiny, poor Albanian immigrant became one of the most admired women in history. She was awarded honorary degrees and global prizes and ultimately beatified by her church not because she had accumulated wealth but because she lived with purpose and loved others deeply with little regard for herself.

Few of us are called to the life of Agnes Gonxha Bojaxhiu. Her life isn't a good example because of her sainthood or Nobel Prize. She never sought either of these accolades, only seeking to live a life of service to others. But the lesson of Mother Teresa and those she served is that our wealth does not determine our worth. One reasons so many ancient faiths and historical traditions, including Stoicism and Buddhism, warn of the temptations of wealth is that money can so easily become an obsession and a metric to understand our value. Because it's quantifiable and can afford luxury and power, money is easy to seek, measure, and become obsessed with.

This obsession can become quicksand that consumes us. Money is a wonderful tool. The Missionaries of Charity relied on the financial resources of those who worked in other professions and were generous toward Mother Teresa's work. And she and her sisters must have been incredibly grateful to the bankers and bakers alike who dedicated a portion of their paychecks to their work in Kolkata. Their mission took both on-the-ground servants and those who supported them to make a difference.

But too often we ignore the example of Mother Teresa and allow money to become a measuring stick for our own worth or the worth of those around us. I've worked with many people who became insecure when their social circles expanded to those richer than them. I've met those who are positively dismissive of people less wealthy than them. In all honesty, I've occasionally felt myself slipping into each of those bad habits, too.

Most of us do, at some point. But the truth is that none of the wealthiest people I've met will ever have a legacy that compares to that simple, poor woman from Albania. And most of us will never find the peace she found in serving the poorest among us—people whom she unfailingly viewed with dignity and respect—unless we somehow learn to view others in the same way.

When money becomes a way of measuring human worth, it grows psychologically and materially destructive. It drives people to make bad decisions in their own lives, to live with deep insecurity, and to judge and disregard others. These are traps. They dehumanize those who believe them and too often justify the abuse of those who lack material means. But freeing yourself of this belief, knowing that your worth and the worth of others around you has little to do with wealth, is liberating and encouraging. Money can be taken away. Core human dignity—the idea that each person is "created equal . . . endowed by their Creator with certain unalienable rights, that among these are life, liberty and the pursuit of happiness"—is intrinsic. It is inviolable. Our core human dignity reminds us that our worth is not our net worth, and neither is the worth of anyone around us.

This is a simple lesson. It is a truth championed by almost every serious belief system in the world. But remembering it is a constant struggle. And the heart of Good Money is a mindset that relegates material wealth to its proper place in our lives.

Chapter 3

Earn with Purpose

A s noted earlier, there are four things you can do with money: earn, spend, give, and invest. Of all those categories, we spend the vast majority of our time earning. If we don't think about our work in a way that creates a positive impact on others and flourishing in us, we're missing a core opportunity to live with purpose and joy.

The Southeast Lineman Training Center (SLTC) is a fascinating business based in Trenton, Georgia.[1] Originally founded by George Nelson in 1999, SLTC was established to train people to enter the line-work industry. Line workers come in a variety of shapes and forms, but most commonly they work on overhead electrical lines, maintaining and repairing them even in the most dangerous conditions. When your power goes out in a hurricane or a blizzard, line workers are the ones standing by to go out into the storm and try to restore power. Each year, there are memorable images, as there were in 2024 with Hurricane Milton, of parking lots full of line workers and their trucks ready to brave the hazardous conditions to keep everything, from hospitals to homes, functioning.

Today, SLTC is one of the most successful apprentice line worker training programs in the United States. Co-led by David Powell and his brother-in-law P. J. Nardy, SLTC is exemplary not just because of how it has turned the work of training line workers into a purpose-filled pursuit but also because, in doing so, it is enabling thousands of people to earn a living with purpose.

Its offerings are straightforward. In its electrical line worker training program, SLTC recruits an incoming class of aspiring line workers, including GED holders and former military service members.[2] For fifteen weeks, the center trains them both in the field and in the classroom. It then sends them out to be placed with electrical utility companies and similar organizations around the world. At a time when many are questioning the value of a four-year college education, SLTC charges $22,995 to attend (sometimes paid for by a future employer) and places nearly all its graduates in jobs where the average salary is $94,000 (the average US salary more broadly is only $63,795).[3] With such a strong value proposition, the program itself could be bare-bones, but Nardy and Powell have crafted it into something unique.

They care not just about the future earnings of their students but also about their life success, and they want the graduates to be both proficient in the technical aspects of their jobs and balanced and flourishing. Evidence of this goal is everywhere on campus and in their programs. Nardy and Powell employ inspiring language like "Put it all on the line" and "Toward the storm" to inspire graduates, constantly reiterating the importance of the profession and acknowledging the risks these brave individuals take. A central feature of campus is a movie theater, where the SLTC team shows professional-grade short films that portray line workers as the true action heroes they are. The center also has an on-site company store with a host of line worker equipment and other swag with the program's most inspiring mottos. SLTC even filmed a television series, *Woodwalkers*, which was released on Amazon Prime and reflects the heroes' journey the students take. As Powell explains, part of the excitement for prospects is how purposeful the field can be: "The draw, too, is to make a difference. They typically desire to have impact in some way, to do something that matters. We forget that our society functions because of linemen. Electricity is fundamental to our society, and it works because of people who are in the electrical trade, so these people make an impact in the world."[4]

Beyond keeping purpose and inspiration front and center, SLTC tries to care for its students in the fifteen weeks they are on campus. In addition to teaching them line work, the center incorporates life skills and financial management into the program. After all, many of the students will make more than anyone else in their family has at an incredibly young age. SLTC also teaches them proper financial stewardship to make money good in their lives. The program pairs up the line workers with local families to provide housing and community while they are in town, and it has a chaplain on campus.

My favorite feature is the "graduation and rodeo" the center puts on at the conclusion of each class. Way more fun than a college graduation, it's a day of celebration, competition, and camaraderie. The graduates bring friends and family members so that hundreds or thousands of people are in attendance. It's a giant outdoor party with food, country music, classic rock, and event competitions where the graduates climb up poles carrying eggs in their mouths to test finesse or perform simulated rescues with heavy human dolls. The graduation is like a rock concert with thousands attending and celebrating the students' accomplishments. As one mom put it, "The rodeo and graduation ceremonies were like nothing I have ever seen. So amazing!"[5] Everyone has an incredible time sending these new graduates into careers that will be challenging but satisfying and financially secure.

Nardy and Powell get great purpose from the work they do. More importantly, they do so by helping others achieve both financial freedom and a sense of belonging. Sean O'Connor, a graduate of the program, says, "Going to SLTC was one of the best decisions of my life. . . . Like anything, you get what you put into it. I put my all into it. . . . I'm the best that I could be for myself."[6] And instructor Justin Marro spoke of his experience working for SLTC and how line work impacted his life:

> [When] I went to school I was probably one of the few that was just kind of trying to figure it out. . . . Then finally becoming a lineman gives you a little bit of joyfulness. . . . And it has paid dividends over dividends. . . . It makes you learn new friends and new people. Even though it's a big world out there, you know the lineman world is very small. . . . It's like a small

family and small community. It's more family oriented even though there's long hours. You just feel grateful at the end of the day to see your family and come home to them knowing that you're going to provide a good life for them. . . . I mean I wouldn't take anything back. I'd do it again.[7]

Many people today don't have that kind of inspiring work environment, and they content themselves with never finding it. They end up working for the money, but whether they are a middle manager or a millionaire business owner, they find that the money won't make them happy, absent purpose. This is an existential problem in the world today. And so, any book on the habits, mindsets, and values for financial flourishing needs to address earning with purpose.

Our Crisis of Purpose

We are living through a crisis of purpose that is affecting people globally from all walks of life. Although the world is richer, safer, and healthier than it has ever been, people aren't happier or flourishing more, and a great deal of that has to do with the lack of purpose so many feel in their professional lives.

The evidence for this decline in flourishing is widespread. Gallup does perhaps the most comprehensive surveys on emotions and happiness globally, and in its 2024 report on global emotions, it found that its composite negative-experience index remained near all-time highs despite a small turnaround in 2023. This negative index shows that although prosperity has grown, happiness and life satisfaction haven't grown with it (figure 3-1).

Leading the world in negative emotions are the countries you might expect—those that, like Afghanistan and Sierra Leone, were suffering desperately through violent conflict or unimaginable poverty. Surprisingly, it isn't rich countries that dominate the positive-emotion index, but it's places like Indonesia, Mexico, Paraguay, and the Philippines. The results reflect our general observations about money: When you don't have enough money (or health or safety), life is genuinely worse. But after a

FIGURE 3-1

Negative experiences are growing worldwide

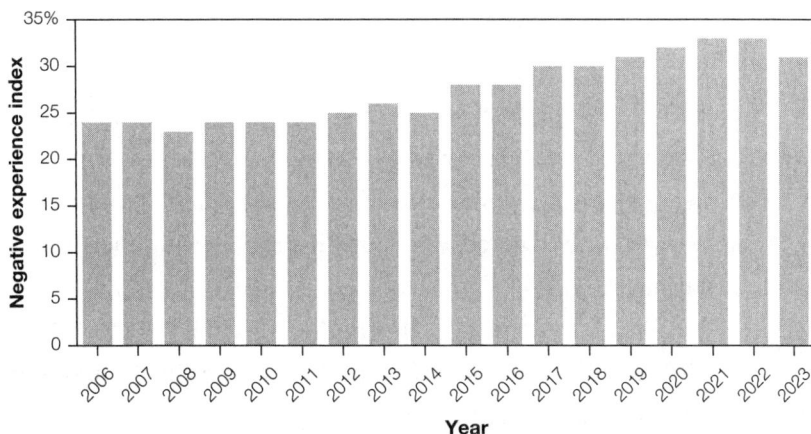

Source: Data from Gallup, "Gallup Global Emotions 2024," 2024, https://www.gallup.com/analytics/349280
/gallup-global-emotions-report.aspx.

certain threshold, it's what you do with that money and how you fashion
your life that matters most to flourishing.

These surveys are complemented by real-world data documenting an
unprecedented rise in things like mental illness and so-called deaths of
despair—deaths from things like suicide and alcohol or drug abuse. A
recent study of global mental health, for example, documented a remarkable rise in various types of mental illness around the world, with anxiety, substance abuse, and depression skyrocketing—a situation only
exacerbated by acute spikes in these conditions because of the Covid-19
pandemic.[8]

These trends are concordant with decades of data that document a rise
in loneliness and isolation among many people. Particularly troubling is
the data that shows the vast majority of people across the globe lack a
sense of purpose and meaning from the places they spend the majority of
their time: work.

According to recent global surveys, while nine out of ten people would
trade money for more meaning in their work, only around 15 percent of

employees globally feel engaged at work.[9] That's a shocking number. More Americans still carry a checkbook.[10] If you think about what that means, in any group of twenty people in a work environment, only three feel truly engaged. In a recent polling of Americans, of all their sources of meaning, people ranked jobs and careers below caring for pets and reading.[11] According to another recent global survey from Pew Research Center, in no country in the world do a majority of people list work as a significant source of meaning in their lives, and in some countries that number is single digits—with only 6 percent of South Koreans feeling their work is meaningful (figure 3-2).

As a leader, I find those results catastrophic. Company leaders should aspire to cultivate cultures that help people flourish at work and allow them to leave at the end of the day more joyful and motivated than when they came in. But the majority of people in workplaces around the world are leaving work disengaged and demotivated. And while there are a multitude of reasons that people are less happy, more stressed, and more lonely today than twenty years ago, a lack of purpose at work seems to be a central factor in these broader trends.

Is this you? Do you feel disengaged at work or think that you are struggling to find meaning in the work that you do? Are you feeling lonely and isolated, stressed or demotivated? Does your work offer satisfaction and meaning, or do you view it with resentment, a necessary evil to achieve your financial goals? If so, you might be earning without purpose—working a job without crafting meaning into that work in a way that offers you both flourishing and financial stability.

This is the reason the SLTC story is so inspiring. Most of us desperately want our work to matter. We want to know that the one-third of our lives we spend on our profession made a difference to others and helped us to flourish in the process. And leaders want (or should want) that for everyone over whom they have responsibility every day.

What can be done? Fortunately, the problem is imminently solvable on an individual and company basis. The solution starts with an understanding that optimizing our careers for money doesn't work. No matter how much we make, we will always fall short of true joy if money

FIGURE 3-2

Low rates of meaning at work around the world

Work is commonly cited as a source of meaning in life.

Percentage who mention their occupation and career when describing what gives them meaning in life.

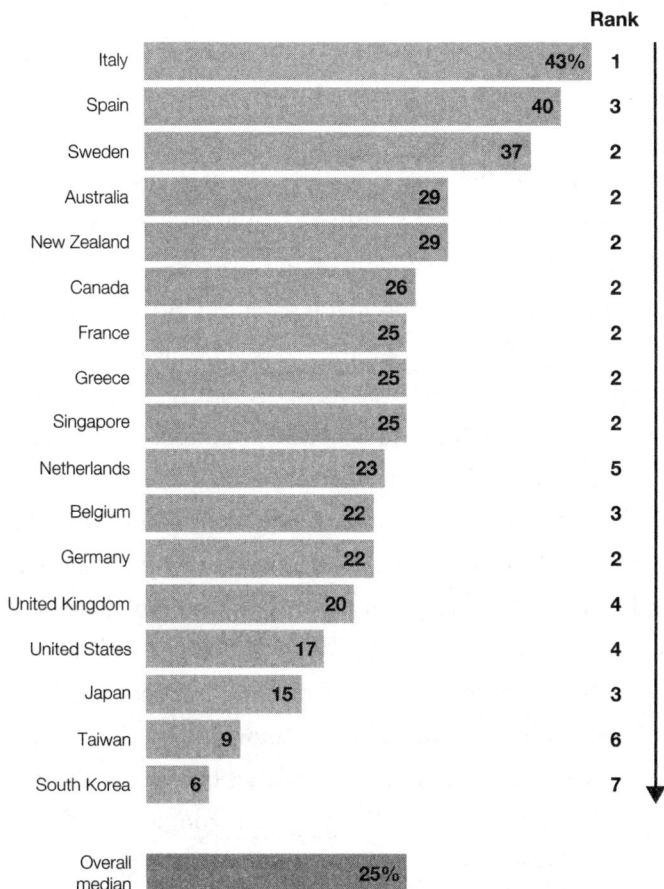

	Percentage	Rank
Italy	43%	1
Spain	40	3
Sweden	37	2
Australia	29	2
New Zealand	29	2
Canada	26	2
France	25	2
Greece	25	2
Singapore	25	2
Netherlands	23	5
Belgium	22	3
Germany	22	2
United Kingdom	20	4
United States	17	4
Japan	15	3
Taiwan	9	6
South Korea	6	7
Overall median	25%	

Note: Open-ended question. Rank reflects where the topic fell in a list of seventeen sources of meaning that were coded.
Source: Pew Research Center, "What Makes Life Meaningful? Views from 17 Advanced Economies," Global Attitudes Survey, spring 2021, Q36.

is the goal. With that in mind, we can learn to sow greater purpose into the work we do—to see it differently as Nardy and Powell do in their work at SLTC—and to make career choices that allow us to earn in a way that leads to a meaningful life and not just a financially successful one.

Don't Take a Job Just for the Paycheck

When I graduated from college, I was focused on creating financial security. Like a lot of people who experienced some measure of financial insecurity as children, I was paranoid about ending up with less than I needed. I was convinced I could do just about anything if the financial rewards were there. That mindset, combined with an impulse to perfectionism, almost derailed me.

For my first real job out of college, I interviewed at all the right places—investment banks, consulting firms, and investment funds—to find a role that could set me up for financial success. I had no background in these things. I had a typical liberal arts undergrad degree and a penchant for reading old books. But I ended up taking a job at a quantitative energy trading firm. My job was to figure out how to trade something called transmission rights and to build mathematical algorithms and computer programs to do so successfully. I had never programmed in my life. I was better than average at math but far from a savant. But the paycheck was right, the offer was in hand, and I thought I could put my head down and work through anything for the right financial reward.

I was wrong. This is not a criticism of the firm. I had some colleagues who genuinely loved and seemed to find great purpose in their work, and they were good at it, too. But I was not among them. For months, I put in twelve-plus-hour days. I read programming books and math textbooks to try to figure out the work. I struggled through even the most basic tasks my colleagues excelled at. And I had a hard time in the culture of the firm, which was a bit more introverted than me and lacked any sort of formal training program to get people up to speed. For a few months, I fought hard, and I hated every minute of it. I'd always been a successful student, but I found learning programming painstaking. It was so unenjoyable for me it was difficult to maintain the focus I needed to excel. I also regularly encountered failure on the job as I was hopelessly behind the computer science and physics majors I worked with. Eventually I resigned. It was one of the hardest, scariest, and most demoralizing moments of my life. The firm was gracious and offered me time in their consulting wing until I could start my new job. I found a position at McKinsey & Company, which was much more in line with my passions and talents. I learned the hard way that even if the money is right, if you don't have passion and find purpose in what you will do, you will never excel at it or truly flourish. Those few months I spent grinding for a paycheck were some of the most miserable of my life, both in and away from work. I periodically have to relearn that lesson; each year it hits home more and more.

The truth is we can't just do anything for money, even if we are technically capable of being excellent at the work itself, as so many burned-out lawyers and bankers can testify. Trying to do so damages our souls. I often write about the Harvard Grant Study, the oldest longitudinal study in the world, which followed male Harvard graduates over decades of their lives up to this very day.[12] Many of the results were published in a book, *Triumphs of Experience*, and some of the saddest stories were those of men who had chased financial wealth—far more than was needed to support their lives—and had broken their families, their friendships, and their own spirits in the process.[13] I see this situation every day in the work I do with dozens of companies and in counseling friends. From those just making money to get by to those accumulating mountains of wealth (which too often becomes central to their identity), many people feel a resignation that they are cashing a paycheck but not living with purpose. And that's the kind of destructive habit that causes the crisis of meaning and purpose we explored earlier in this chapter.

Worse yet, the treadmill of earning will never stop. That temptation is particularly acute among the wealthy, as we saw earlier. Money becomes an easy scoreboard to measure success, and a vicious cycle can erupt. A person who sacrifices the good things in their life—health, relationships, experiences, love—for money has a hard time dealing with their personal failures and places more and more emphasis on the one thing that they can measure and quantify and that tells them they have made it: their net worth.

But it's never enough. And those who make money an end worth pursuing often find themselves deeply self-conscious and making bad decisions to continually chase financial goals that will always be just out of reach.

One of the saddest instances I've witnessed of what I perceive as this misdirected mindset happened to the former managing partner of Mc-Kinsey & Company. Rajat Gupta's story, as told in the press and in courtrooms, serves as a cautionary tale.

Gupta was a legendary managing director (CEO) of the firm. Born in Kolkata, Gupta found himself orphaned before he turned eighteen after his mother and father (a journalist) passed away prematurely. He earned his way into undergraduate studies at the hypercompetitive Indian Institute of Technology and then to graduate studies at the Harvard Business School, joining McKinsey & Company's New York office in 1973. His trajectory at the firm was exceptional, and in 1994, he was elected the managing director of the entire firm—the first non-American to be named to that position. The firm prospered under Gupta, who was re-elected twice in 1997 and 2000, serving the maximum three terms as the firm's head. In the process, he became a global business phenomenon. McKinsey at that time had an almost-mythic stature, and Gupta had access to more CEOs than perhaps any other person on the planet. He was compensated well ($5 million to $10 million annually by some estimates). He was one of the first Indians to break through the glass ceiling and lead a major multinational firm. Gupta became renowned for his business acumen, philanthropy, and leadership. He advised the prime minister of India, the UN secretary general, and members of the World Economic Forum.

On leaving McKinsey, he was also appointed to some of the most prestigious corporate boards in the world, including Procter & Gamble and Goldman Sachs. Then it all came tumbling down. In March 2009, the Securities and Exchange Commission filed an administrative civil insider-trading complaint against Gupta and Raj Rajaratnam, a hedge fund manager, and another McKinsey partner, Anil Kumar. That charge was eventually dropped, but in 2010, Preet Bharara, the US attorney in New York, charged Gupta criminally and arrested him. Allegedly Gupta provided Rajaratnam with insider knowledge from his board service, which allowed Rajaratnam to reap additional returns of more than $20 million. A jury convicted Gupta of securities fraud, and he was sentenced to two years in prison. He has maintained his innocence and says that he did not profit from any of the alleged misconduct.[14]

But assuming the jury and courts are correct, why would a man of wealth and power like Rajat Gupta risk everything to commit securities fraud? I don't know his mindset specifically, but I've observed similar (though legal) behavior in many others I've encountered. The money and the status are never enough. When a millionaire spends time with a centi-millionaire, or a centimillionaire with a billionaire, they feel inadequate. They want more. When they see the scoreboard that says they are losing, they want to find ways to catch up or to impress the person who is ahead—whether they be a hedge fund manager, a CEO, or a small business entrepreneur. When we prioritize money as an end and a source of flourishing, its pursuit becomes endless and it can destroy the things that really matter in our lives.

The opposite is also true. Some people have a better sense of flourishing that allows them to turn away even from vast sums of money and to careers and pursuits that are meaningful. P. J. Nardy and David Powell regularly sacrifice a little short-term shareholder value to pour money into creating meaning for the people in whom they invest.

Recently, I've had the privilege of investing alongside someone like this. Kelly Merryman Hoogstraten is one of the most dynamic and important voices in media and entertainment today. Hoogstraten has led an extraordinary career that's put her at the heights of the entertainment industry, serving as vice president of content acquisition for Netflix and vice president of content partnerships for YouTube. These roles allowed her to operate at the top of her field and created a great deal of financial success. But something was missing. Hoogstraten increasingly felt called to create more content that she felt good about sharing with her kids. Noticing how much of today's entertainment glorified values she didn't feel wholly comfortable with, she made the bold decision to take a major pay cut and join a fledgling startup, Wonder Project, founded by filmmaker Jon Erwin. Wonder Project's mission (which Hoogstraten helped craft) is "to entertain the world with courageous stories, inspiring hope and restoring faith in things worth believing in."[15] Its content is intended to be family-friendly and enjoyable as cross-generational viewing, highlighting stories of love, hope, joy, and optimism in an industry that can often focus on what is dark and broken. There's financial upside, certainly, as there is in any new venture. But it comes with risk—risk an established executive like Hoogstraten didn't have to take and perhaps wouldn't have taken if she were optimizing for money alone rather than the purpose she could realize in her work. She describes her transition to working for a purpose:

> I've been fortunate to work in senior positions at leading companies during times of transformational change: Sony Pictures during the earliest days of digital home entertainment distribution. Netflix during that company's industry disrupting shift from physical DVDs to the Netflix we all know today. YouTube during a pivotal moment of global expansion that demanded a win-win partnership structure for both IP owners and the platform itself. After building all of that, managing hundreds of people and traveling the world, my achievement cup was full. My purpose cup, less so. That's why Wonder Project is an amazing next chapter for me. I have young children, so I have a personal stake in wanting to bring more courageous storytelling to a global audience—and I get to do so while solving a practical problem for millions of parents by giving them high quality films and series that they can feel great about watching with their kids. It's a win-win, and getting to build a mission driven organization from the ground up has been the most fulfilling experience of my career so far.[16]

If optimizing for money isn't the right choice in a career, what should we be optimizing for? How can we make our jobs more purposeful?

Aim for Success with Significance

In 1995, Bob Buford wrote the bestselling book *Halftime*, which popular-
ized the concept of "moving from success to significance" in the second
half of life.[17] Buford realized that many businesspeople work their whole
lives to achieve material success only to find their happiness and sense of
purpose wanting when that success comes. And he rightly encouraged
those people to seek out meaning and impact in their later years.

That success-to-significance framing is well intended, but it has become
misused. The point was to encourage people who have spent a career accumulating resources—money, power, status, and achievement—to redeploy
their time and talents in service of others. But to some, this framework also
implies that professional success and a happy, meaningful life are mutually
exclusive. In reality, there is no success without significance.

If you read Bronnie Ware's brilliant *The Top Five Regrets of the Dying*,
the Harvard Grant Study, the pioneering work of Daniel Kahneman and
Angus Deaton on happiness and income, or the teachings of nearly every
ancient religion or philosophy, you'll discover that few people, at the ends
of their lives, care about money, fame, or power as much as they think
they will.[18] And almost everyone regrets a deficit of meaningful relationships or a lack of meaning in their work and life.

I've spent the last decade writing about leadership and personal development, particularly the topic of purpose, and have been investing in,
consulting with, or leading hundreds of companies. One key insight from
that work is the hollow nature of material success when it lacks meaning.
Success without significance—which I define as purpose, service, and
meaningful relationships—is not really success at all. And whether you're
at the beginning of your career, at your professional peak, or contemplat-
ing the latter parts of your working life, it's never too early or too late to
begin identifying, emphasizing, and crafting the significance in your
work.

Few of us have thoughtfully considered the mainstream concept of
success before we have pursued it. We often default to the material and
financial trappings of accomplishment that the world prioritizes. We

may be thoughtful about selecting a job or career by thinking about what we're good at or the paths of those we admire, but over time, that job can dominate other meaningful parts of our lives or we may lose sight of what made that career purposeful in the first place. Too often, we chase material progress—raises, bonuses, promotions—without truly asking why.

Instead, we need to properly reflect on how we can live a life intensely imbued not just with the superficial trappings of success but also with deep purpose and joy in all we do. As psychologist Martin Seligman has framed it, true flourishing involves some element of accomplishment, certainly, but also involves meaning, positive emotions, engagement, and relationships. Reflecting on this more profound definition of success challenges us to adopt a fundamentally different path than the one championed in popular culture.

In the *HBR Guide to Crafting Your Purpose*, I propose that a flourishing life is full of purpose—including meaningful love, avocations, beauty, a worthy occupation, religious or philosophical beliefs, and service to others. The best time to conduct these reflections is often in the midst of a life transition like graduation, marriage, having kids, or divorce; when considering a new job; or at or before retirement from your primary profession. The process can also be used to rejuvenate an existing career or set of activities when things have gotten stale. Importantly, this kind of reflection is not just for the young. It can and should be conducted throughout a career and life. And it doesn't necessarily require switching jobs. Often simply identifying the latent sources of meaning in our professions, emphasizing them, and adapting our work can allow for greater meaning and fulfillment.

As you get started thinking about a deeper vision for significant success, ask yourself a few questions:

- What is the core purpose of my work and how it makes the world better, and how can I lean into that purpose in my day-to-day work?

- Where is purpose and meaning lacking in my work today, and how might I correct that?

- Who are the key relationships in my life, both inside and outside of work, and how can I deepen and enrich them?

- Who am I serving in my work and outside of it, and what more can I do at work, at home, and in my community to serve others?

- How am I becoming better each day? How can I pursue meaningful craft in my personal or professional life?

Many people who wait until the second half of their lives to consider these questions find that their ability to experience true success has been diminished by several decades of following an emptier course. But it's never too late—or too early—to turn to a life of significance. Regardless of your age or professional tenure, it's imminently possible in your life today. It may involve changing the way you view your work or investing in more fulfilling, positive relationships. You may choose to deepen your service to others or your pursuit of new and worthwhile avocations, or you may make a bigger change in your profession, location, or lifestyle. But whatever the change looks like, it will include your stopping right now to take serious stock of your life and reflecting deeply on whether the path you're on leads to where you want to go.

Wherever you are on your journey—whether you are fifteen, twenty-five, or fifty-five—start this process now and put serious thought into what will make your life meaningful, joyful, and fulfilled.

Make Your Job More Meaningful

In 2011, I wrote a leadership book with two coauthors, Oliver Segovia and Daniel Gulati. We were in business school at the time, and our generation had just lived through a number of catastrophic failures in leadership—the dot-com bubble, Enron and related corporate scandals, terrorism, two major wars, and, finally, the global financial crisis. My coauthors and I wanted to paint on the back side of these leadership failures a picture of how our generation might lead differently moving forward.

What resulted was a book with thoughts on globalization, diversity, and a host of other trends, but the red thread throughout was the desire of our generation for meaning and purpose at work. We and our peers had seen what optimizing for wealth and power at all costs led to, and we hoped to live lives that were fundamentally different. We titled the book *Passion and Purpose* because almost every leader we spoke to articulated a desire to live with those two traits.

My very first speech on the book showed me I had done almost no serious reflection on the nature of purpose at work. After I concluded my prepared remarks, a young woman stood up and asked the most obvious question in the world: "How do I find my purpose?"

I had just been through three years of graduate school, including classes on leadership. I had listened to hundreds of lectures by successful leaders. Prior to school I had served nearly a dozen companies as a consultant. And I had written a book with *purpose* in the title! But I was totally unprepared for the simplest and most obvious question anyone could ask about meaning in life—the same question I'd asked myself a thousand times.

I can't recall what I said that night (I've repressed the memory!). But I know it wasn't satisfying to me, to her, or to anyone else in the room. Over the next five years, I reflected deeply on the topic through dozens of speaking engagements, working with hundreds of leaders, and writing a number of articles with HBR. I finally came to believe the question itself was flawed.

That question—the same one I asked—assumed three things to be true:

1. *Purpose is found:* We believe purpose is a pot of gold at the end of the rainbow. We believe in the hero's journey, where we wander through life until we stumble on one thing to build that life around. And our fear is that we are never lucky enough to find it.

2. *Purpose is a single thing:* "How do I find my purpose?" assumes a singular source of meaning in our lives. It assumes we need to find *one big thing* that will give us hope and focus throughout our careers—a single calling or vocation that transitions us from emptiness to fulfillment.

3. *Purpose is stable over time:* We implicitly assume that one big thing will be our one big thing forever—that we will find some professional job that will be endlessly fulfilling for the next fifty years of our lives (or more).

Each of those assumptions was wrong. Purpose is largely made or crafted, not found. True flourishing happens when we understand there are multiple sources of purpose in our lives at any time and that building a web of purpose around us leads to true human flourishing. What's more, purpose—particularly professional purpose—changes over time. Our professional purpose looks a lot different when we are college students, early-career entrants, middle managers, in the peak of our professional careers, or in the later years of those careers, transitioning gracefully to less demanding work.

In retrospect, these ideas seem almost intuitive. They even reflect the way most of us live day-to-day. But not recognizing them consciously creates anxiety and indirection in our lives.

I won't belabor each of these points individually, but even in a book on money, it's worth a brief aside on these questions: If money can't be the primary goal of purposeful work, what can? And if we have the power to craft meaningful work, not just find it, what are the best ways to do so?

At the highest level, I believe that creating purpose in work involves at least four distinct practices. Engaging in each will make you not only happier and more flourishing at work but also more likely to achieve financial success in your chosen profession.

Craft your work

Craft as a concept has a double meaning as we build more meaningful jobs. *Job crafting*—tweaking work to make it more engaging, fulfilling, or fun—is especially popular now, and for good reason. It is essential to craft your work, adapting your job in small ways to make it more intrinsically meaningful. This is taking the raw material you find in a job and adjusting your work to spend more time on and emphasize the things you find most rewarding while simultaneously making your whole job more impactful to others. It's taking the job you have, and making it the job you want. And here's the secret: job crafting often makes you more successful professionally—potentially leading to both greater engagement and better financial outcomes.

Make work a craft

Meaning also comes from treating your work as a craft—taking pride in the excellence of a job well done and becoming expert in whatever you do. There's almost nothing like watching the work of a true craftsperson.

One of the companies we are invested in sells fire trucks. James Wessel, the leader of that organization, is more focused on his craft than almost anyone I know. He eats, sleeps, and breathes fire trucks and firefighters. He has personally been a mechanic on hundreds of trucks. He knows seemingly every small-town fire department in the United States and has memorized every fire truck model. Once at a conference in Washington, DC, he started texting me at 3:00 a.m. because a fire had started nearby and he ran out of his hotel to observe the firefighters and their equipment. He approaches everything he does to be the best at that activity and in turn is the best in the entire world at his job.

Each of us has that same call to be a craftsperson at whatever we do: sales, spreadsheet models, product design, architecture. Making our work meaningful involves both job crafting and treating our work as a craft. And unsurprisingly, those who perfect their crafts are often rewarded both personally and financially for that work.

Connect your work to service

Research has shown definitively that we are happiest when we are serving others. Each of us, in some way, is serving someone else at work. Those in client roles see, very clearly, that they are there to empower and serve clients. People working in technology are serving their colleagues, and those in management positions are serving those over whom they have authority. If nothing else, we're each working for some reason—to support a family, parents, friends, or causes we love—and those acts of service constitute the reasons most of us work.

Finding ways to mine our daily experiences for opportunities to serve can help us generate greater value in everything we do. Each day, we have the chance to show generosity and service to others. When we do take that chance, we are more fulfilled and more likely to succeed professionally as well.

Invest in positive relationships

Few things matter to happiness and meaning in life as much as the relationships we have. Study after study has shown that those who live life enmeshed in a series of positive relationships are more fulfilled and purposeful. And the need for such relationships doesn't end at the office door. While work relationships are, by necessity, of a different character than personal ones, they are essential to fulfillment at work. Cultivating positive relationships outside of our primary work can be the buttress that makes all our experiences more meaningful. The web of positive relationships we build over time can enable our financial goals—whether the relationships are with clients, colleagues, vendors, or anyone in between. Good relationships are the right thing to do and wholly aligned with business and financial success.

. . .

Each of these four approaches to more meaningful work could be broken down in much more detail. For our own purposes here, it's enough to say that dispelling the myths about professional purposes and embracing the opportunity to craft purpose in these four ways can help us to earn with purpose while potentially earning more financially as well. A core proposition is that most jobs can be meaningful if we make them so, and we don't necessarily have to leave a job to earn with purpose.

I'll close this topic with a simple example. One of my most valued colleagues is a woman named Elise. Elise joined our firm straight out of college to be an executive assistant for my business partner and me. That job can be difficult, demanding, and sometimes tedious. Our calendars are tough to wrangle. The people we interact with aren't always as kind as we would want them to be, and even my partner and I have days when we are probably not the most pleasant to deal with. But Elise has not only excelled in the role but also transformed it. First, she perfected the core roles assigned to her, treating her administrative job as a craft. She learned the areas we lived in and the work lunch locations we preferred. She educated herself on the people we most frequently interact with and their priorities and preferences. She helped research better technologies to make those roles easier and implement them and approached every job, big and small, with attention to detail and a commitment to excellence.

She has also crafted her role to be much more than we initially hired her for. In a small firm, there's a lot of opportunity for those who take it, and Elise has risen to every challenge and leaned into her unique talents. As one example, Elise is gifted at hospitality and organizing events. Our firm decided to put on a major summit for our most important clients. Running such a summit would be a sensitive role for anyone. But Elise raised her hand to run the event, with me sponsoring and helping direct it. She nailed the challenge. The event was a huge success, and many attendees commented that it was one of the best they had attended. In the lead-up, she was exceptionally prepared and, at the event, a veritable field general exercising maturity far beyond her tenure—escorting CEOs, important investors, and even a former vice president of the United States throughout the summit. She loved the activity, and though it wasn't in her formal job description, she leaped at the chance to craft her work in more meaningful ways. Elise describes her own job crafting: "Something I enjoy about my job is that there are always ways to be creative and proactive. I find satisfaction in being helpful to others and identifying new ways to do so. As my work is always evolving and changing, I like to ask the question, 'What can I do that would be most helpful?' or 'What is happening just around the corner that I can get ahead of and tackle?' In addition, the relationships I have formed through my job are such an encouragement to my work."[19]

In all of this, she creates positive relationships and acts with an attitude of service. She has a deep sense of joy that influences everyone she interacts with and a talent for owning mistakes and staying calm under pressure. She invests time with all our team members and with important clients, becoming a friend and treasured colleague in the process. Elise is always looking for ways to serve and support even those whom she doesn't directly work for. "So much of what I do in my role is in service of others," she says, "whether it be managing calendars and scheduling for our leadership or hosting events for our partners. When I focus on the individuals I am serving through administrative work or planning events, it brings purpose to the long hours or tedious, sometimes monotonous tasks at hand."[20]

This orientation only deepens the relationships she builds and the positive impact she has on others. Of her work, Elise says, "The best part of my work is getting to care for others, particularly those who I have built meaningful relationships with over the course of my time at the company. I am deeply loyal to my colleagues and those who I work under, so it's a joy to lift administrative burdens and make their day-to-day easier through scheduling and planning for them, knowing that they can work diligently and still prioritize family dinner. I love that I have a part in helping them use their time and talent well."[21]

Not every person hired to be an executive assistant could or would engage this way. But Elise has transformed the role into one of the most impactful in our firm and has gotten greater purpose and meaning from it in the process.

Jobs should be about more than money. Every job can be purposeful with the right mindset. And we should never waste the opportunity to try to craft greater meaning and purpose into our work.

Explore Meaningful Change (If Needed)

Almost any job can be meaningful if crafted properly. Every job has opportunities for craft, service, and relationships. Our work, even if stale, can often be tailored to be more personally purposeful and fulfilling. But there are times when we have exhausted the meaning in a current profession and need to seek out a professional environment better suited to our needs. This change may come with financial trade-offs, whether we are starting over in a new field, launching a company, or shifting to nonprofit or governmental work. But as we've seen previously, past a certain earnings or wealth threshold, those financial considerations should take a backseat toward more intrinsically motivating factors at work. And making the leap can sometimes pay huge dividends to the purpose we feel in our work.

I first met Anand Kesavan when we were both graduate students at the Harvard Kennedy School of Government. Kesavan is brilliant, likable, and a great communicator. We hit it off as we were both crafting careers in finance and shared a passion for public education. Kesavan was a successful investment banker for UBS, working on government and nonprofit projects, before moving to another firm where he helped lead investment banking for public finance, particularly for K–12 schools. For many, this level of engagement with his passions would have been enough. Kesavan had crafted purpose into his work in much the way I described earlier. He took a job that can be grueling and money focused—investment banking—and found a way to shape it into supporting the passion he cared most about, providing high-quality public education for kids. But when Kesavan came to believe he wasn't as fully committed to this cause as he could be, he reshaped his whole life in its pursuit.

Kesavan left investment banking and became the chief financial officer for a charter school network, KIPP Texas–Austin, working directly in schools to help them successfully educate kids. He then took a position at the prestigious Charter School Growth Fund, a highly respected institution creating equal opportunity to higher education in the United States, leading its structured finance capability. Again, he was pushing further and further into purpose in his career, irrespective of the financial cost to him. But even that wasn't enough. He saw a unique opportunity to be a social entrepreneur solving one of the greatest challenges in the world of charter schools today: facilities funding.

Although charter schools are public schools, often serving even more diverse and economically disadvantaged student populations than conventional public schools in their area, their funding formula is different. Each state has a different formula, but the schools typically receive only partial funding from federal, state, and local sources for the students they educate. In almost no state do charter schools get full funding for their facilities. These buildings are expensive, sometimes costing $15 million or more. Charter school founders have to find creative ways to fund acquisitions and leases on top of their other obligations and without student-based revenue to do so—raising external funds or pinching pennies in other areas of the budget to make their leases or facilities payments work. Years ago, a market emerged for charter school bonds to help fund these facilities with lower-cost debt, but even that market rarely funded the full cost of a facility or offered rates that made payments affordable.

That's where Kesavan saw an opportunity. Starting a new enterprise, the Equitable Facilities Fund (EFF), he raised philanthropic capital from generous groups like the Walton Family Foundation. This first-loss capital on these facilities would allow the schools to get better rates and more funding in the bond markets. He also raised enough capital to create diversified pools of facilities to raise these bonds. Markets like diversification, and bond markets would often rather fund a pool of twenty high-quality schools than one, since the diversity naturally lowers their risk of loss. Through EFF, Kesavan has found a way to raise more than $1 billion to help charter schools around the country lower their facilities costs, providing better classrooms for kids and more financial resources that can be devoted to teachers and instruction.

You don't need to go into education or leave lucrative careers to create transformational change through philanthropy. Quite the contrary. What makes life so beautiful and endlessly fascinating is that the diversity of people in this world perfectly mirrors the diversity of opportunities for work. Everyone finds joy, meaning, and fulfillment in different things. I've met investment bankers who were miserable and investment bankers who absolutely loved their clients and calling. I've met teachers who found their calling in helping kids and those who realized the job was not for them. I once worked with a man who absolutely loved his work stocking shelves at a major grocer. He was smart, insightful, remarkably hardworking. So much so that when my team and I were in a position to elevate him professionally—something I communicated to him—he wanted none of it. He loved the simple craft of his work, finding small ways to be more efficient, learning every stock-keeping unit, and helping customers. He also knew that the responsibilities that came with promotion would ruin this joy.

While almost any job can be crafted in such a way as to be more meaningful, there are certain jobs that are a better fit for you. I'm conscious that for some, changing careers may be a luxury you can't afford. There are plenty of people who can't leave jobs because of the financial hardships that a change would impose. Crafting work to be more enjoyable is the only option they have.

If you do have the privilege of options and financial security to pursue a new profession (even if it requires a bit of short- or long-term belt tightening), it's worth putting in the time and effort to consider that thoughtfully. If you want to change jobs to be more meaningful, it can often be within the same company. Sometimes the change doesn't necessitate a financial trade-off. But sometimes a change is more dramatic, and it's something you, like Kesavan, have to be willing to consider.

Mentors and friends can help expose you to options. Internships or classes can help you to explore them more deeply. But picking the right one also rests on brutally honest self-understanding.

I found this to be true when I switched careers while writing my book about purpose in 2020. I was working in a very large company but had been feeling more disenchanted and out of place for some time. I finally made the decision to transition into something dramatically different, and as I embarked on that journey, I created a simple grid to help guide my decision-making. In one column, I listed all the traits I might seek in a new job. Immediately next to this, I assigned that row a weight to help me see which of these characteristics were more or less important. It looked like table 3-1 (though some categories and weightings have been changed).

TABLE 3-1

A values-based framework for evaluating a career

Characteristic	Weighting	Opportunity 1	Opportunity 2	Opportunity 3
Prestige	10%	7	6	6
Financial upside	10	7	5	10
Culture	10	8	8	5
Challenge	5	8	9	5
Adventure	10	5	8	5
Flexibility	10	8	9	5
Leadership opportunities	5	8	7	4
Mentorship	5	8	7	5
Growth opportunity	10	8	8	6
Merit based	10	7	6	4
Ability to use talents	10	6	8	8
Interesting and changing environment	5	6	8	8
Total		86	89	71
Average		7.2	7.4	5.9

Then I tried to score every new job I considered according to these criteria. Obviously, other things mattered. At a minimum, I had to have the skills and experience to succeed in the job (although if I was willing to take a step back financially and in my title, I could relearn a profession with hard work). That type of work had to be available to me. But ultimately, the grid was incredibly helpful. It helped me think through options with my endlessly supportive wife, who even enthusiastically talked about changing our lifestyles to allow me more financial freedom to pursue a job I loved.

I ended up doing just that, making a radical change to a smaller, values-aligned firm that posed more financial risk than some of my other options but also offered greater autonomy, entrepreneurship, financial upside, values alignment, hands-on work, and fun. It ticked almost every box, so making the immediate financial trade-off was easy—and if it worked, the trade-off wouldn't even be sustained.

If you'd like to undertake this exercise yourself, consider grabbing a notepad or opening up a spreadsheet and making a chart like table 3-1. Begin to reflect deeply on what characteristics matter to you in a job (keep these to ten to fifteen things or fewer), and then think through how much each of those characteristics matters to you—assigning it a percentage with the totals adding to 100 percent. This exercise is better done with input from others who know you well. But keep the circle tight and make sure your assessment is brutally honest. Don't change categories or weightings to be inauthentic just because you fear judgment from those with whom you share your grid. In my case, I only shared all the details with my wife and best friend, people with whom I have total trust and comfort. And I spoke in more general terms with other mentors.

Once your grid is complete, start to review different professional opportunities (even radically different ones) against it to look for surprises in which some jobs, companies, or fields start to stand out. Tweak the grid as you learn more about yourself. Even include your current job to see if it's truly structurally misaligned or if there are less radical ways to rejuvenate the purpose and fulfillment you need to feel at work.

My advice to those struggling to earn with purpose is, consistently, to try to craft your current work first. Make sure it can't be the right job for you with a change in mindset, responsibilities, or position before you make the dramatic decision to do something new. Sometimes you are in the wrong job or in the right field but with the wrong company. Approaching a search thoughtfully can be an important opportunity for self-reflection as well as a chance to think through how much wealth you really need. Targeting only opportunities that pay as much as, or more than, your current work may cut you off from something remarkable. Now that I lead a smaller, more entrepreneurial firm, I see it all the time—people who know they aren't happy but are convinced they need their current income to make life work. The inertia of their financial lives and their unwillingness to take risk or change lifestyle make a more fulfilling career impossible to achieve.

Importantly, don't become locked into your work by your finances. If you've set a financial finish line and maintained a modest lifestyle (which we'll cover in the next chapter), you'll have a clear view of what you actually need to make things work. And if your lifestyle has creeped beyond what you truly need, the option of changing it is always available to you. Embracing that mindset may open a world of professional purpose you didn't know existed. Anchor yourself not at your current income but at the income that can enable the other things you and your family need to flourish in life. And beyond that, consider the importance of the other, more intrinsically meaningful parts of the work you might do.

Nonprofits Aren't the Only Path to Purpose

As I've discussed, being clear on what you love and what matters to you is essential to earning with purpose. Working toward achieving that purpose, in small or grand ways for an aligned organization, is critical. But many people assume that to have real purpose, you need to work in a nonprofit.

That's not always so. While one group of people assumes that maximizing their pay will maximize their purpose, another makes the opposite mistake. The final word I'll offer on the connection between earnings and flourishing at work is that sometimes, indeed, you can have both together.

The truth is, the world needs teachers, social workers, and international aid administrators. It also desperately needs neurosurgeons, auto mechanics, technology entrepreneurs, and nurses. Each of those jobs can be incredibly purposeful to the right person while not necessarily involving financial trade-offs. Nursing pays well but is also critically important to patients who need quality health care. Entrepreneurs often found companies that revolutionize the world in positive ways. Hollywood actors and directors at the top of their games may be well compensated, but they can also use their platforms to tell beautiful and uplifting stories that affect millions.

These people have every bit as positive an impact on the world as those in other sectors, and their being well compensated for that doesn't change this fact. As a bonus, these financially successful people may then be in a position both to give back to their communities (as the many charitably minded people in this book have) and to help lift up and encourage others pursuing their dreams.

Kazuo Inamori is a legendary Japanese business leader who was born in 1932 in Kagoshima and raised in an era of war and poverty. In 1959, he founded a company that would become Kyocera, manufacturing things like television tubes and silicon transistor headers.[22] Kyocera would go on to employ more than seventy thousand people.[23] In 1984, he founded another company that would become KDDI, the second-largest telecommunications company in Japan.[24]

Inamori is a titan of postwar Japan, acclaimed widely for his unique business philosophies, philanthropic interests, and life path. In 1984, he founded the Kyoto Prize, honoring people who make "extraordinary contributions to science, civilization, and the spirituality of humankind"—philanthropy that could continue to grow and expand over time into new areas.[25] His unique management philosophy emphasized optimism and self-confidence grounded in reality and harnessing and creating passion and purpose in the work of those in his employ. These philosophies stemmed from his dedication to Zen Buddhism and its core tenets. Among Inamori's well-known list of twenty maxims, several reflect this focus:

> A clear and pure mind can feel positive energy, while a selfish heart sees complexity and chaos.
>
> . . .
>
> Instead of looking for a job you like, it is better to like the work you already have; rather than pursuing fantasies, you might as well fall in love with your immediate work.

. . .

Concentrate on one line and one industry, don't get bored, don't worry, work hard, your life will produce beautiful flowers and bear fruit.

. . .

The colder the winter, the more open the cherry blossoms. The same is true for people. Without suffering and troubles, it is difficult to have great development and will not grasp true happiness.[26]

So deep was Inamori's dedication to these practices that in 1997, he became a lay priest at Empukuji Temple in Kyoto, leaving his business career behind.[27] In an earlier section, I discussed how purpose can shift over time. Inamori's life is a fascinating reflection of that observation, as he shifted between business, philanthropy, and even life as a priest, embracing the fluid nature of the work that gave him purpose over time. But even as he had embraced a life immersed in his religious tradition, he never saw the false boundary between his business interests and his personal life— eventually leaving the Empukuji Temple in 2010 at the age of seventy-seven when the government of Japan requested he rescue bankrupt Japan Airlines.[28]

Like Casey Crawford, Kelly Merryman, and so many other great business leaders across sectors, Inamori realized that there can be great purpose in almost any work. He also demonstrated that a person dedicated to a life of purpose can navigate this aim across multiple spheres of work after deep reflection and a dedication to maximizing the positive impact they have on the world. Inamori's companies employed hundreds of thousands of people in meaningful work. His philanthropy allowed him to drive positive change in other sectors. And his religious practice anchored him in a deep understanding of his views of the world.

Ninety percent of the jobs in this world can be made purposeful and societally useful in the right hands. My admiration for those who make genuine financial sacrifices to serve others through nonprofit work is enormous. Those who serve in public office, lead humanitarian charities, or have important roles in the field are to be admired and appreciated. They have often given their lives over to others without reserve. But not everyone is called to, or capable of, that path. Earning with purpose doesn't always mean earning less. Making a change to optimize professional purpose may not involve financial trade-offs. It may instead involve your getting comfortable with accumulating and using wealth the right way.

Money can be a tool for opportunity creation. Its accumulation is not, in itself, a bad thing and is often a sign of positive contributions a person has made through their work. Earning is the central way in which each of us brings in the money we have. And earning with purpose—whether in the private, public, or nonprofit sector—is a critical component of making money good in your life. We should never wait for success to achieve significance, because there is no true success without significance. But significance can be found in almost any profession with the right mindset in play.

Chapter 4

Consume Wisely

One of the most life-changing things my oldest son and I did was take a vision trip to a Central American country a few years ago. He was nine at the time and had never traveled to a lower-income country or experienced poverty other than the kind we might see around us every day in a major US city. Through one of my partner's foundations, we signed up to travel abroad for one week to see the work of the foundation and contribute in small ways. The trip was remarkable.

Our experience on the ground was twofold. First, we were accompanying a nonprofit led by a man named Brian Copes. With the help of his high school students, Copes builds rudimentary prosthetics for people who have lost limbs in the developing world. Typical prosthetics are prohibitively expensive for most people in most parts of the globe, often costing tens of thousands of dollars. The loss of a limb in much of the world is akin to a death sentence. Where the majority labor is manual, losing a leg or an arm often means losing your ability to provide for yourself. These men and women frequently then lose their wives or husbands. They fall into poverty. And they lose hope. Copes and his high school students create simple, cheap prosthetics that can offer these people some of their mobility back, and the nonprofit gives them away for free.[1]

Second, we were visiting the churches and hope centers established by this foundation to serve the local community—particularly kids. At each stop, we would help check in on the progress of those centers and celebrate with the children and adults there by singing, dancing, enjoying a cookout, and bringing toys for the kids.

At first, the trip was really hard on my son. He was shocked to see the poverty in the area we visited. He began crying when he saw the homes and schools of the kids we met—small, crumbling, exposed to the elements, and unprotected. He found it difficult to get off the bus when we met the first group of amputees—a frightening concept for a child. He had dozens of questions. He wondered why these kids couldn't have lives like those we experienced back home. Hearing how the amputees had lost limbs because they were often too far from formal medical care to receive professional treatment, he worried that the same might happen to him.

But as the initial shock wore off, the trip transformed him. He learned that these kids, trapped in poverty, were exactly like him on the inside. He and the other American kids on our trip quickly integrated into the communities we visited, laughing, playing soccer, and singing together (even when they didn't speak a common language). He experienced joy at seeing those who had been devastated by their injuries walk for the first time in years. He bonded with the group we were traveling with, debriefing at the end of each day about what we were learning and feeding the local iguanas that visited our rental home. As a dad, I was so proud to see his heart for others, even as my own heart broke at the daily reminders of the suffering so many live through in the world. The trip cost us money, but the return was incalculable.

Our lives and relationships are defined by experiences. Little League baseball games. Hikes. Honeymoons. Semesters abroad. Service opportunities. Theme parks. Pilgrimages. While our phones, cars, and clothes seldom leave an indelible mark in our lives, the experiences we have with others do.

Spending is a huge component of our relationship with money. We work to gain the financial resources to purchase food, a place to live, transportation, and medical care. Then on top of these necessities—the essentials of life—we layer our discretionary purchases.

There's almost no category that influences more whether money is a good or bad thing in our lives than spending. Spend on the wrong things, and those outlays simply breed further insecurity, needs, and wants. Spend too much, and you can find yourself crippled by debt and deeply unstable. But spend on the right things at the right levels, and money can be a tool for some of the most memorable moments of your life.

In this chapter, we'll explore further how Good Money can lead to financial flourishing by laying out some basic principles for consuming wisely: choosing experiences not stuff, understanding that the best experiences need not be expensive and should be enjoyed with others, living within our means, and refusing to associate spending with status. To begin, we will first seek to understand a crucial topic: hedonic adaptation.

Why Spending More Doesn't Make Us Happier

Briton Keith Gough hit it big when he and his wife Louise won a £9 million (roughly $16.4 million) lottery. The Shropshire resident had been a baker and a man of modest means, but the massive jackpot meant he and his wife could have everything they had ever wanted. In short order, that's exactly that they tried to acquire. He bought and bet on racehorses, purchased luxury cars, and purchased an executive box at Aston Villa for the local football club. After two years of this new lifestyle, Louise and Keith ended their twenty-five-year marriage. He developed an alcohol problem and ultimately died alone, his windfall resources completely exhausted. "My life was brilliant," Gough told a British paper. "But the lottery has ruined everything. What's the point of having money when it sends you to bed crying?"[2]

In 1988, William "Bud" Post III won a $16 million lottery jackpot in Pennsylvania. When he won, he had just $2.46 in the bank and was living on disability benefits. He elected an annual payout of nearly $500,000, and within two weeks, he'd spent $300,000. He was $500,000 in debt within three months and was soon tied up in litigation with a girlfriend who claimed a third of his winnings. Over the coming years, Post would purchase multiple homes, a luxury sailboat, a twin-engine plane he couldn't fly, numerous cars and trucks, and a variety of other luxuries. His brother hired a hit man to kill him (unsuccessfully). His poor financial decision-making eventually led to his downfall. He was convicted for assault after firing a gun on a debt collector and served twenty-four months in prison. Post passed away in 2006. In the end, he had a clear perspective on the experience: "Everybody dreams of winning money, but nobody realizes the nightmares that come out of the woodwork. . . . I was much happier when I was broke."[3]

I hesitate to tell too many cautionary tales in my written works (and in both cases, the protagonists of these stories have passed away), but with money, we sometimes need to see vivid examples of the damage bad money can bring. Its love and misuse can be the root of all kinds of evil. And the rapidity with which it can destroy lives is breathtaking. The point of telling the Goughs' and Post's stories isn't to paint a poor picture of them. It's to emphasize that many of us would respond in similar ways, our psychologies torn apart by a host of issues that accompany wealth, particularly sudden riches. One famous study of lottery winners found that almost one-third are bankrupt within three to five years, and the stories of despair and tragedy seem more common than stories of success.[4]

It's a trend we see in many people who come to wealth, whether they acquire it suddenly or slowly. Professional athletes suffer the same consequences. A *Sports Illustrated* article once claimed that 35 percent of NFL players are bankrupt or experiencing financial distress within two years of retirement, and an enormous percentage of National Basketball Association (NBA), NFL, and Major League Baseball players are similarly distressed within five years. Given the opacity of the data, some of these numbers have been disputed, but even conservative estimates by the National Bureau of Economic Research found that roughly 16 percent of NFL players were bankrupt within twelve years.[5] By contrast, only 0.12 percent of average Americans go bankrupt per year despite much lower earnings than the average professional athlete.[6] The tragic stories of celebrities and their heirs who get hooked on luxury purchases or illegal substances are commonplace. Actor Jim Carrey expressed his views on the phenomenon this way: "I think everybody should get rich and famous and do everything they ever dreamed of so they can see that that's not the answer."[7]

There's a lot to unpack in those examples. For instance, sudden wealth is deadly if you don't consider capping your lifestyle, because it's easy to overspend in the present without understanding the limits of your future earnings. Lottery winners spend as if they have $10 million now, not $10 million to last a lifetime. Athletes often adjust their annual spending to their annual income, not realizing their careers may end in a few short years. The same temptations hold true for lawyers, dentists, IT consultants, and so on, but the problems often happen more gradually because of their longer careers. When we define our lives through material things, we lose sight of our true value.

At the heart of what drives such escalations in lifestyle is a principle called hedonic adaptation—sometimes termed the hedonic treadmill. Hedonic adaptation describes the way we quickly reset our lives and expectations when we experience an inflow of money.

Hedonic adaptation refers to the "reduction in affective intensity of favorable and unfavorable circumstances."[8] Put differently, human beings adapt to changes in their lives remarkably quickly, and, once adapted, that life is their new baseline. Some of this flexibility is good. It's what's remarkable about the human spirit and why people can sometimes live so bravely in the midst of unimaginable circumstances like war or famine. Our adaptability is also why people in poor countries often rate their happiness higher than those in rich ones. It's one reason my wife and I were so happy in our first cramped apartment, even though returning to that home now would be a challenge. Human beings are psychologically flexible. We are resilient. We adapt to our surroundings.

This adaptability can even have a positive impact on achievement. Once we achieve something, we want to set new goals, chasing the next experience of accomplishment. In day-to-day life, this tendency can be beneficial. It can motivate us in our work or help us maintain an exercise habit or keep practicing writing or art. It can also have a dark side, though, the kind of disillusionment so many feel when they reach the top of their field and realize there's nowhere left to climb. It's a peril for high achievers like astronauts and professional athletes and can lead to challenging psychological problems and insecurity.

That same psychological impulse makes us uniquely vulnerable to the perils of wealth, particularly when we fail to consider it carefully and we use it recklessly to acquire stuff (or, worse, seek new hedonic experiences through drug use or other maladaptive pleasures). That's the root of the term *hedonic treadmill*, which adds a layer onto this more basic reference to human psychological flexibility. With our flexibility comes the danger of how we adapt to new pleasurable experiences and new material circumstances: we always desire more.

As soon as we get a new home—maybe even a dream home!—we get used to it and start noticing the problems or how much better we like our friend's slightly larger, better house. We've dreamed of a new car, but often shortly after we get it, we begin to dream of a new one. Like drug users, we can fall into the temptation of chasing a new high through acquiring stuff, only to find that once we achieve that high, it fades quickly and we need a new fix. How much land is enough? A little more. How much stuff is enough? A little more.

With this mindset, we can drive ourselves to insecurity, unhappiness, and even financial ruin. That's a hard truth. And it's why there's little relation between prosperity and happiness at either the macro (national) level or the micro (personal) level. Spending on stuff is a trap. It seems like the stuff will make us happy. But spending is a race without a finish line; it can ultimately run us to death unless we consciously step off the treadmill with our spending habits.

So what are habits that can help us spend wisely? Let's review a few.

Spend Less Than You Make

Earlier in my career, there was a scandal involving someone employed by a branch of the company I worked for. This man managed the accounts of individuals with ultrahigh net worth and became enamored with their wealth and status, though his own means were far less. To build a life that looked like the lives of his clients—cars, properties, vacations—he started spending more than he had, borrowing money from these trusting clients to pay for it and ultimately ending up deeply in debt to them before tragically ending his own life.

Money is good when it works for us but bad when we work for it. And when we owe money to others or have expenses higher than our income, we are serving money, not having it serve us. Unfortunately, today, many people are living their lives serving their next payment. In 2019, the Aspen Institute estimated that more than 10 percent of US households (13 million families) had a negative net worth, meaning their debts were greater than their assets.[9] A survey by Credit Karma, meanwhile, estimated that more than half of Americans don't know how to calculate their net worth, and 30 percent of Americans have a net worth of $0 or less.[10] Pew Research Center estimated that 54 percent of Americans have secured debt, things like mortgages and car loans. And 56 percent of those households carry unsecured debt such as credit card debt. The same survey found that the average household had a debt-to-assets ratio of 30 percent, and a debt-to-annual-income ratio of 84 percent.[11] Total household debt in the United States has skyrocketed from just over $8 trillion in 2004 to nearly $18 trillion in 2024, and while that increase is dominated by mortgage debt (perhaps the most understandable and safest form of household debt), auto loan debt is $1.6 trillion, and credit card debt, the most dangerous debt the typical person carries, is now north of $1.1 trillion.[12]

Meanwhile, Americans are carrying more than $1.7 trillion in student loans (up from $0.5 trillion in 2006), with the average graduate owing more than $40,000 in loans—starting adult life at a disadvantage.[13] Global statistics are a bit less available, but a number of countries boast even higher indebtedness than the United States—including Canada, the United Kingdom, Sweden, and Australia.[14] As a result, many people end up working simply to keep up with prior decisions made about purchases. More than 450,000 Americans declared personal bankruptcy in 2023, unable to climb out from underneath the mountain of obligations they have accumulated.[15]

There are always examples of those for whom this kind of spending and indebtedness is due to bad fortune—particularly those who suffer catastrophic medical problems. But the vast majority of this indebtedness is poor financial decision-making. It's spending money we don't have on things we don't need. It's attending an expensive private university to pursue a degree that won't pay off or choosing electronics, clothes, or even experiences we can't afford. We burden our finances in the future with poor decisions in the present and then pay (in the case of credit card debt) nearly 23 percent per year just to cover the interest on those decisions.[16]

I have a radical and countercultural piece of advice: never let your net worth go negative. Your net worth is simple to calculate. It's the value of your assets (like your cash, investments, home, and car) minus your liabilities (like your credit card debt, student loans, and mortgage). If you have more in liabilities (debt) than you have in assets, your net worth is negative—you've effectively obligated your future self to pay for the things you are buying today. This is a vicious cycle, as the interest rates on debt often make a negative net worth challenging to escape.

Instead, create financial flexibility and security for yourself by always maintaining assets greater than your liabilities. There was a time in US and world history when the advice to never owe more money than you have or spend more money than you make would have seemed almost confusingly blasé. Before the advent of complex credit markets around mortgages, college, private schools, cars, consumer spending, and everything in between, people throughout history mostly sought to avoid being a debtor.

But today, many people live on debt. This situation is largely due to two categories of spending. One affects almost everyone: consumer credit. The advent of credit cards has led many people to acquire things they can't afford in hopes they can pay them off later—all while accruing the crushing burden of double-digit interest rates from which it can be difficult to overcome. This kind of debt is obviously bad, and there are many books and programs dedicated almost entirely to fixing this mindset and helping people extricate themselves from the burden. I won't rehash those practices here. I'll simply say that if you are carrying a credit card balance of any kind, you should stop. And if you can't afford to fully pay for something (absent a home or potentially a needed car) in your current pay period, you probably shouldn't buy it.

More controversially, don't get into significant debt for your education. Many people will debate this recommendation. But almost nothing is limiting the financial futures of people under forty (in the United States at least) more than education debt. Nearly forty-three million US borrowers have student loan debt, with each borrower averaging between $38,000 and $41,000 but expecting an average starting salary of only $52,000.[17] The average law student graduates with $130,000 in student debt, despite the fact that only 80 percent go into law, and those students have a median starting salary of $85,000.[18] The median debt for a master's degree is $84,000, while a PhD racks up $126,000 in debt.[19]

These numbers hide wide disparities. Although the average college student owes around $40,000, the average four-year state school student spends barely more than that on their total tuition costs (four-year private colleges are almost three times as expensive).[20] Some disciplines, like engineering, pay far more to new graduates than do some others. But overall, many people dig a nearly insurmountable financial hole for themselves before they have even taken their first job.

This is not meant to be a screed against college. I have graduate degrees and went to a four-year private university. I actually serve on a private college board of trustees. But these observations about debt are a jeremiad against the idea that it's OK to simply borrow to pay for college when you absolutely don't have to. Student loans are one of the primary reasons so many Americans are unable to generate a positive net worth. As a matter of principle, only go to a school you can afford to pay for, whether that's a community college, a state school, or an Ivy League school. That affordability may be because you've won scholarships or attend a less costly institution.

Work throughout college and during summers to build financial stability. At my alma mater, Berry College, almost every student works on campus (I worked seven of eight semesters). This work forms a habit of discipline and mitigates financial need.

And don't pursue degrees you don't need—particularly graduate degrees. Many US college students default into graduate school if they are not certain what else to do, and as previously described, their debt often more than doubles when they do so. Meanwhile, people practicing trades and eschewing formal four-year degrees often end up more than $140,000 ahead of their four-year-degree peers by graduation.[21]

Modern society, particularly US society, encourages us to debt-finance almost everything—homes, education, cars, phones, and furniture. Sometimes, this approach might make sense. When we buy a home, for example, the asset is worth its debt (assuming an appropriate down payment) and may appreciate. A modest car needed for work can make sense if the expenditure is within your means and you plan to keep it for a long-enough time. But developing a habit of consuming only what you can afford now, even on big areas like education, will ensure that you never lose the freedom of a positive personal balance sheet. The sidebar "Good Debt" discusses which types of debt might ultimately provide financial flexibility.

Pay off any credit cards you have monthly. Think carefully about what vehicle you can afford, borrowing only where prudent if it is an essential (rather than a luxury) purchase and carefully making sure the interest rate available is low and reasonable (wait for the 0 percent financing options!). Only take out a mortgage when you can remit a significant down payment that assures the value of your home is always higher than the loan you have on it, and ensure you have sufficient income to make your monthly payments with a cushion. (A rule of thumb is to only allow your mortgage payment with taxes and insurance to be 20 percent of your gross income.) Debt is readily available today, but to build wealth, you must have a mindset that avoids debt and rejects spending on what you cannot afford. Spend less than you make, save for the future, don't dig a financial hole for your future self. Simply swear off the idea that you can consume something today and pay for it later.

So now that you know how to limit your spending, what should you spend your money on when you have it?

Good Debt

Not all debt is bad. Investors often use debt to finance business activities they couldn't otherwise afford—buying new equipment, financing new inventory, or simply using lower-rate debt to finance a profitable and growing business with less cash. Individuals can use debt in similar ways, like using a reasonably priced mortgage to finance a home. But in evaluating whether to take on debt, you might keep a few simple principles in mind.

Use debt that is asset-backed

When you borrow to finance a home, you are taking on debt (a mortgage) but receiving an asset (the house). If you make a substantial down payment up front (on the order of 20 percent or more), the asset is immediately worth more than the debt (the 80 percent you borrowed), and in a pinch you could sell it to cover your loan. This practice is not without risk. The value of your house could decline by more than your down payment, as so often happened during the financial crisis of 2007–2010. But it's at least safer than borrowing to purchase a good or service that has no sale value. And in the case of typically appreciating assets (like homes), the loan has the potential to become a good investment. Financing a car you need for a job might fall into this category as well, though unlike homes, cars decline in value over time. For this reason, cars may require a larger down payment than a house or another growing asset, and you should have a clear-eyed view of what you can sell it for in the future.

Be sure to have the cash flow to cover payments

Whenever you take on debt, you are obligating your future self to pay for something you are purchasing now. It's critical that you have reasonable certainty that you can cover the payment on that debt over time so that you don't experience financial distress or risk truly damaging outcomes like bankruptcy. It may make sense to finance a car at 0 percent interest on a special deal, for example, even if you have the cash to pay for it up front, as your investments may be consistently growing more quickly than 0 percent and you know you can repay the debt over time. It may make sense for a small business to take on debt to fund new equipment or inventory if doing so will drive revenues that will adequately cover the payments. But any time you take on debt, you need to understand the cost to repay it over time, the consequences if you don't, and the likelihood that you can cover its costs.

Focus on opportunity creation, not consumption

The most pernicious form of debt is consumer debt—particularly credit card debt. Buying clothes or concert tickets with a credit card you can't pay off exposes you to debt with a high interest rate and with no asset to support it. Doing so also indicates you are living beyond your means. A home, a work car, or a business loan are intended to help you build income or purchase an asset that may grow. Creating future opportunities by investing today can be an appropriate way to increase, not decrease, your financial flexibility over time. A piece of furniture, a new phone, or a nice sweater decreases your flexibility. Just avoid all consumer debt. Live within your means. Use cash to engage in consumption.

Student loans are a gray area. Investing in education is a good thing. But students often fail to understand the payments required for their loans over time or the career prospects (and risks) that might make repayment a challenge. The better choice is to invest in an education you can afford today in a field of study likely to help you enter the career you want with a solid and predictable financial benefit. There are cases where modest student debt may make sense. But you're better off buying the education you can afford right now to give yourself flexibility for the future. Carefully estimate the total cost of the education in your field and then the salary you are likely to earn. If there's a mismatch between the two, pause and pursue your opportunities on a more affordable path.

Choose Experiences, Not Stuff

When Jamaican-born Ike and Natalee Anderson of Palm Beach, Florida, took a DNA test and found out they had genetic lineage from thirty-two countries, they made a radical decision. They sold many of their belongings and took their three young children on a global adventure, intending to travel for a year to explore the broader world and their cultural roots.

The couple ran their marketing agency remotely and determined that trading some financial stability for a unique set of experiences together would be worth any cost. Ike explains how he made this decision:

> I see this journey as a quest to find out who we are, and what we can leave behind. I was thinking to myself one day, "What legacy do I have? What will I leave for my children?"
>
> It's great to leave money behind, but I thought travelling and having the opportunity to learn and giving them an open mindset would be a better gift for them.[22]

The couple homeschooled their kids on the road, visiting places as varied as Cancun, Mexico; Edinburgh, Scotland; Karnak, Egypt; and Bali, Indonesia. What began as a yearlong pilgrimage turned into something more. The Andersons found they loved their journey, which they extended to thirty-six months before settling down in Ghana, West Africa.[23] According to Natalee, "We chose to make Ghana our home, as this was to be Mission Central for the next step of our journey—being of service to a community and a cause greater than ourselves."[24] They turned their experience into a business, arranging similar pilgrimages for others, providing coaching and mentorship, and even starting their Rite of Passage program to help young adults of African ancestry experience the continent.[25]

The Andersons seem to have no regrets about the things they gave up to fund the journey. Natalee has advice for other families:

> I recommend that other families do what we do—the exposure and bonding is just priceless.
>
> I have realisations about our family and how much we've grown. For families who think they may argue or not enjoy the experience, I still think they should try it—you should go towards your biggest fear.[26]

The Andersons' decision isn't right for everyone. It's hard to uproot your kids and travel the world. Even the Andersons eventually settled down. But at the heart of their story is the idea of giving up the things you are often told to prize—particularly, material things—and instead directing your resources toward meaningful experiences shared with others.

When you look back at those purchases that gave you real and lasting joy, what were they?

For me, the most meaningful expenditures have never been on jewelry, TVs, new phones, or other gadgets. Universally, they have been on experiences. Going to the zoo with my daughters, looking for giraffes and monkeys. Enjoying an outdoor concert with my wife and our friends. Going fly-fishing with old classmates. Doing a road trip from San Diego to San Francisco in a rented convertible the winter break I asked my wife to marry me. These moments were ephemeral, but unlike all the physical things I've bought in my life, they have lasted a lifetime. There's research to support the idea that for all of us, it's almost always smarter to spend money on experiences, not stuff.

I first encountered the research behind this principle in the work of Elizabeth Dunn and Michael Norton, whose book *Happy Money* documents five habits for happier spending. Dunn and Norton are respected academics at the University of British Columbia and Harvard Business School, respectively, and their research has focused on what habits of spending make people the happiest. In their book, the very first chapter encourages readers to "buy experiences."[27] The evidence they outline—in both their research and the research of others—is overwhelming. Not only does spending money on experiences rather than things make us happier, but spending too much money on material things can actually make us less happy.

Dunn and Norton demonstrate this in a variety of ways. First, as we've seen, stuff doesn't seem to make people happy. We think it will. We often think new furniture or a new outfit will improve our mood and well-being (so much so that *retail therapy* is a catchphrase for those who process emotions by shopping). But the overwhelming evidence is that shopping does not—even for the types of stuff we often associate with happiness, like a dream home. Dunn and Norton show, for exam-

ple, that homeowners are no happier than renters and that better versus worse housing doesn't result in greater happiness with life overall.
More broadly, they find that in self-reported studies, "57 percent of
Americans reported that experiential purchases made them happier
than material purchases, while only 34 percent reported the opposite."[28] These experiences often tie closely to other aspects of human
flourishing, including happiness, well-being, health, and relational
connection.

In fact, Dunn and Norton highlight several principles that can maximize the impact of the experiences we purchase—whether it's a beach vacation, a night at a concert, or a tasting menu at a Michelin-starred
restaurant (or an equally tasty hole-in-the-wall). Their principles suggest
that experiences are best with any of these characteristics:

- The experience brings you together with other people, fostering a
  sense of social connection.

- The experience makes a memorable story that you'll enjoy retelling
  for years to come.

- The experience is tightly linked to your sense of who you are or
  want to be.

- The experience provides a unique opportunity, eluding easy
  comparison with other available options.

The length of the experience doesn't necessarily matter a great deal,
from a monthlong hike on the Appalachian Trail with a friend to an after-
noon at the theater with an aging parent.

In the summer of 2024, for example, I took my son to watch the Boston Celtics clinch the NBA championship over the Dallas Mavericks. I
was a high school basketball player and have loved the game my whole
life. My then eleven-year-old son was getting interested in basketball,
playing in a league, and watching games with me on TV. Partly because
my wife is from New England and we lived in Boston for several years, he
has grown to love the Celtics, especially his favorite NBA player, Jayson

Tatum. We were on vacation near Boston when the Celtics brought their series with the Dallas Mavericks back from Texas with a 3-to-1 lead. And even though I'd never paid so much for an athletic event, I booked two seats for my son and me. It was one of the best experiences of both of our lives. He was over the moon—singing, cheering, and standing the whole game. We high-fived each other and everyone around us as the crowd watched their home team dominate from start to finish. We waited for the confetti and postgame awards, then fought our way out of the Garden through thousands of revelers to our car. My son fell asleep within five minutes of hitting the road, exhausted from the excitement of the moment.

Using Dunn and Norton's framework, my son and I had a deep social connection (the deepest!). It's a story we tell often (he told it daily for weeks). It's tightly linked to our sense of self—as lovers of the game, as a son and a dad. And it was a unique, once-in-a-lifetime opportunity we may never replicate. Everything about it made the money I paid worth every penny.

So often we are tempted to believe that a physical thing will make us happy. But physical possessions never do. What truly drives happiness is adventure, experience, connection with others, and memories. Those kinds of priceless things are worth the price we pay.

Spend on Time, Health, and Relationships

Choosing experiences and not stuff will certainly offer a happier life. But it might not clearly cover all the areas in which it's best to consume. There are at least three more areas in which consumer spending—spending that is not on an asset or an investment—can be wise: health, time, and relationships. Each of these categories may overlap with experiences, like taking in a baseball game with your daughter (a choice for both experiences and relationships). But sometimes they are discrete. Think of these wiser spending choices as shown in figure 4-1.

We've discussed experiences in depth. Now let's spend a bit of time digging into the other three areas and seeing how they are all interrelated.

FIGURE 4-1

Four key areas for more-meaningful spending

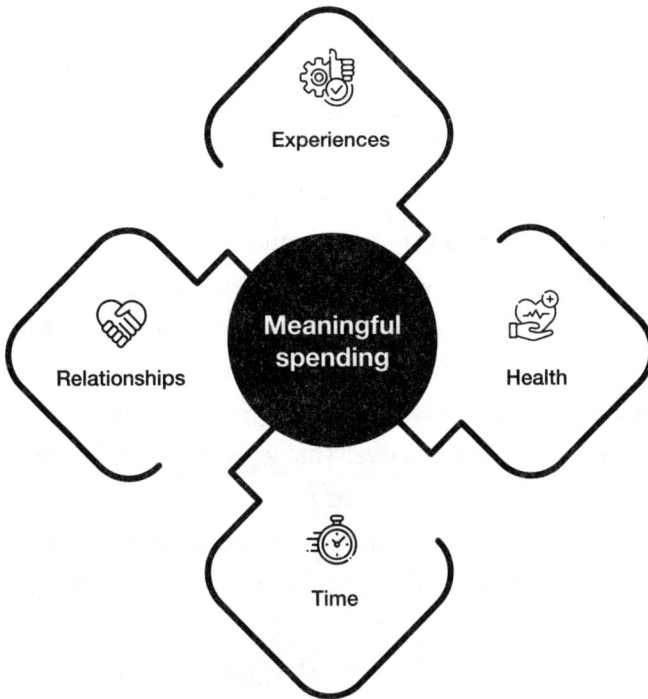

Health

One of Tyler VanderWeele's five key areas of human flourishing is physical and mental health. It is challenging (though not impossible) to live a flourishing life devoid of mental, physical, and spiritual health. They are at the core of how we experience life, enabling engagement in purposeful work and the opportunities to build meaningful relationships. When we do have the money available to spend, starting with wellness is usually a wise decision.

Globally, and particularly in rich nations like the United States, people are plagued by poor mental, spiritual, and physical health. In 2019, one in every eight people (nearly 1 billion) in the world experienced a mental health condition, including anxiety, depression, post-traumatic stress disorder, or other issues. That number skyrocketed as much as 30 percent during the Covid-19 pandemic.[29] Half of all the people in the world will experience mental illness in their lifetime.[30] Mental disorders now account for more than 14 percent of deaths globally, and current rates of mental illness are more than double what they were in 1990—despite the world being safer and wealthier than at any point in the past.[31]

Spiritually, this downslide in health has corresponded with an epidemic of negative emotions and a precipitous decline in religious observance—the primary way in which people traditionally oriented their values and beliefs. Gallup's index of negative emotions finally ticked down in 2024 for the first time in a decade after dramatic climbs, but the world still remains unhappier and lonelier than in the past.[32] Globally, religious adherence is still relatively stable, with the vast majority of the world expressing a belief in a higher power. But that's largely a result of population growth in the most religious societies in Africa, Latin America, and Asia, while religious adherence has collapsed in North America and Europe.[33]

Finally, many societies globally are struggling with deteriorating physical health—often a result of poor choices related to exercise, eating, alcoholism, or substance abuse. Today, more than 80 percent of adolescents and nearly 30 percent of adults do not meet the World Health Organization's guidelines for physical activity as people become more sedentary and attached to desk work and online screens.[34] The prevalence of lower-than-adequate exercise nearly doubled from 2000 to 2022.[35] In 2022, some 43 percent of adults worldwide were overweight.[36] In one sense, this last statistic is a triumph, as malnutrition and hunger are declining globally.[37] But new problems are arising from poor food quality and sedentary lifestyles, factors responsible for the nearly 10 percent of global deaths from obesity.[38] This number may understate the problem, given that poor eating and exercise habits contribute to the other major causes of death like heart disease, cancer, and dementia. These connections are pointed out thoughtfully in the work of health professionals like Peter Attia and Casey Means.

Further, these global trends are often more pronounced in developed countries like the United States, where, for example, an astounding 42 percent of adults are obese and 74 percent are overweight.[39] The trend in obesity is a crucial reason why the US lifespan remains stubbornly below that of many other wealthy countries and seems to have plateaued. These lifespan figures may actually underestimate the problem. *Health span*, a term referring to the amount of time people are in good health while living, might be more appropriate. With so many people suffering from chronic conditions brought about by unhealthy lifestyles, the gap between health span and lifespan has grown.[40]

It's in this context that spending on mental, spiritual, and physical health can be a cornerstone of broader financial flourishing. In this section, as in others, I approach the topic humbly. Many people do live paycheck to paycheck. Many lack the resources for quality medical care or even high-quality fresh foods. That is a challenging and tragic obstacle to overcome. But many people who do have the resources nevertheless choose to spend on poor food or consumer goods rather than healthy choices that could transform their lives.

Some healthy choices can be relatively inexpensive. Joining a local YMCA, for example, is often the cheapest gym option for a whole family in an area, and membership gives access at YMCA locations across the United States. Relatively affordable monitoring devices like the Oura Ring help people be more conscious of their sleep choices, stress, and physical activity. We can reduce our reliance on Uber Eats, DoorDash, or dine-in restaurants by buying healthier whole foods (fruits, vegetables, meats) from the grocery store to reduce costs while improving our health. For mental health, counseling services are becoming more affordable and are often covered by health insurance. A membership in a local church, mosque, or synagogue that invests in spiritual health is free and can provide both relational community and spiritual care. Almost anyone can take more time to read the research on physical and mental health in books like *Blue Zones* and *Outlive*. Or they can listen to excellent podcasts from practitioners and academics like Andrew Huberman or Peter Attia to think through good habits, diet, exercise, and health supplements.

Additional diagnostics recommended by these sources, like calcium scans and bone-density scans, can provide real data to manage health span and lifespan alike.

Many of these tools are free or covered by health insurance. Many are also available for less than the cost of one Uber Eats delivery per month. Their benefits to human flourishing are remarkable. Taking care to exercise regularly, to eat healthy, to monitor major health conditions, to access treatment proactively when those conditions develop, and to access resources for mental and spiritual health is the very foundation of a flourishing life, allowing any of us to live longer, happier, with less pain, and with more energy. And spending on these areas—coupled with the personal discipline to prioritize them—is often well worth it in the benefits it provides to flourishing.

Time

In August 2017, Dunn and Norton, along with a number of coauthors, published an article in the *Proceedings of the National Academy of Sciences* titled "Buying Time Promotes Happiness." The conclusions were intuitive: when we can use money to eliminate things that we don't enjoy but that take away our time, we are happier. Noting the rising prevalence of "time scarcity" in modern society—the feeling that so many of us are harried and overcommitted—the study showed that those who used money to eliminate tasks from which they did not receive joy, whether that be housecleaning or tending to the yard, were happier as a result.[41] Norton and Ashley Whillans examined several studies on this issue in a *Wall Street Journal* article titled "If You Want to Feel Better, Spend Money on Saving Time."[42] Their observations were later echoed in Dunn and Norton's previously described excellent book on wise spending. While it's helpful to have the data to support the idea that spending money to regain time is wise for flourishing, the concept itself is intuitive.

Sometimes the mundane activities in life—folding laundry or gardening, for example—can be cathartic or enjoyable. Not every day-to-day task needs to be eliminated. Some should be delegated to children as a part of their maturation process (which we will discuss later). Often, we simply can't afford to eliminate tasks from our lives. Hiring someone to come wash and dry the dishes, cook every meal, do the laundry, and clean up after pets would be amazing for almost all of us—but also cost prohibitive. Those who use private jets often refer to them as "time machines," reveling in the moments they save that would otherwise be wasted in TSA lines and connections.[43] But the cost of private jets makes them unavailable to most of us.

Where we can marshal the resources to save time on an activity we don't love—even if it crowds out some consumer spending—that's often a good idea. It's particularly important if it makes room for us to invest in activities deeply linked with human flourishing, like relationships.

Early in our marriage, my wife and I decided we would gladly forgo material things in order to get time together. We have four young children whom we love. But we also know it's important for us to have one-on-one time as a couple, and we try to have one date per week where it's just us. These dates are often cheap or free—a hike in the park, a few hours at the museum, or a grocery shopping trip together where we have the space to talk. But given the ages of our kids, they always require babysitting, which can be expensive. We made the choice that we could buy cheaper clothes and cars to make room in our budget to get childcare for the kids so that we could spend alone time together. And we've never regretted the decision.

In 2017, I remember reading research on the relationship between commuting and happiness. We live in Atlanta, a city known for its difficult traffic. There were many studies documenting what we all know—sitting in traffic on long commutes can make us frustrated and unhappy. At that time, though, one study showed that adding twenty minutes to a commute led to as much unhappiness as a 19 percent pay cut.[44] And while there are cheap ways to mitigate the mental costs of a tough commute in the modern world—including podcasts, audiobooks, and Bluetooth-enabled calls—the fundamental truth is that time spent in the car commuting to work or school is time spent away from loved ones or fulfilling work. So, when we moved in 2018, we decided we would pay a little more for a house if we could find one that optimized the commutes we each had to work and school. We found a home five minutes from the kids' school and only fifteen minutes from my work. This location made it easier for each of us to catch dance recitals or to make it home safely to have dinner as a family. We "bought" time by reducing our commute, and that gave us more space to engage in the relationships we hold most dear.

Time is one of life's most precious commodities. And time savings are within reach, particularly if we consciously control our spending on less fruitful items. Hiring someone to deep clean once a month, securing babysitters occasionally to get time out of the house, or ordering groceries from a grocery delivery service, for example, are often feasible for those who budget consciously. Spending a little money to avoid things we don't want to do and to make free time for things we enjoy can lead to greater fulfillment.

Relationships

Nothing in life drives fulfillment, happiness, and flourishing as much as the depth and breadth of our positive relationships. This is echoed in the works of Seligman and VanderWeele and was the primary finding of Harvard's legendary Grant Study, the key conclusion of which was that "happiness equals love—full stop."[45] Central to Dunn and Norton's work on happiness and money is not just the idea of choosing experiences rather than stuff but also the concept of focusing on the experiences we enjoy with others. What's better than a trip to the Grand Canyon? A trip to the Grand Canyon with our spouse or partner and kids. What's better than a tour of Europe? Doing that tour with three of your closest friends. How can you improve a theater outing? By taking it with a parent or sibling, laughing together at the performances.

The best time we can buy is time with those we love. Using that time to take a son to a chess tournament or to watch a daughter's diving practice is priceless.

As a general rule, every experience is better when done with someone we care for. Expenses are worthwhile when they deepen or broaden relationships. Even for the introverts of the world, there is no substitute for living in community with others.

A wise approach to spending, wherever possible, is to spend in ways that give us more time with others and deepen our positive relationships in the world. Invite someone else to join you on a special trip. Pay the extra cost to get tickets for your kids to the art exhibit you've been wanting to see. Forgo a little extra pay if the alternative gives you the time to spend with loved ones.

Relationships are at the very center of human flourishing. They have been shown not just to increase happiness but also to improve longevity, a connection noted in numerous studies and in Dan Buettner's book *Blue Zones*, which reviewed the areas of the world with the most centenarians.[46] That book concluded that a key factor in living longer was living in community with others.

Smash Your Idols

The 1956 movie *The Ten Commandments* is a classic cinematic epic. Based on the story of Moses leading the Israelites out of slavery in Egypt and attempting to help them re-form their nation, the film is headlined by unforgettable performances by Charlton Heston and Yul Brynner. One climactic scene toward the end of the film stands out. The Israelites have finally escaped bondage in Egypt and are now seeking to renew their national identity and shape the future. Moses goes up on a high mountain to receive instruction, which he records on two stone tablets as the Ten Commandments. But when he returns from the mountain, he finds his people not worshipping the God who freed them but an idol—a golden calf. Enraged, Moses smashes the idol with the stone tablets and the golden calf explodes, killing the worshippers nearby.

We human beings often go astray when we obsess over the wrong things at the expense of those things that can truly lead to human flourishing. When we find that some material thing—or consumption itself—

has become an idol like the one that enraged Heston's Moses, the right answer sometimes isn't just to deprioritize it but to smash it. Rather than limiting that thing's influence over us, we must eliminate it entirely by deciding ahead of time that we won't pursue it.

In his remarkable article (later a book), "How Will You Measure Your Life?," the late Clayton Christensen laid out a host of important principles. One of the most compelling to me is "100 percent of the time is easier than 98 percent of the time."[47] Christensen, a Mormon, observed the Sabbath—a concept common among a number of faiths that one should rest one day per week and not engage in any work. Early in his life, Christensen played on a basketball team. The team had a championship game on a Sunday (Christensen's Sabbath day), and Christensen was tempted to play but made the difficult decision not to. He realized that throughout life, there would always be temptations to break his Sabbath "just once" for an important event, and if he started making exceptions, he would never stop. So, he set a hard-and-fast rule to keep Sunday clear, no matter what. He realized that such a rule was easier to keep than a flexible one.

In the same way, alcoholics who idolize drinking often need to swear off alcohol entirely. Even though some nonalcoholics can have a glass of wine or beer with no issue, an alcoholic recognizes the uniquely tempting and distorting influence of the substance in their lives. They realize that controlling its influence is easier 100 percent of the time than 98 percent of the time—because that 2 percent will inevitably lead to more. When you find yourself idolizing something that is difficult to control, sometimes the best thing is to simply put that thing behind you, to smash it. And material consumption can be very much like that.

In the academic literature, such an approach is often referred to as *precommitment*, and it's one of the most widely confirmed and helpful psychological tools any of us can employ to make better decisions, limit temptations, and offer ourselves freedom. Precommitment is deciding, in advance, to limit your future choices. The topic has been written about in books as diverse as Dan Ariely's *Predictably Irrational*, Angela Duckworth's *Grit*, and Jon Elster's *Ulysses and the Sirens*. Elster uses the vivid example of the Greek hero Ulysses (Ulysses is the Latinized term for the Greek hero Odysseus) in Homer's classic work, *The Odyssey*. In that tale, the Sirens are dangerous figures who lead sailors to their deaths by luring them into shipwrecks with their irresistible songs. In that sense, the Sirens are a metaphor for all temptation. Ulysses is warned of the sirens by a sorceress, Circe. To avoid the perils of the Sirens, Ulysses has his men plug their ears with beeswax and binds himself to the mast of the ship, telling his crew: "She [Circe] said we must avoid the voices of the otherworldly Sirens; steer past their flowering meadow. And she says that I alone should hear their singing. Bind me, to keep me upright at the mast, wound round with rope. If I beseech you and command you to set me free, you must increase my bonds and chain even tighter."[48] Elster uses this scene as a demonstration of precommitment. Sometimes the only way to deal with something that we know is too tempting to enjoy even minimally in our lives is to precommit to not having it at all.

Of course, that approach doesn't work with all consumption goods. We often become obsessed with consumer goods that in their basic forms are necessities: cars, phones, clothes. We can't precommit to not having those things without living as hermits or bypassing contemporary conveniences. But we can precommit to eschewing an obsession with those items by smashing our idols and dedicating ourselves to the least nice versions of them that are minimally functional.

For instance, what if you find you're obsessing over the latest mobile phone—whether yours is nice enough, what it says about you, and which of your friends' is better? Buy the oldest functional phone you can, and eliminate any aspiration in that category (keep the cracks in your screen, too). Self-conscious that your nice car isn't as nice as one of your friends' vehicles? Fully commit to not caring, buy a used minivan, and precommit that nice cars aren't the way you measure your self-worth. Spending more money on clothes than quality food or time with your children? Sell the nice clothes on eBay, and buy a new wardrobe from a secondhand shop. Nothing is inherently wrong with a well-made car, phone, or jacket (though many luxury goods today aren't well made but are transparently poorly made status symbols). These items become problematic when they become idols that distract you from the more important things in life, that is, significant things that lead you and those around you to flourish.

In 1913, Arthur "Pop" Momand launched a comic strip that ran until 1940. Called *Keeping Up with the Joneses*, the strip tells the story of the McGinis family, who obsess over social status and spend all their time trying to match the material wealth of their neighbors, the eponymous Joneses (who actually never appear in the strip). The humor of the strip was in the obvious social climbing of the McGinis family. Their actions, far from making them happy, made them miserable. The strip was written at a time when Americans were thinking deeply and publicly debating about whether we were overly concerned with the trappings of material wealth. In 1899, economist Thorstein Veblen coined the term *conspicuous consumption* in his *Theory of the Leisure Class*. The book put a label to the habit (which was really a permanent fixture of human nature) of buying things—flashy clothes, houses, or other items—that are valuable to us not because they truly make our lives better but because they signal to others our economic power and status. These idols have little real worth. They are false measures of self-worth that we worship because we think others do. They lead us down a dangerous path of comparison, materialism, and insecurity.

No material thing defines your worth as a person. And an overfocus on what certain objects say about your status relative to others' is a path to perpetual insecurity and unhappiness. There will always be someone richer. There will always be a nicer car or watch. There will always be a better house. Most of the time for most people, that doesn't matter. We are happy with our cars and unworried whether our neighbor has a nicer one. We enjoy our homes, phones, and clothes and don't think about them too much. But if you find yourself idolizing something that won't lead to flourishing, sometimes the best answer isn't to moderate your consumption of that idol. Instead, let it go entirely, precommitting to abstaining from it or, when it's a necessity, obtaining only the thing's most basic version that can work for you. Doing so can even be a fun, contrarian way of living that allows you to challenge the societal norms that tell you to live a life of endless consumption.

Consume Less

A captivating part of Walter Isaacson's biography of legendary Apple founder Steve Jobs is his portrait of Jobs's minimalism. Famously single-minded about simplifying design and life (a preoccupation that allowed Apple to craft some of the most elegant and beautiful hardware in computing), Jobs was similarly fanatical in his personal life. He liked to wear the same outfit every day to eliminate choice, buying multiples of the same shirts and pants. Even when he was fabulously wealthy, he kept the furnishings in his house incredibly sparse, only purchasing things that were essential.

This minimalism was probably both an ingrained piece of Jobs's personality and an outgrowth of his adopted Buddhist faith, which emphasizes simplicity and the idea of enjoyment without attachment, which we explored earlier.[49] Buddhism advocates leading a simple life and avoiding materialism, embracing instead a form of minimalism in which you only buy what you need and give away what you do not.[50] In a modern world in which stuff is so often equated with status and is more readily available than at any other point in human history, this has ignited a contemporary movement toward minimalism—the idea of buying and owning less.

Overconsumption is particularly acute in the United States, though the culture of acquisition is spreading globally, an outgrowth of historical levels of prosperity and the innate human desire to own more. In 2015, *Time* magazine wrote a feature on Elinor Ochs's decade-long study on hyperacquisition. The first house Ochs's team analyzed had 2,260 visible possessions . . . in just three rooms. The article noted that while US kids are 3 percent of the global child population, they buy 40 percent of the world's toys, even as their parents spend tens of billions of dollars on self-storage to try to declutter their homes and garages, which are literally bursting at the seams—so much so that the average move in the United States weighs 8,000 pounds.[51]

These things don't make us happy. And they crowd our lives in counterproductive ways. Americans have so much stuff, we buy books, tools, and other gadgets to help us deal with the clutter. Americans aren't the only culprits, as the average British woman owns thirty to thirty-five pairs of shoes (the average British man, eighteen pairs).[52] And our ongoing desire for more stuff seems insatiable even as we recognize the problems with such limitless acquisition.

In the preceding sections, I laid out things better to spend money on than stuff—experiences, health, relationships, and time. But there's one more overarching lesson: just buy less, period. Most of us are at the point where we do not need more clothes, shoes, gadgets, furniture, art, or other material things. To be sure, some people struggle with deprivation, as the rising homelessness crisis in many US cities shows. There remains desperate poverty for hundreds of millions of people around the world. But for billions of others, the question is really how to be happy in the midst not of deprivation but of excess.

One study of millennials out of the University of Arizona, for example, found that young people who saved more and spent less reported higher well-being and lower stress.[53] This is concordant with a study from the University of Minnesota that showed that having fewer choices for consumption items can generally increase happiness.[54] In a review of much of the academic literature on the subject, four academics reached a simple conclusion: "The majority of selected studies suggest that reduced consumption is associated with higher levels of well-being or that there is not a significant relationship. Others indicate potential negative effects. The results suggest that reducing consumption does not typically have a negative association with the well-being of consumers in wealthy nations."[55]

In October 2009, Joshua Fields Millburn lost his mother to lung cancer, and his marriage to divorce. From this existential crisis, he began to embrace a movement called minimalism and became one of its chief evangelists. It started with his mother's possessions. Rather than renting a storage unit for them, he donated them. Millburn connected with a childhood friend, Ryan Nicodemus, and the two began to downsize their lifestyles in radical ways—moving into smaller homes, decluttering, giving many of their things away. They helped launch a movement of minimalism that has caught fire with many around the world. Millburn and Nicodemus found that far from making their lives more difficult, this process of consuming less was freeing practically, spiritually, and emotionally.[56]

Millburn says that the goal of this change in lifestyle is to fight the temptations and pressures of consumption and, by doing so, to make room for the things that matter. I've articulated these things earlier in this chapter: experiences, relationships, health and well-being:

> Minimalism starts with reducing our material possessions, but the purpose of minimalism has to do with the benefits we experience once we're on the other side of decluttering. Hence, removing the clutter is not the end result; it is merely the first step.
>
> Sure, we feel a weight lifted right away, but we don't experience lasting contentment by just getting rid of our stuff. Minimalism doesn't work like that. It is possible to get rid of everything you own and still be utterly miserable. That's because consumption is not the problem. Compulsory consumption is the problem. And we can change that by being more deliberate with the decisions we make every day . . .
>
> As a minimalist, I don't focus on having less, less, less; I focus on making room for more: more time, more passion, more experiences, more growth, more contribution, more contentment. More freedom. Clearing the clutter from life's path helps make that room.[57]

Minimalism of the type Millburn and Nicodemus embrace is an admittedly radical lifestyle change, and it's not for everyone. But the core of its insights is well supported by both the scientific literature on the topic and the admonitions of philosophical systems as varied as Buddhism, Stoicism, and Christianity: love of stuff, like love of money, is a dangerous path. It's an endless pursuit that can make life more complex and difficult rather than more fulfilling. Learning to care less for material possessions and be much more deliberate in our pursuit of them can yield far more lasting joy.

Regarding stuff, Steve Jobs is right: less is more. Consuming less gives us the money for more fulfilling purchases, investments, or giving. It allows us to savor those things we do buy, emphasizing quality over quantity. We could all benefit from a new motto of "buy less, enjoy more." Almost anyone reading this book should consider halting new purchases for a while and decluttering what they have, making mental and physical space for the things that are truly valuable in our lives.

Chapter 5

Give Generously and Well

Yvon Chouinard was born in Lewiston, Maine, in 1938. His father was a handyman, plumber, and mechanic who transplanted the family to Southern California when Yvon was nine years old. Yvon started rock climbing in 1953 as a fourteen-year-old member of the Southern California Falconry Club. A club leader, Don Prentice, taught the boys how to rappel down the cliffs to the falcon aeries.[1] Chouinard was hooked, eventually becoming a leading figure in the golden age of Yosemite climbing. He made daring first ascents on the North American Wall (Yosemite National Park, California), the north face of Mount Edith Cavell (Alberta), and the north face of Mount Sir Donald (Glacier National Park, British Columbia), among many others.

To save money on equipment, he taught himself blacksmithing and made his own climbing tools.[2] In 1957, he bought a used coal forge, an anvil, some tongs, and a hammer and began making pitons. When friends wanted to buy them, he built a small shop in his parents' backyard in Burbank, and he started selling them out of the back of his car. He lived hand to mouth, "[taking] pride in the fact that climbing ricks and icefalls had no economic value."[3]

In 1965, he formalized the business with fellow climber Tom Frost, founding Chouinard Equipment and redesigning various climbing tools to make them stronger and lighter. In 1967, they moved the business to a rustic tin shed in Ventura.[4] By 1970, Chouinard Equipment was the leading supplier of niche climbing equipment in the United States. Chouinard started to sell rugby shirts to grow the business in 1972 and started to experiment with new materials for climbing and outdoor clothing at that time, just as he had with pitons and other climbing equipment fifteen years earlier.

Alongside Chouinard Equipment (which eventually became Black Diamond Equipment after a bankruptcy in 1989), Chouinard founded a company for his experiments in clothing in 1973, and he named the company Patagonia.

From its start in that shed in Ventura, Patagonia was a different company. It was an innovator, focused on new materials to enhance performance and reduce environmental impact and introducing vibrant colors to the outdoor clothing space—previously dominated by tans and blacks. Employees could wear whatever they wanted to work, even coming barefoot, and often surfed or played volleyball on breaks. Patagonia sponsored ski and climbing trips, had a cafeteria for healthy food, and insisted on on-site daycare for employees' children. Chouinard committed 10 percent of its profits to philanthropy in 1986, ultimately pledging 1 percent of revenue (profit or not). And over the decades, Patagonia became a leader not just in innovating the outdoor clothing and equipment space but also in committing itself, corporately, to improving the environment.[5]

It also became one of the largest and most successful clothing companies in the world. By 2022, Patagonia, still a private company owned predominantly by Chouinard, was making $1.5 billion in revenue per year, was employing three thousand people, was earning perhaps $100 million in annual profits, and was worth an estimated $3 billion.[6] It was at that point that Chouinard decided to give it all away.

Chouinard (along with his wife and two children) put all the company's stock into a charitable trust designed to fight climate change. Every dollar in profit made by the company, beyond that needed to reinvest in the business, would be given away to environmental charities via the Patagonia Purpose Trust and the Holdfast Collective. Chouinard explained the decision at the time: "While we're doing our best to address the environmental crisis, it's not enough. We needed to find a way to put more money into fighting the crisis while keeping the company's values intact. . . . Truth be told, there were no good options available. So, we created our own."[7]

Chouinard wasn't the first entrepreneur to take such a dramatic step. Kristin Groos Richmond and Kirsten Saenz Tobey did that with Revolution Foods. They created a B Corp dedicated to building a healthy, financially sustainable company to provide high-quality food to public schools but to do so while giving back philanthropically to education systems.[8] Bea Dixon did that with the Honey Pot Company, a women's plant-based hygiene company that dedicates a portion of its profits to charities involving women's health.[9] Casey Crawford, mentioned in a previous chapter, had done the same with Movement Mortgage almost from its inception. Alan and Katherine Barnhart had done the same with Barnhart Crane—eschewing personal wealth and opting instead for giving collectively alongside their employees.[10] But Chouinard's decision at Patagonia was one of the most widely heralded and one in line with all his prior focus as a company. The man who loved climbing because "it had no economic value" proved he wasn't in business for the money but was in it for his love of the outdoors and the impact his work could have.

Examples of giving well don't come only from billionaires or entrepreneurs. Ronald Read, for example, was born in 1921 and was a US Army veteran who had served honorably in World War II. After the war, he settled in Vermont, where he spent twenty-five years as a gas station attendant and mechanic and then seventeen years as a janitor at J.C. Penney. After his wife died, he never remarried, and he retired in 1997—possessed of simple habits and hobbies that kept him occupied. After retirement, he used to read at the coffee shop attached to Brattleboro Memorial Hospital, and when it closed, he switched to the Brooks Memorial Library. His life seemed unremarkable—at least until Read's death in 2014, when this retired janitor's estate was found to be worth $8 million. Two million dollars went to his stepchildren and caregivers, and the remainder went to the hospital and library that had provided him so much comfort.[11]

I'm sure Chouinard is no pauper, and he and his family live comfortably. But what Chouinard, Read, Dixon, Groos Richmond, and so many others have realized is a salient fundamental point about money: there is no better use of it than helping others.

Money can buy you lots of material possessions. But none of those things can match the fulfillment you get by dedicating your resources to worthwhile causes and people. These don't always have to be charities, as we will see. You can help someone directly when they are down on their luck in even more powerful ways than giving formally to charity. And you don't have to give everything away. Most faith and philosophical traditions simply articulate a percentage of your income that must be given to others—a precommitment strategy echoed in the tithe that Chouinard originally made at Patagonia and that Dixon implemented at the Honey Pot Company.

But regardless of the method you choose for helping others and regardless of how much of your money you dedicate to it, the act of selflessly giving is one of the most important core values of a flourishing financial life. Money simply cannot be good in your life without the essential act of helping others.

The Foundations of Generosity

Generosity is the foundation of Good Money. Each of us has an opportunity to live in a way that loves and cares for others financially. All of the anecdotal and scientific evidence we have indicates that doing so allows us to thrive more fully even as we invest in the flourishing of others. Giving also forces us to end any unhealthy attachment to money.

The command to help others is nearly universal among major belief systems. In Hinduism, generosity is termed *dana* and is a firm part of followers' dharma, or religious duty. The Bhagavad Gita goes further, stating that the right type of giving is done with no expectation of return.[12] Buddhism, sharing some roots with Hinduism, similarly explains that giving, or dana, "is about generosity, openness, and our capacity to embrace others with compassion and love."[13] The Koran instructs followers to give freely to others—not just money but also time, help, and kindness.[14] In

Proverbs 11:24, King Solomon noted, "A generous person will prosper; whoever refreshes others will be refreshed." And Jesus commanded his followers in Luke 12:33, "Sell your possessions and give to the poor. Provide purses for yourselves that will not wear out, a treasure in heaven that will never fail, where no thief comes near and no moth destroys."

Other great thinkers, considering morality apart from religion, similarly highlight the importance of generosity. Utilitarianism reasons that those with stable material possessions—the threshold levels of wealth we explored earlier—should dedicate their resources to helping others.[15] And utilitarianism's most famous (or perhaps infamous) modern strain, effective altruism, is an entire philosophy dedicated to material generosity.[16] Immanuel Kant, meanwhile, argued that charity is restitution for past injustice, writing that "charity therefore is an act of duty imposed upon us by the rights of others and the debt we owe to them."[17]

Why does almost every serious strain of moral thinking agree on this topic? Perhaps selflessness, generosity, and love for others are essential not just to individual flourishing but also to the flourishing of our families, communities, countries, and the world more broadly. Without these traits, life is truly, as Thomas Hobbes once described it, "nasty, brutish, and short."[18] As modern social science has developed, the evidence has proven the wisdom in these ancient traditions: helping others, including with our financial resources, is as good for us as it is for those we serve.

In a report titled "The Science of Generosity" prepared for the John Templeton Foundation, Summer Allen, a researcher at the University of California, Berkeley, conducted a thoughtful literature review of both the impact of generosity on people and generosity's origins in our species.[19] Allen notes the benefits of generosity across almost all dimensions of human flourishing. Serving or giving to others has identifiable benefits to physical health, including things like "blood pressure, hearing, sleep quality, and other conditions." Volunteering delays death, and (perhaps morbidly) when you study couples where one spouse volunteers and the other doesn't, the service-minded one lives longer.[20]

These benefits are, if anything, even more pronounced in psychological health and well-being. Allen notes that the psychological effects of generosity start early in life: "One study found that toddlers younger than two exhibited more happiness when giving treats to a puppet than when receiving treats themselves and were even happier when they gave some treats from their own bowl." Another study of 632 Americans found that "spending money on other people was associated with significantly greater happiness, regardless of income, whereas there was no association between spending on oneself and happiness." This association held for as little as $5.[21]

Unsurprisingly, generosity has major benefits for relationships. Multiple studies have found that a mindset of generosity (financial and otherwise) and small acts of kindness benefit marriages and romantic relationships more broadly, leading to great relational satisfaction. Others found that generosity can break the cycle of antagonism when relationships go wrong and can build higher levels of trust between people.[22] Across the board, generosity is linked with greater mental and physical health, more happiness and life satisfaction, and better, more trusting relationships. As Jenny Santi wrote in a *Time* magazine article titled "The Secret to Happiness Is Helping Others":

> Scientific research provides compelling data to support the anecdotal evidence that giving is a powerful pathway to personal growth and lasting happiness. Through fMRI technology, we now know that giving activates the same parts of the brain that are stimulated by food and sex. Experiments show evidence that altruism is hardwired in the brain—and it's pleasurable. Helping others may just be the secret to living a life that is not only happier but also healthier, wealthier, more productive, and meaningful.[23]

So why aren't we more generous? The aggregate studies reveal that despite an intellectual understanding of the benefits of helping others, we are incredibly stingy with our giving. The United States is the most charitable nation on Earth in terms of charitable dollars given as a percentage of GDP, but Americans still only donate 1.44 percent of their

FIGURE 5-1

Charitable giving as a percentage of GDP in selected countries

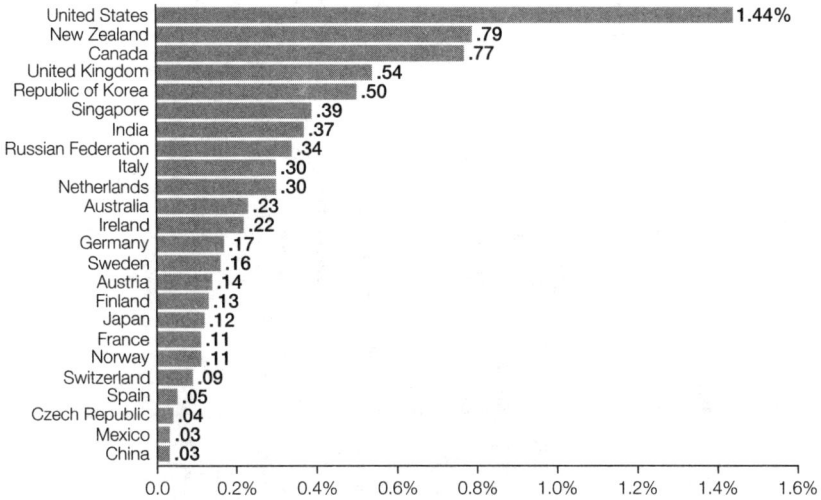

Country	Percentage
United States	1.44%
New Zealand	.79
Canada	.77
United Kingdom	.54
Republic of Korea	.50
Singapore	.39
India	.37
Russian Federation	.34
Italy	.30
Netherlands	.30
Australia	.23
Ireland	.22
Germany	.17
Sweden	.16
Austria	.14
Finland	.13
Japan	.12
France	.11
Norway	.11
Switzerland	.09
Spain	.05
Czech Republic	.04
Mexico	.03
China	.03

Source: Charities Aid Foundation, "Gross Domestic Philanthropy: An International Analysis of GDP, Tax and Giving," January 2016, https://www.cafonline.org/docs/default-source/about-us-policy-and-campaigns /gross-domestic-philanthropy-feb-2016.pdf.

GDP each year. The second-most generous country, Canada, gives less than half that percentage, and only .03 percent of Chinese GDP goes to charitable causes.[24] This data is from a 2016 report, as global surveys are conducted infrequently (figure 5-1). More recent US statistics show that by 2023, charitable giving was relatively flat, hovering around 2 percent of GDP, even when both individuals and corporations are taken into account.[25]

Formal charitable giving as a percentage of income or GDP, of course, is only one measure of generosity. The 2023 World Giving Index focuses on broader definitions of giving—including not the percentage given but instead the percentage of those who give, volunteer, and help others. It ranks Indonesia as the most generous country, with 82 percent of adults donating money and 61 percent engaging in volunteer service—compared with 61 percent and 38 percent, respectively, in the fifth-ranked United States.[26] But even those are paltry numbers, and they only get worse in the

FIGURE 5-2

Three components of global charitable behavior: Top ten and bottom ten nations

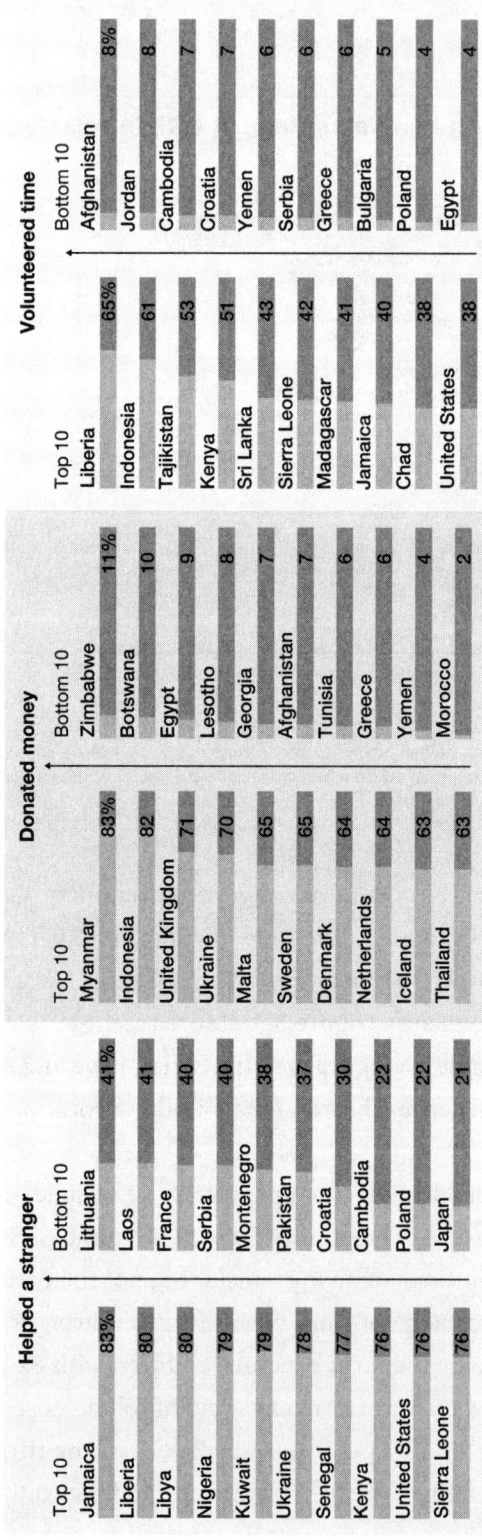

Helped a stranger

Top 10		Bottom 10	
Jamaica	83%	Lithuania	41%
Liberia	80	Laos	41
Libya	80	France	40
Nigeria	79	Serbia	40
Kuwait	79	Montenegro	38
Ukraine	78	Pakistan	37
Senegal	77	Croatia	30
Kenya	76	Cambodia	22
United States	76	Poland	22
Sierra Leone	76	Japan	21

Donated money

Top 10		Bottom 10	
Myanmar	83%	Zimbabwe	11%
Indonesia	82	Botswana	10
United Kingdom	71	Egypt	9
Ukraine	70	Lesotho	8
Malta	65	Georgia	7
Sweden	65	Afghanistan	7
Denmark	64	Tunisia	6
Netherlands	64	Greece	6
Iceland	63	Yemen	4
Thailand	63	Morocco	2

Volunteered time

Top 10		Bottom 10	
Liberia	65%	Afghanistan	8%
Indonesia	61	Jordan	8
Tajikistan	53	Cambodia	7
Kenya	51	Croatia	7
Sri Lanka	43	Yemen	6
Sierra Leone	42	Serbia	6
Madagascar	41	Greece	6
Jamaica	40	Bulgaria	5
Chad	38	Poland	4
United States	38	Egypt	4

Source: Charities Aid Foundation, "World Giving Index 2023: Global Trends in Generosity," https://www.cafonline.org/docs/default-source/updated-pdfs-for-the-new-website/world-giving -index-2023.pdf.

vast majority of countries in the world, where charitable giving and volunteering outside the bounds of the family are often quite uncommon (figure 5-2).

In large and small ways, most people have some impulse for generosity. But given the overwhelming evidence that generosity makes our lives better in almost every way, the fact that Americans donate less than 2 percent of their productive output to others—and that's as charitable as anyone in the world—means there is great room for improvement. We all seem to know it's better to give than to receive, but we find it exceedingly difficult to actually act on that. Through this failure, we are actively handicapping our own ability to achieve true flourishing.

The previous analysis is incomplete because it simply focuses on the good that comes to us when we are generous—the way our own happiness, satisfaction, health, and relationships improve. It doesn't adequately capture how generosity can transform the lives of those around us. In my conversation with Tyler VanderWeele, he noted that true human flourishing is communal, meaning it's difficult to claim that we as individuals are flourishing if we are not in some way contributing to the flourishing of the individuals and communities around us. That's where those fixated on individual well-being but closed off to helping others fall so desperately short. It's difficult to say we are truly living purposefully, relationally, and healthfully if we are not making others' lives better. And that's where giving is the most powerful. It's a force multiplier that has the power to make the lives of the giver, the recipient, and the community better all at once.

When I was a high school senior, I knew that I needed scholarships to attend college (which I would supplement by working). I was very fortunate to receive support from generous donors, and I never forgot the opportunity they provided. My wife and I now have the opportunity to similarly donate in our own limited ways to student scholarships at my alma mater Berry College, particularly to the Griswell Scholars, named in honor of a wonderful philanthropist named Barry Griswell. The scholarship supports young people who have overcome the most difficult circumstances in life. We know firsthand how that

act of generosity, small but meaningful for us now, can be transformative in the life of a young person. Even more dramatically, we get to see
how financial generosity can transform the poorest lives and communities. Many of the most profound leaders I know of are dedicating
their lives to serving needy people and communities in the world:
Zaman International's Najah Bazzy, CARE International's Sofia Spre-
chman Sineiro, International Justice Mission's Gary Haugen, and
World Vision's Edgar Sandoval Sr. I've had the great privilege of seeing
how their sacrifices and those of their donors are breaking the barriers
of homelessness, poverty, and human trafficking to allow otherwise-
desperate people and communities the opportunities to flourish and be
generous to others.

Generosity is powerful, but how can we do it well? We'll explore simple
tools and strategies to be more generous and make money good in the remainder of this chapter.

Simply Put, Give More

The first step to giving generously is just that: giving more. If, on average,
most of us give 2 percent or less of our income to charity, there is ample
room for the vast majority of people globally to allocate a greater portion
of their income and wealth to serving others. There are at least four ways
to do this. I call these approaches the four Ps of giving: percentage, passion, partner, and participate (figure 5-3).

Become a percentage giver

As explored in chapter 4, precommitment is a powerful psychological
tool. First explored by economist Robert Strotz in 1956, precommitment
is the idea that when we decide ahead of time to do something and take
meaningful action to do so (e.g., informing someone about our decision
or asking someone to hold us accountable), we are more likely to follow
through on that commitment.[27] If we want to abide by a budget, it's better
not to make decisions on spending in the moment. We're better off doing

FIGURE 5-3

The four Ps of better giving

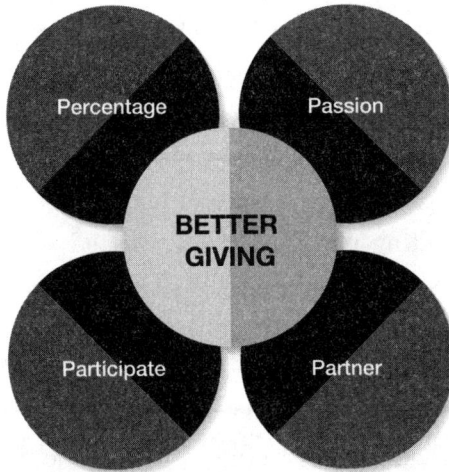

so ahead of time, often with the support of a friend or financial adviser. If we want to get healthy, we may enter into a competition with friends, buy a gym membership, or work on a plan with a personal trainer. And if we want to behave more charitably, we can commit a percentage of our income ahead of time and take meaningful steps to ensure that we actually set aside this income. We can build charitable giving into our budget. We can do so while telling a religious leader, a spouse or partner, or a friend about our plans. Or we can even take steps to set aside monthly a certain amount of money that we cannot touch and that is given directly to charity.

This is particularly possible with the advent of modern donor-advised funds (DAFs). Pioneered in 1931 in the United States, DAFs allow givers to donate consistently to a fund held in their name and then to remit those funds to charities at the right time.[28] The DAF structure is significantly less costly and complex than a private foundation and is easy to use. It enables you to be a consistent percentage giver (a DAF, for example, can simply withdraw a predetermined percentage of your income from your bank account every month) and then thoughtfully distribute that to underlying charities as decisions are made. Once funds are deposited in a DAF, they can't be taken back—hence the precommitment—but givers can base their giving out of the DAFs to carefully evaluate the charities they want to support.

In this way, a DAF works almost like income tax withholdings—a strategy used by the federal and state governments in the United States to minimize the psychological pain of taxation on taxpayers by automatically withholding pay in each pay period without the taxpayer having any say in that decision. DAFs also have the virtue of preventing givers from scrambling at busy times of the year, like Christmas, to do their annual giving, perhaps contributing less than they should or giving to charities they haven't properly evaluated. By donating to a DAF each month and then carefully selecting the charities you choose to support on an ongoing basis, you end up precommitting to charity, giving more than you might otherwise, and having the time and space to thoughtfully evaluate the charities you want to support. You avoid decision fatigue in your charitable giving and give more freely and joyfully.[29]

Pick things you are passionate about

This may seem obvious, but it's easier to give to things we are passionate about than things we are not. Many people around the world give tactically, not strategically. We round up a purchase at the grocery store or give to a cause a friend asks us to. We buy a seat or table at a charitable banquet. We give impulsively when asked by someone on the street. None of those actions are necessarily bad things, but they are rarely the right way to develop a mindset of generosity and build a habit of giving.

To become passionate about giving, you must be passionate about the causes you are giving to. My wife and I, for example, are passionate about opportunity creation, particularly through education. Both of us know how impactful education has been on our lives, and we have seen how transformational it can be on the lives of others. As someone born into a home with few material resources, I benefited from the good schools and teachers who gave me the opportunity to pursue a career I could never have otherwise contemplated. My wife, as a researcher on child development and psychology, a former classroom teacher, and a child counselor, has seen how the right educational environments can transform the lives of kids from even the most challenging of circumstances. Giving to children and to educational causes in service of hoping to create equal opportunity in their lives has become a passion of ours.

Giving to charities in these areas is far from a burden and ignites our passion. That doesn't mean we don't believe in charities supporting cancer treatment, clean water, or animal welfare, for example. Far from it. Each of those causes is worthy. But we focus our time and attention on the things we are most passionate about. Doing so helps us to give more cheerfully, to engage more deeply, and to make a stronger commitment to them.

This combination of your time, talent, and resources is often the most powerful way to give—and it's only possible when we have a personal passion for the causes we support. The Philanthropic Initiative, a nonprofit advisory firm, found in its report "Passion: Discovering the Meaning in Your Philanthropy" that high on the list of motivators for increased charitable giving among the wealthy was "finding a passion." In the report, the initiative's founder, Peter Karloff, underscores this observation: "The alignment of one's passion to one's giving is often elusive, but worth the search. The reward is that your gift giving becomes the best possible articulation of your core values and belief systems and at the same time becomes a direct link to those issues within community and society that you deem to be of greatest significance. The payoff is in the immense personal satisfaction that comes when your generosity is grounded in what you feel is the most important."[30]

What are you passionate about? What causes have impacted you or your family directly? What could you pour not just your money but also your time and talent into? Finding the areas you are most passionate about will ensure that you give consistently and tirelessly. If we all do that, worthy charities of all types will thrive.

Partner with family and friends

One of the charities my family and I support is called Compassion International. We have four young children and care deeply for child welfare, education, and health. Founded by Everett Swanson in 1952 (though the current name took shape eleven years later), Compassion International allows people to sponsor children in impoverished areas by focusing on holistic childhood development. Kids sponsored by this charity receive financial support from families who help to pay for things like food, education, and health care with the intent of creating opportunity for those who might otherwise not have it. Even better is that one of the key ways to give is to sponsor an individual child. A family matches with a specific individual in another country and gives monthly to that child throughout their entire young life. For us, this has looked like sponsoring a child for each of our own children. We find someone the same age as that child in another country, and then we make our son or daughter their sponsor. Compassion International then allows our kids to exchange letters with their friend overseas, to offer them appropriate gifts on birthdays and holidays, and to grow up alongside them, witnessing how someone from a very different circumstance lives. Importantly, this practice allows our whole family to give together and allows my wife and me to have important conversations with our kids about the importance of helping others while giving them a vibrant, real-world opportunity to do so.

Habitat for Humanity is another charity that offers this kind of personal connection and relationship building. Founded in 1976 by Millard and Linda Fuller and brought to prominence with support from President Jimmy Carter, Habitat for Humanity seeks to address the problem of inadequate housing and homelessness by building and repairing homes for those in need. While it works internationally in a variety of ways, one of the most prominent is allowing groups of people—church groups, businesses, and other organizations—to sponsor a Habitat house, paying for part of the house itself and then volunteering to build it (partnered with experts). That act of physically working together for the benefit of others in community is one of Habitat's core impacts. I've since come to know Habitat's CEO, Jonathan Reckford, one of the kindest and most thoughtful people I've ever met. He has helped me understand how Habitat builds communities globally—not just by erecting homes and neighborhoods but also by bonding with those who commit to these builds.

The same logic of togetherness in volunteering is behind community food drives, school fundraisers, and college days of service. When we work together with others for the benefit of others, our lives and communities improve immeasurably. There is almost no greater experience in the world.

In my work with wealthy families, I've noticed consistently that those who are best adjusted choose to give together as a family. They often make a big deal of the decision to give, spending whole days presenting new ideas and celebrating giving decisions together.

There is a benefit to giving quietly and out of the spotlight, like Ronald Read, whom we met earlier. Many traditions encourage anonymous giving. But there is real power in giving as a community. Create a family tradition of giving. Work with your place of worship or company to sponsor a Habitat house, a local school, or a Compassion International child. Host a fundraising event or banquet for a worthy cause in your community. Introduce a day of service to your workplace. Doing good work with others creates joy for those who give and receive alike.

Participate in the causes you care about

Giving is about time as much as money, and integrating the two is a way to make generosity both more personal and more impactful for others. In graduate school, I became dear friends with a remarkable man named Rye Barcott. Barcott would go on to distinguished service in the Marine Corps before founding Double Time Capital and With Honor, a nonpartisan political action committee supporting military veterans across party lines in Congress. But in college at the University of North Carolina at Chapel Hill, Barcott took a transformative trip to the slums of Kibera, Kenya, to study youth empowerment and ethnic violence. What he experienced in Kibera moved him so much he cofounded (alongside Kenyan counterparts Salim Mohamed and Tabitha Festo) a nonprofit, Carolina for Kibera, now CFK Africa. The nonprofit was intended to connect Barcott's resources at the University of North Carolina and in the United States to the needs of the people in Kibera. Since 2001, the organization has mobilized millions of dollars and large numbers of people in the United States to improve the lives of their peers in some of the poorest parts of East African cities. CFK "empowers tens of thousands of youth in African slums through sports, education, and public health."[31]

Barcott is still deeply involved as the volunteer chair of the board. He has written papers and articles on Africa and even a book, *It Happened on the Way to War: A Marine's Path to Peace*, which documents his journey as a marine and social entrepreneur. But what's kept Barcott motivated to give so generously over the years is his deep connection to the people of Kenya and his experiences in that country over time. Barcott frames his journey this way:

> I've found the greatest fulfillment in life through service. After the Marines, when I was about 30, I set a goal to make enough money so I could give the best hours of my days to mission-oriented work. Thanks in part to a great business partner, I hit that goal by creating a successful business that financed solar power. I've been able to stay active volunteering on the board of CFK Africa for nearly 25 years because the organization is locally led. Local leadership is the essential ingredient to driving sustained growth in impoverished communities. There are few things as gratifying as working with talented partners on successful missions that matter.[32]

Similarly, my wife Jackie cares deeply about children and education. She serves on the boards of Skyland Trail (an initiative for juvenile mental health at a wonderful facility in Atlanta) and our kids' elementary school. She is also deeply involved with CureGRIN, a nonprofit serving the families of those with a series of rare genetic disorders called GRIN. Those who suffer from these disorders—predominantly children—experience seizures, cognitive impairment, serious behavioral problems, physical disabilities, and even death, as we've tragically seen in some of the families we've come to know and love in this community. CureGRIN organizes the families of those suffering, funds research, and connects families and researchers to spread the news of new treatments.

Like Barcott, she has also developed the ability to give well as she participates more broadly in the causes she is passionate about—her expertise lining up nicely with the causes she is supporting. Jackie makes sure that the dollars and time we contribute go toward solving social problems rather than ending up wasted on organizations that are not genuinely creating progress (a problem endemic to parts of the charitable sector that we will address later in this chapter).

Like building a Habitat home or writing letters to children you sponsor through Compassion International, participating directly in the causes you are giving to creates more sustainable engagement and buy-in and smarter philanthropy overall.

Make Sure Your Generosity Is Put to Proper Use

Bob Morin spent nearly fifty years as a librarian for the University of New Hampshire. A frugal man, he drove a 1992 Plymouth and often had a breakfast of Coke and Fritos, a cheese sandwich for lunch, and a frozen dinner at home. He read every book published in the United States between 1930 and 1938 (minus a few categories), and he averaged three videos or movies per day—holding a dual passion for books and cinema. He loved students, smoked a pipe, and was dedicated to the school.[33]

Through saving and investment, Morin amassed a $4 million estate by the time he died in 2015. He bequeathed this fortune as a gift to his beloved employer. It's a remarkable story of generosity. Morin lived a life with few luxuries and then gave back all he had made and more over his fifty-year career to the place he'd called his working home. He left most of the gift unrestricted, earmarking only $100,000 for the library and library science scholarships.[34] What happened next drew national headlines.

The University of New Hampshire, which compensates adjunct professors with $3,000 per class, elected to use $1 million of Morin's donation to purchase a new video scoreboard for its football stadium ($2.5 million was used for a career center). The university claimed the gift was appropriate because Morin, in his last fifteen months in an assisted living facility, developed a love for the school's football team.[35] But people around the world wondered whether donating the quiet librarian's life work to a video scoreboard demonstrated appropriate empathy for his legacy and other passions. Many wondered why the school, with all its priorities for this remarkable gift, could choose something so seemingly trivial and unrelated to its core mission. The story raised questions about both the responsible use of donor dollars and the preservation of charitable intent.

These questions have long existed among those interested in philanthropy. There has been active and wide discussion of the idea that philanthropy often perverts incentives and has unintended consequences that end up hurting those whom the givers are trying to help. In a 2014 article in the *New Republic*, Michael Hobbes told the story of PlayPump International, a charity that installed water wells in rural Africa where water was scarce and attached the pumps to merry-go-rounds. Every time a kid took a spin, the pump would activate and fill a nearby container. The rig even had space for advertising that could be sold to pay for maintenance. Except that in the aftermath, the pumps broke down quickly. They sat in disrepair, sometimes leaving the villages worse off because they had replaced their prior hand pumps and occasionally even resulting in the use of child labor.[36] Hobbes's article is full of such stories, with a solid grounding in Nina Munk's *The Idealist*, which chronicled her own efforts following economist David Sachs on his quest to end poverty. His efforts often resulted in disastrous consequences that proved the sometimes-devastating impact of foreign aid on local people and economies.

These examples don't mean all charity is bad. Philanthropy has made a dent in global diseases like malaria, HIV, tuberculosis, and polio. It has helped to fund remarkable medical research, supported orphanages, and provided much needed food and medical care to some of the most desperate people in the world. It has been used to counter human trafficking and to send talented young people to schools to better themselves and their communities. For every bad story, there is certainly a good one. But the evidence says we should be considerate and deliberate about the uses of our philanthropic dollars to make sure they make the world better, not worse.

The same can be said of the problem of donor intent. We will never know if Bob Morin would have approved of his university's spending $1 million on a scoreboard with his life's savings. Certainly, many family foundations or the charities they give to begin to stray from their original intent as they evolve. This is particularly true over long stretches of time, where some claim that many large endowments and foundations now act in ways the original founders of those organizations never intended.[37] But it can be true in the shorter term as well. Universities and charities sometimes go as far as to break the law (with real consequences) to stray from their donors' initial guidance. Philanthropy Roundtable and other organizations have documented such cases extensively.[38] A recent journal article from the University of Chicago Press, titled "You Did What with My Donation?!," highlighted not only the prevalence of donor intent problems but also how these betrayals deter givers from further charity and make them cynical about the potential giving they might otherwise do.[39]

This misuse of funds can even play out in more direct charity to friends, family members, or needy people we encounter on the street. In a later chapter, I'll delve more into how we should think about helping our kids with our financial resources, but a simple rule is to always think through how the money could be used in destructive ways before giving. Carefully considering that question and weighing the risk of that scenario against the potential positive uses of that money can ensure that it's used for positive rather than negative purposes.

What can the average person do to be generous while making sure that their generosity is put to proper use and implemented in such a way that actually helps others rather than hurting them? There's no silver bullet,

FIGURE 5-4

The TRUST framework for better giving

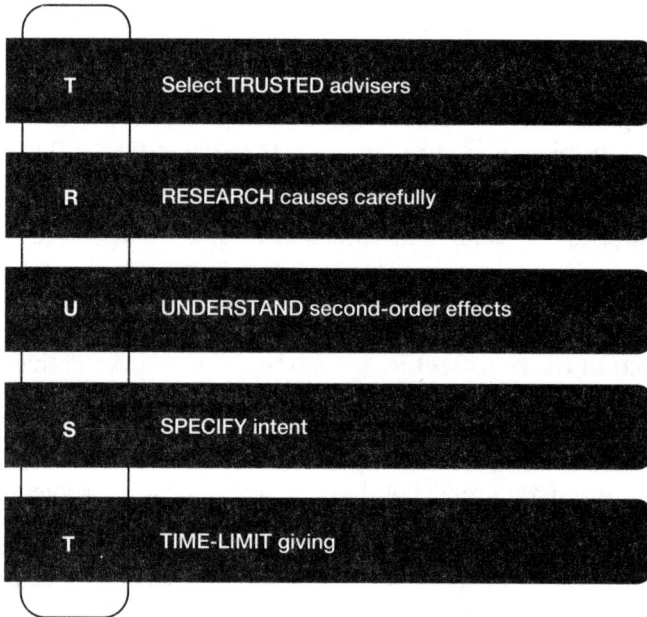

T	Select TRUSTED advisers
R	RESEARCH causes carefully
U	UNDERSTAND second-order effects
S	SPECIFY intent
T	TIME-LIMIT giving

but a few principles might be helpful. We can remember these using the acronym TRUST (figure 5-4).

Select trusted advisers

Giving is best done in community, as we've already seen. For most of us, that starts with close family. But beyond family members, you might considering giving with a wider circle of friends, researching causes together, serving together, and pooling capital to make a bigger impact. Engaging in this more collective approach introduces elements of community and relationship building while offering an individual giver the opportunity to more carefully consider the causes they support.

Some givers, particularly those giving larger amounts of money, may consider formal advisers to consult. People with charitable foundations, for example, are often well advised to recruit a board of knowledgeable, values-aligned individuals who can process opportunities to help others collectively. There are giving organizations that, like Philanthropy Round-table and AmPhil, offer resources, community events, and even paid consulting and research services to more thoughtfully select charitable causes. A good financial adviser can often partner with an individual or institution to help them think through not only maximizing their giving responsibly but also how to add new causes or cease giving to old ones. In general, no giver should act in isolation. One of the best ways to assure a positive impact from donated capital is to consult trusted advisers and give in community with others.

Research causes carefully

In 1998, Pat Dugan took his pharmaceutical sales company PDI public and suddenly had more wealth than he'd ever imagined. Concerned over high-profile scandals he'd seen involving what he previously considered reputable charitable organizations, Dugan began looking intensively for resources to help him evaluate the effectiveness of charities to which he was considering contributions. "I really didn't want to throw my money down the rat hole," he said. "Nothing really existed that met my needs to reassure me that the money was going to be well taken care of."[40]

Dugan launched a new rating organization, Charity Navigator, in 2001. Initially, it featured only eleven hundred charities and simply used their publicly available 990 forms (public tax filings that list how organizations use their funds) to assign ratings to the charities and offer donors better transparency into their financial management. Over time, Charity Navigator's ratings have become more complex, and by 2018, some eleven million visitors were checking Charity Navigator each year.[41] The group currently rates more than two hundred thousand charities. There are a variety of other competitors now seeking to do something similar for prospective donors.

Giving away money without wasting it or having it create unintended consequences can be challenging. One of the best ways to assure care in doing so is to research your causes carefully, particularly when you are not already closely involved in an organization. For most individuals and families giving more modest amounts of money, this care probably involves checking websites like Charity Navigator, looking for online reviews, and reading an organization's 990. Simple online searches can often reveal supportive or critical news articles that offer additional context for a charity and can help a donor understand it.

Givers should also consider a more personal approach. I'm a fan of more concentrated giving to causes we are passionate about and engaged with. If you'd like to begin donating to a charity like Habitat for Humanity, call friends in the housing space to get their thoughts. Consider volunteering at a site alongside an initial donation to get a feel for the organization. And speak with someone at the nonprofit to ask questions directly. Giving money away doesn't mean wasting it. You worked hard for the resources you've gained, and the point of philanthropy—whether you're giving formally to a nonprofit or informally to a friend or relative—is for that money to make a positive impact. Careful research can help ensure that this is the case.

Understand second-order effects

As a college student, I participated in a student organization called Hunger and Homelessness Outreach, Programs, and Education. We helped to educate other students about these problems in our college's community, and we worked with local shelters and soup kitchens to provide housing and food for people in need. One of the first principles we learned (common among organizations dedicated to these causes) was to only rarely give directly to those we encountered experiencing homelessness and to instead focus our financial efforts on supporting organizations serving these communities full-time. The rationale was that in all but a very few cases, those organizations can better understand the root causes of a person's suffering and more fully address them. People who are unhoused and hungry often struggle with other variables like mental health issues or addiction, and giving money to them directly can sometimes contribute to their problems, not their recovery. A shelter or kitchen, meanwhile, can make certain their deeper needs are addressed by knowledgeable professionals.

That principle holds true in many other areas. If the purpose of financial giving is to enhance flourishing for others, we would never want our dollars to be underutilized or to make someone's life worse and not better. But sometimes our charitable giving can exacerbate rather than solve problems. I experienced this dilemma in my own work in Afghanistan in 2011. While many people around the world wanted to help people in need in that war-torn country, the influx of charitable causes and organizations in Afghanistan created a series of poor incentives that compounded its struggles. Smart Afghan individuals were often learning English to go to work for these charities or to apply for grants, for example, rather than turning their talents to entrepreneurship and building sustainable enterprises that could have helped the country in the long term. Working the charitable system became more profitable than creating native industry with value. And while that was certainly not true of every charitable organization, the second-order effects of this influx of charity (rather than investment) were broadly observed—a phenomenon seen elsewhere in the developing and developed world alike. In the example at the beginning of this chapter, PlayPump was well intended and attacked a real problem, but the second-order impacts of the way the charity attacked that problem led to poor results.

Charitable giving is essential. But it can have dire impacts if not thoughtfully considered. Before you give directly to any person or organization, consider carefully the second-order effects of that giving.

Specify intent

Often, nonprofits prefer gifts without specified intent—so-called unrestricted giving—because it gives them maximum flexibility to use the money as they see fit. Indeed, for some givers to some organizations, unrestricted giving is the best course. The consulting firm Bridgespan Group, for example, has documented what it calls the "nonprofit starvation cycle." In this cycle, donors worried about nonprofits' misuse of funds restrict their giving to specific uses, but recipients can't pay core overhead expenses needed for these uses.[42] Charities need some flexibility, and they need core staff and infrastructure to operate.

But sometimes it pays to be more specific. It's one reason we love Compassion International, which allows us to sponsor health and education for specific children. We're confident the whole organization is doing worthwhile work, but seeing our money go directly to a child in need is more fulfilling personally for our family and guarantees we are 100 percent supportive of the use of the funds we offer.

Some charities, historically, have been criticized for misusing funds in ways that are counter to the intent of their donors. Famously, for example, Greg Mortenson, author of *Three Cups of Tea*, misused millions of dollars from his charity, the Central Asia Institute, and was forced by Montana's attorney general to repay part of this amount to the organization.[43] Similarly, the Wounded Warrior Project endured a period of scandal when it was discovered that much of the money given to the charity was not being used to help wounded warriors but was spent on lavish conferences, travel, and entertainment for staff.[44] Donors carefully specifying the use of their funds can't always be sure that their requests will be honored, but specificity (or working with charities that clearly define the use of donor dollars)—whether that be funding a particular scholarship for a student or sponsoring a child through an organization like Compassion—can do more to make certain the money is well spent.

Most charities are out to do the right thing. They have clear missions and motivated, wonderful people. They are impacting the world in various remarkable ways. But donors, particularly as they begin to donate more and more consistently, are often best served by making sure the intent of their gifts is spelled out properly and that they and the recipient enterprise understand it fully. Such clarity is often best for all parties involved.

Time-limit giving

Bernie Marcus was one of the most charitable individuals in history. The cofounder of Home Depot, Marcus never wanted to simply accumulate wealth but wanted to deploy it in a way that served others with generosity. He founded Autism Speaks with Bob and Suzanne Wright by providing a $25 million commitment for them to launch the organization. Now, the Marcus Autism Center treats more children with autism than any other clinic in the world.[45] His dollars have helped enable high-quality public education for students in places like Home Depot's home state of Georgia. And he was very careful to specify only a few areas into which his immense fortune could be deployed: medical research and health care; Jewish causes; free enterprise; veterans initiatives and national security; the health and welfare of children, with an emphasis on civics education; and targeted community support. The Marcus Foundation has donated more than $2.7 billion since its founding in 1989, with every grant approved by Marcus himself.[46]

But Marcus also chose to do something still somewhat unusual with the foundation. He elected to sunset it over a relatively short period after his death. Vibrant to the end, Marcus passed away at ninety-five years old in 2024. His foundation will now distribute all its assets to charity, directed by a board, over twenty years. What Marcus had witnessed was that over time, many endowed foundations not only strayed from the original intent of its founders but also came to be self-serving power centers for their eventual leaders, not entities truly dedicated to affecting the world for good. In an interview with Bridgespan, Marcus explained:

> I don't want people to be here in perpetuity. I think it's a terrible thing to do. It's a power base for people. People use it for power. I mean, when you have millions of dollars to give away a year, you're a powerful person. And many people use that for their own benefit. And so here's the guy who made the money, you know, this idiot is now laying in his grave, and some imbecile, you know, thirty, forty, fifty years after he dies, is living

off his money. Got a great salary, great benefits, all the things that they care for themselves. It goes on for perpetuity. They give away 5 percent. They never give away more. They want to keep the principal and they want to keep it going for succession. And they pick their successors, and it's a payoff for people they love. I think [it's a mistake] to let a foundation go on forever.[47]

Some might put it less colorfully than Marcus, but an increasing number of donors are choosing to give away all their money while living, to sunset their foundations, or to fund only operating grants (rather than endowments) while they live. Michael Moritz, for example, donated more than $30 million to Ohio State University to fund four professorships and thirty student scholarships, only for his son Jeffrey to find out the university had begun charging an annual fee to the endowment, redirecting $3 million to fund their broader development operations over fifteen years.[48] And while some causes are best endowed permanently, there is a growing debate over the wisdom of locking up pools of capital in perpetuity that can either outlive their original purpose or come to be abused.

For most giving and most causes, time-limiting gifts, such as giving annually rather than contributing to an endowment, may be the wisest course. For an individual making donations, this can look like making single, rather than multiyear, commitments to a charity you support. It can also look like giving money for operating funds rather than endowments or endowed programs to make sure those endowed funds don't one day go astray. An increasing number of family foundations are following Bernie Marcus's model, with 8 to 12 percent of foundations now including sunset provisions.[49] These time limitations can help ensure fidelity and effectiveness of the charities that donors give to and the preservation of intent for a donor's wishes. They are principles that givers of almost any size can adopt.

The TRUST framework, diligently executed, can help you to give more and better.

Give More Than Money

In December 2021, Sophia Jackson was watching the news when she saw the story of Vadrien Alston, a New York City Police Department officer with two children who was in desperate need of a kidney transplant.[50] Alston suffers from renal failure. Twelve years earlier, she had received a kidney from a friend, but that organ had started to fail and she was forced to shut down her life and go on dialysis. Jackson was so moved by this story, she volunteered to be a living donor for Alston. Unfortunately, she was not a match—but Jackson then explored something creative.

Through the National Kidney Registry donor voucher program, Jackson "swapped" with another donor—donating her own kidney so that someone who was a match for Alston would donate theirs. Alston was floored by the news. "It was like coming home and telling my family I'd won the lotto," she said. "That's how I felt, that she still decided to donate just for me. Even if it couldn't benefit me directly, she was still willing to help. It was one of the best feelings that I've ever experienced." Jackson's selflessness ended up saving not one life, but two, as she encouraged another donor to get in the game.[51]

This is a book about financial flourishing—the habits, mindsets, and values we need to make our money Good Money. As a result, we won't spend a great deal of time on the things in life that create flourishing but don't intersect with money. We won't explore in detail, for example, good marriages, close friendships, proper parenting, or personal health and well-being. But generosity, such a core topic for financial flourishing, is at its heart a mindset as much as a practice. Financial generosity is core to financial flourishing. But you will be more likely to be generous if generosity isn't just something you simply do with your paycheck but is a deeply held core value and a mindset you take into everything. It's important to talk about the various ways in which you can give, over and above financial generosity.

Generosity can take many forms. It can look like selflessly serving others in the workplace—one of the key ways that we can craft greater purpose at work. That same attitude of service will indeed make you a better spouse, partner, parent, friend, and mentor. When we learn to think of others first—before prioritizing our own interests—we develop a mindset of generosity that permeates all we do. Instead of constantly thinking "How can I help myself in this situation?," ask "How can I use the gifts I've been given to improve the lives of others?" In this way, we will experience more gratitude and joy while simultaneously improving the communities and lives around us.

Our generous action may not look like donating an organ (though it might). But it can be manifested in a host of wonderful ways. By partnering our time and talents with our treasure for the causes we care about, we can enhance both our commitment to financial generosity and the benefits we give and receive.

Capital Group vice chair Jody Jonsson is extraordinarily financially blessed. A leader within Capital Group for more than three decades, Jonsson is one of the most senior members of an organization that manages more than $2 trillion in assets. When she turned fifty, she decided to become a pilot, and over the subsequent decade, she achieved a number of instrument ratings that allow her to fly a variety of aircraft. Watching Jonsson speak of this at a conference in 2023, I could tell how fulfilling this avocation was for her personally. But it has also allowed her to get involved in a charity called Angel Flight. This organization flies people in desperate need of medical care (often cancer patients) to the facilities that can treat them. "Really, what I love about it is I'm inspired by the patients," Jonsson says. "It's very humbling to hear their stories and [it] makes you grateful for good health. But it's really a treat to be able to help people in this way."[52] Angel Flight pilots like Jonsson donate their time, their talent, and the financial resources to operate the planes to make these trips a reality. And in so doing, they create a deep personal connection to those they serve while meeting a need that would be nearly impossible to satisfy with solely financial resources.[53] Jonsson probably has the means to simply give money to causes like this. It would certainly save her time that she could spend at work or with her family. But there's something special about putting your whole self to work for something you feel deeply passionate about.

My friend Davis Smith, the founder of outdoors brand Cotopaxi, is the same. Smith grew up in various countries in Latin America, falling in love with the region. When he founded his apparel company in 2014, he named it after one of Ecuador's highest and most beautiful volcanoes. As a B Corp, Cotopaxi has a dual mission: to create financial value for its stakeholders and to "do good" (one of the brand's mottos) for others. This parallel commitment to entrepreneurship and social impact has always been at the core of Smith's identity.[54] He has always been financially generous with others both through his own resources and through those of Cotopaxi. But in 2022, he was called to do more. At the height of his success at Cotopaxi, Smith's church asked him to leave his day-to-day work at the company he had created and to lead the church's mission in Brazil. Smith, his wife Asialene, and their four children were asked to move from Utah to Recife, Brazil, to oversee the Mormon missionaries who serve in that country—and that's what they did. Completely uprooting their lives and finding ways to reduce his day-to-day involvement in the brand he was building, the Smiths moved to Brazil, where they have been living and working since. Of his new work, Smith says, "Cotopaxi was built on purpose and mission, and my job as CEO and founder of the business has been to evangelize that mission and purpose. Sharing the gospel of Jesus Christ is the greatest cause, and we get to be a part of it."[55]

We may not be called to give a kidney, earn a pilot's license, or move abroad. But we each have talents that can enhance our service to others. I'm able to do this through nonprofit board service, for example, and through organizing events that connect nonprofit leaders to one another and to sources of capital that make their work easier. I have friends who serve as Big Brothers or Big Sisters, offering mentorship and care to young people, and the wife of another friend dedicates a great deal of her time to the Humane Society in our city, personally caring for animals in need. A private equity firm I know, Halifax Group, recently organized a day of service for both firm members and their clients so that they could give of their time together—an unforgettable experience for team members and their limited partners alike.

Notably, using our financial resources to "buy time," as we saw in the previous chapter, can create the space for us to be more generous with the time we dedicate to service. If you find ways to shorten your commute, deliver groceries more efficiently, or bypass mundane household chores, you may find you have the time for more meaningful service-oriented involvement in your community.

Using our time and talents to help others is no substitute for financial giving. We should give financially at whatever level we can. Doing so helps us loosen our grip on money and change our relationship with it. It helps us realize that even when we have little financially, money does not define us and generosity can transform us. But financial giving without heart—without personal dedication and passion—can be similarly hollow. It's in combining the two, giving more than just money, that we can realize the deepest and most lasting impact on ourselves and others.

Chapter 6

Invest for Impact

T here's an old adage that "Compound interest is the eighth wonder of the world. He who understands it, earns it. He who doesn't, pays it." And any discussion of investing must start with a simple understanding of compound returns.

Compounding is a miracle that is often difficult to grasp, and it's at the heart of why we invest at all. Compounding works like this: if you are twenty years old and invest $10,000 today in the S&P 500, which has a recent long-term return of around 10 percent, and you simply leave that money in markets without touching it for forty-five years, over that period your returns on that initial investment will look like the graph in figure 6-1.

Now let's say you have one friend investing at a 2 percent rate of return, one at 6.5 percent, yourself at 10 percent, and another friend at 15 percent over the same period. What would each of you have when you turn sixty-five? Take a look at figure 6-2.

After forty-five years, your friend investing at 2 percent annual rates of return will have just shy of $25,000 (not adjusted for inflation). Your friend investing at 15 percent will have almost $5.4 million—$4.7 million more than you, even though you earned a healthy 10 percent. And notice that if your friend had encountered an expense they had to pay for after twenty-five years, they would have missed out on 90 percent of the growth

FIGURE 6-1

The miracle of compound interest: A simple compounding investment over time

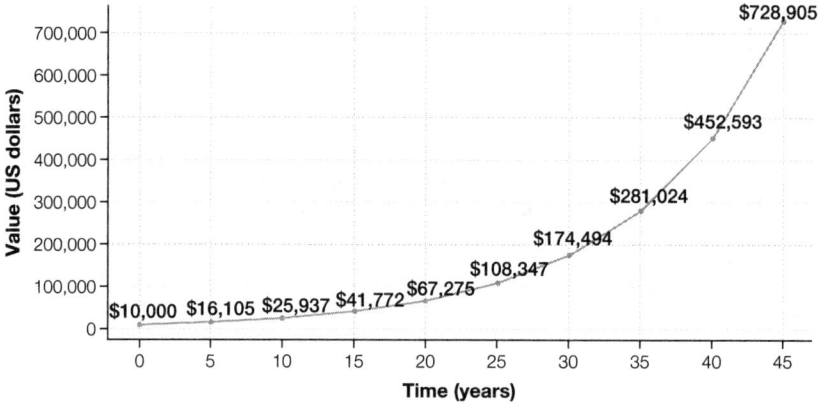

FIGURE 6-2

The miracle of compound interest: A simple compounding investment over time at different rates of return

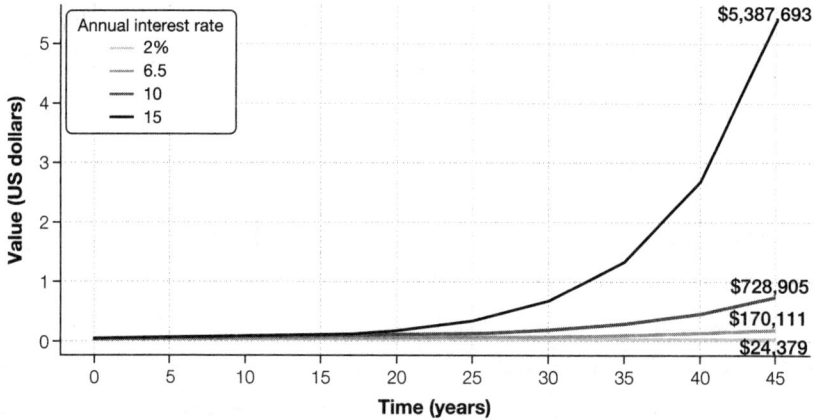

in their assets. That's "the eighth wonder of the world" the previous adage refers to. Even small amounts of money, invested at decent rates of return over long-enough periods, can be life-changing.

Many of the wealthiest people and families in history engaged in the simple practice of investing consistently and wisely from a young age. Investor Warren Buffett, currently worth approximately $150 billion, made his first million dollars at thirty-two and didn't become a billionaire until age fifty-five, but his incredibly stable investment philosophy made him one of the wealthiest people in the world.[1]

The practice of steady, early investment isn't, of course, just for the wealthy or financially sophisticated. Many of the tools for this practice are available for almost any investor today, and they often outperform investors who structure more complex investments. For an entertaining example of this principle, look to the Buss family's recent partial sale of the Los Angeles Lakers in 2025 (still pending at the time of this writing). Jerry Buss, a very good businessman, invested around $68 million to buy the Lakers in 1979, turning the team into one of the most successful sports franchises in history. In 2025, his family announced the sale of the team for approximately $10 billion—the highest price ever paid for a sports franchise in the United States. This would seem an amazing return, wouldn't it? The only catch is that if Buss had invested the same amount in the S&P 500 index that year (an index available for investment to almost anyone at any level), the outlay would now be worth $13 billion— significantly more.[2]

The overarching mindset you need around savings and investments is simple: put every dollar you reasonably can into an investment as soon as you can, and if you do so and manage your risk well, you will transform your financial life. So, save as much as you can. Hold an emergency fund of cash. Then put the rest in investments seeking to deliver a high risk-adjusted return (consult a financial adviser as you do this). Many people are intimidated by the importance and complexity of these decisions, but the basic habits are simple, and there are many qualified professionals available who can help with the more complex aspects of this process. Just invest.

There are a nearly infinite number of financial instruments you can explore for your investments. In my prior positions, I was an executive at a firm managing more than $1 trillion across hundreds of products, so I had a bird's-eye view of the options. The average person might do well to stick to the basics—money market funds, public equity securities or exchange-traded funds, publicly traded fixed income, or similar investments. On the other hand, a wealthier person with more financial security and sophistication can begin to explore options, futures, private equity, private credit, venture capital, real estate, asset leasing, litigation finance, movie productions, and dozens of other categories. Many of these tools aren't available to the average investor (because of regulations and suitability) and require greater care in selection. But they can come with unique features to enhance returns or lower risks and make a person's capital grow more safely or at higher rates over time. Again, this level of complexity requires real focus and a partner or an adviser who understands the things you don't. I am the CEO of an alternative investment firm today, but I still have a financial adviser who manages much of my portfolio, is involved in my tax and estate planning, and serves as a knowledgeable person I can talk to on more complex topics, giving my wife and me peace of mind.

If you are not saving money to invest today, you should be. Read up on the basics of investing to become more knowledgeable, and consult wise counsel on your portfolio—whether they be a formal financial adviser or family member or friend who understands these topics and can get you started. Never invest in something you don't understand, but keep saving and investing more each year and resist the urge to raid your investments for expenditures over time.

Earlier in this book, I highlighted the importance of earning with purpose and spending less than we make. Doing so can give us the extra capital each year to transform our financial lives through the miracle of compounding returns. What's missing from this advice is the remarkable impact your investment dollars then have on the world. Fluid capital markets, with individuals and institutions working together to fund companies, build new real estate, make loans to growing businesses, and even finance new movies, enabling enormous creativity and growth in the world. Almost every company today uses investor money to grow and build. And almost every office tower or multifamily housing development in your city does the same. Our investment dollars create dynamism in the economy—the kind of dynamism that leads to financial returns for investors but also creates jobs, housing, innovation, and opportunity. Therein lies an entirely different way to view your investments, not just through the lens of investment returns (which are important) but also through the influence those assets have on the world around us.

Good Money creates the financial foundation to pursue flourishing, and investments reinforce and grow that foundation. There are thousands of books you can read on tax strategy, different investment vehicles, and other tactical investment topics. In this book, we move beyond the standard advice and focus instead on how the investments you accumulate can reflect the values you hold dear along the way and, in doing so, impact the world around you for good.

All Investing Is Impact Investing

As a young professional, James Tieng was straight out of central casting to become a leading figure in the world of high finance. A Princeton graduate with internships in asset management and investment banking at Morgan Stanley and J.P. Morgan, Tieng went on to management consulting at McKinsey & Company out of undergraduate school before proceeding into private equity. He then pursued an MBA at Harvard Business School, landing a coveted private equity job at Apax Partners.

But something was missing. Tieng had always had two professional passions: education and investing. He was indulging in a great deal of investing but not in education, at least in his day job. In business school, he had taken classes on innovating the education system. And this child of immigrants believed firmly that education is one of the primary gateways to opportunity for those who otherwise lack opportunity.

Taking a risk, Tieng took a new position at Quad Partners, a private equity investor focused on education. He could now both pursue his passion for investing and try to transform the world by investing in entrepreneurs building new and innovative approaches to education and learning. Tieng loved his new role, and eventually he partnered with his friend Victor Hu, who led education investment banking for Goldman Sachs, to cofound Lumos Capital Group. This growth-stage private equity firm focused on innovative approaches to education and human capital development across the global landscape.

Alongside its financial metrics, Lumos has a set of impact criteria and judges each investment both on the merits of its potential return and on its potential for social impact. Tieng and Hu don't believe, in this case, that there is a trade-off between the two. Tieng describes Lumos this way: "At Lumos, we believe that our financial returns not only align with our mission-drive focus on access and equitable outcomes but there exists a natural collinearity between successful business results and societal impact. Furthermore, Victor and I strive to build on a foundation set by purpose and faith as we look to grow a firm that can provide for our team's families and create value for our investors."[3]

To be good, money should be aligned with the habits, mindsets, and values of flourishing. In chapter 1, we explored the idea that we really only encounter money in four ways: we earn, spend, give, and invest. That last category, investing, is often the one we neglect the most.

We often naturally think of our values in the first three categories. We prefer to earn money in a profession that aligns with our talents, passions, and sources of purpose. We think carefully about spending, trying to make sure the ways we spend are aligned with what will make our life more meaningful and fulfilled. When we give money, particularly to charity, we think deeply about whether that charitable cause is something we believe in and get meaning from supporting. Yet when we invest, we often intentionally park our values at the door, seeking only to understand the risk and return of our investments. Alternatively, because of the perceived complexity of investing, we outsource the management of our money to others without fully understanding how it's used.

This is a surprising approach, given that for the average person (at least in the developed world), investments are greater than annual spending, giving, or earnings. Median household income in the United States was about $75,000 in 2022, for example, and average expenditures were about 77 percent of that (at least according to one study with slightly different income numbers).[4] Giving is a paltry 2 percent of GDP.[5] But the median American household has more than $192,000 in net worth.[6] And while some of that is tied up in real estate through owning a home, 61 percent of US adults own stock.[7] Of course, this percentage varies a great deal by age and income bracket, but the typical American (particularly as they age) has as much in savings and investments as they make in income and more than they spend or give. Those in the top 1 percent have more than $10 million.[8] At that level, they have millions of dollars to deploy in public markets, private equity, venture capital, real estate, and other categories.

While these numbers look quite different in countries ranging from Nigeria to Norway, in the developed world and for those aspiring to financial independence, investments are often the number one category of their financial lives. But people don't as frequently think about expressing their values through investing or understand how that can be done.

All investing is impact investing—every dollar we put to work has an impact on the world, good or bad. Exploring the nature of that impact, who controls it, and how we can make investing a greater expression of, and source of, values in our lives can be as rewarding as doing the same work on the dollars we spend and give.

The Origins of Values-Based Investing

In 1971, the Episcopal Church ignited modern *values investing* when it challenged General Motors' policies in South Africa. In 1971, the apartheid regime in that country was at its height. Apartheid, in that context, referred to institutionalized racial segregation in South Africa and policies that assured domination by the nation's white minority population. The system was brutal, even by the global standards of the day. But many companies and governments continued to support the regime in South Africa despite that brutality.

General Motors was one of those companies. While not formally in favor of the underlying policies of apartheid, per se, GM had extensive manufacturing operations in the country, made possible by the ruling regime. In 1971, the Episcopal Church, owning just 0.004 percent of shares, introduced a shareholder resolution requesting that GM withdraw from the country.[9] Shareholder resolutions are quite common—almost any investor can introduce a resolution at a company's board meeting encouraging it to take action on an issue. Typically, such a tiny shareholder would not gain much attention or favor for one of its resolutions. But GM's lone Black board member, Leon Sullivan, pastor of the Zion Baptist Church of Philadelphia, rallied behind the effort and gave an impassioned plea at the shareholder meeting. "American industry," he said, "cannot morally continue to do business in a country that so blatantly and ruthlessly and clearly maintains such dehumanizing practices against such large numbers of its people." The motion ultimately failed, garnering only 1.29 percent of the vote.

But the activism by the church and Reverend Sullivan so captured the national imagination that GM eventually did withdraw from the country. Moreover, nearly the entirety of corporate America embraced what came to be known as the Sullivan principles, the codes guiding private enterprises' approach to the apartheid regime.[10]

This wasn't the first time people had broached values and investing. Jewish, Muslim, and Christian scriptures all contain sometimes-detailed guidelines on stewarding wealth and investments in a way concordant with faith. Writers like Upton Sinclair brought mainstream and secular attention to corrupt business practices even as governments became more active policing the investments and other business practices of the corporations within their borders. But the church's activism in 1971 roughly coincided with the birth of a modern, mainstream values-based investing movement that was powered by international sovereign wealth funds, US public pensions, nonprofit and religious investors, and individuals alike. The most prominent—but not the only—manifestation of that movement today is known as ESG, or environmental, social, and governance investing.

This book is not an endorsement of ESG or any other particular values approach. While many people see ESG as synonymous with values-based investing, that's far from true. Even within the ESG movement, approaches vary greatly. After recent controversy, the ESG movement is declining and fragmenting, and many values-based investors have little to no involvement with ESG.

But understanding the ESG movement and related movements like sharia finance can show the sheer scope of impact that values-based investing can have and the massive demand for the incorporation of values into investing by entities as diverse as individuals and sovereign nations. These investment approaches are not just relevant at the global scale but important in the lives and accounts of each of us with some wealth to steward. A good grasp of the frameworks by which people can implement their values in a portfolio—and the tools available to do so—is the first step to aligning our investments with our values in a way that makes those dollars good.

The Current Landscape for Values-Based Investing

Globally, managed assets total around $120 trillion. These do not include people's homes or businesses, but they do include the money they have in mutual funds, stocks, bonds, private equity holdings, venture capital investments, real estate investment trusts, and everything in between.[11] And these managed assets touch almost everything in our lives. Individual stockholders, pensions, and retirement plans own the company that produces the Android or iPhone in your pocket. They are the private equity behind your local heating, ventilation, and air-conditioning company and the funding for the company that produced your mobile device, your e-reader, or the paper book in your hands. In many ways, this financial capital is like oxygen—necessary to make modern society function, permeating every corner of our lives everywhere in the world, and influencing the companies, products, and services we interact with each day. Your money is a part of this.

In recent years, people and institutions have become both more aware of the influence of this capital and more inclined to try to consciously craft that influence—in the same way the Episcopal Church did when confronting General Motors over apartheid in 1971. In a recent poll, around two-thirds of Americans say that they want to invest in a "socially responsible way" (though a much smaller percentage do so).[12]

What does socially responsible influence look like? Those who seek to express their values through their investing often adopt a number of approaches, including these:

- *Negative screening:* Investors screen out companies or holdings that represent sectors, products, or services they do not want to support. Common negative screens include gambling, guns or other weapons, fossil fuels, adult entertainment, alcohol, and tobacco.

- *Positive screening:* Investors intentionally invest in sectors they like, such as renewable energy, or in companies with that focus on things like human flourishing, human rights, or environmental impact.

- *Thematic investing:* This approach often involves dedicated funds in areas the investors would like to support. For example, some institutions choose to invest in renewable energy funds, "green" bonds, or venture capital portfolios that back only female founders. Some invest in health care or defense technology.

- *Corporate engagement and activism:* This approach has become a dominant way in which institutions and asset managers engage companies to try to force new policies. This is what the Episcopal Church attempted with Leon Sullivan in 1971. It happens broadly now through *proxy voting*: large asset managers vote for or against company policies using the shares of those whom they manage assets for. Any individual or institution that owns shares of a company can "vote" those shares or introduce resolutions to its board, a potentially powerful practice when done collectively to influence company decisions.

- *Company and cultural formation:* Managers can help shape companies from the ground up as either a significant or a majority shareholder. This is possible especially in private investing, such as private equity and venture capital. Private equity giant KKR, for example, has recently been pioneering an approach to broader employee ownership in its companies, seeking to create more economic sharing and stakeholder buy-in throughout their organizations.[13]

These five approaches may not be fully comprehensive, but they offer a sketch of how values can be expressed in a portfolio. There are a variety of frameworks currently used throughout the world at scale to act on these approaches for people with certain values-based concerns.

The largest and most prominent approach is ESG. Arising out of efforts championed by large sovereign wealth funds, state pension plans, and international bodies, ESG principles are often codified in documents like the UN Principles for Responsible Investing.[14] Initially, the primary focus of ESG was environmental preservation and climate change—still perhaps its greatest focus. But it also encompasses several goals around diversity and inclusion, human rights, and other issues. The goal of this framework is to use the world's financial capital to push companies, countries, and individuals to adopt behaviors and policies aligned with the goals of ESG.

ESG assets have become a huge component of global markets, now accounting for 25 to 35 percent of the managed assets in the world.[15] It's likely that some of the assets you control are in these strategies by default unless you have actively sought to exclude them with your financial adviser. Over the last three to five years, there has been increasingly aggressively criticism of ESG as an investment approach and a push to shift this model. This criticism has come from the political right and left, advocates of a fiduciary standard, regulators, and academics alike and has become evident on a number of fronts. The issues include difficulty quantifying ESG factors, the potential for lower returns, the perception of progressive social and political bias in the ESG framework, greenwashing (false environmental friendliness to attract investment), and a lack of standardization and transparency. But ESG remains a major force in spite of this criticism.

Another dominant approach is sharia-compliant finance, investing that is aligned with the principles of the Muslim faith.[16] Tenets of sharia-complaint finance include the exclusion of companies that are haram (forbidden), like those that produce alcohol and pork; the charging of interest in most circumstances; gambling or speculation; and even certain types of options trading.[17] Globally, Islamic finance totals around $4.5 to $6.7 trillion. It plays a role in the portfolios of both large institutions and individual investors alike through investing in strategies offered by sharia-compliant investment managers and larger investment managers with sharia-compliant offerings.[18]

This approach is echoed, though on a smaller scale, in the Christian world. The consulting firm Brightlight Research, for example, estimates at least $130 billion in strategies aligned with the Christian faith.[19] These approaches are often outlined in formal guidance from denominations, like the US Conference of Catholic Bishops investment guidelines or those of the American Baptist Churches USA.[20] As with sharia finance, these guidelines often focus on prohibited areas of investments but also delve into positive ways in which investments may be used for impact.

Further still are a host of more niche approaches, like Andreessen Horowitz's American dynamism, which focuses on investing in industries that can lead to a more vibrant US culture and economy. I myself work in the values-based investment space and see all the ways these values can manifest themselves.

For almost any person, there are options to invest in a way that embeds their values, avoiding things they do not want to support and contributing to those that they do. Some of these investments will be *concessionary* (sacrificing return for impact), and some will be *market return* (seeking to perform as well as any other similar investment). With the huge number of providers offering values alignment of varying degrees, an investor seeking to optimize investments purely on a financial-returns basis may still find ways to build a portfolio aligned with their values. Several stories showing what this looks like might be helpful. Let's look at some examples.

Values-Based Investing in Action

Now that we better understand the scope of options available to most investors for values-based investing, consider what that can look like at the firm level—both the variety of options available and the way an impact thesis plays out with an individual firm.

Rather than walking through all the potential ways in which a person's investments can have impact, I'll tell three brief stories of different approaches and the tools available to implement these ways. These examples are not intended as endorsements of these funds or services or as financial advice. They are just among thousands of approaches to values-based investing that may inspire your own journey. My hope is that you and millions like you can embrace investing with impact in a way that replaces and improves on the prior frameworks we've explored.

Amee Parbhoo and impact-oriented venture investments

Amee Parbhoo grew up in Charlotte, North Carolina, the daughter of Indian immigrants.[21] Her mother was from Mumbai, her father from rural India in Gujarat. He had been part of a wave of Indians who moved to East Africa for economic opportunity in the 1950s and 1960s—a historical fact that seems to inform Parbhoo's own work in Africa today.

A graduate of Davidson College, Parbhoo has always been interested in serving the global poor:

> I think investing came a lot later for me. The core was always this interest in international development. . . . I remember the first time in middle school I went to India with my family . . . we went to one of the slums in Mumbai with an aunt of mine who was a social worker. Just seeing the impact you could have on the lives of people and the impact my aunt was having through social work, it kind of opened my eyes at a young age. . . . It matters for me to try to think about these big issues, these big challenges of poverty, and I could help solve them.[22]

Parbhoo also developed the belief that while there is a role in international development and poverty alleviation for traditional philanthropy and for government, there is also a role for private industry. She gravitated toward business, first working for a management consultancy and then joining a global microfinance institution, extending small loans to entrepreneurs in developing countries. This experience opened her eyes to the need for more capital in these markets and ultimately led her on the path to investing.

She eventually joined Accion, a global nonprofit that has been operating for decades to extend innovative and responsible financial solutions to underserved people around the world. Alongside its philanthropic efforts, it started Accion Venture Lab, a leading early-stage investor in inclusive fintech startups that are meeting the financial needs of underserved people globally. Accion Venture Lab, which Parbhoo now leads, creates exactly the kinds of capital markets that she thought were needed to unlock entrepreneurship in these regions. Originally funded by Accion's balance sheet, Accion Venture Lab is now partnered with various global institutions and, for a decade, has helped unlock investments around the world.

Accion Venture Lab and Parbhoo believe that in this space, at least, there is no trade-off between the impact and the return they seek to balance. "At Accion and Accion Venture Lab," she says, "we've really built a track record that shows those [the impact and return] don't have to be in tension. [We] can drive both social impact and return at the same time."[23]

As an example, she cites Apollo Agriculture, a portfolio company in which she invested. Apollo seeks to enhance the capabilities of small-scale farmers in the developing world by "providing farmers the financing they need so they can buy better products, increase their harvest, and turn their subsistence farming into commercial farming."[24] The founders were motivated to understand why places like Kenya and Zambia haven't been able to unlock the same agricultural yields enjoyed by many farms in the developed world. After Accion Venture Lab provided the founders with very early funding to explore these ideas, Apollo has blossomed into a business that is both financially successful and incredibly impactful, raising capital from global behemoths like SoftBank and the Chan Zuckerberg Initiative.

When I asked Parbhoo about how others should consider their own approaches to investing in accordance with their values, she offered that the process first starts with reflection. "First of all, it's knowing what matters to you. What are the set of values you want to see in the world?" Then, she says, it's holding yourself accountable to making a difference by thoughtfully measuring impact. "It's really about defining the thesis of an investment," she says, "then thinking about whether you've had that impact all the way through the life cycle of aninvestment."

Parbhoo clearly loves her work—her team, her investors, the companies they partner with, and the impact they are having.

> I feel very fortunate with my team. You know I have a team of thirteen people spread across the globe. Very different backgrounds, different religions, different languages, but we all share the same purpose and mission. And that makes even the toughest days so much more meaningful and powerful. . . . The same goes for the entrepreneurs we invest in. I'm very proud to support the individuals who are building what they're building, because they're good people who are trying to make a difference.[25]

Aimee Minnich and pioneering investing through DAFs

Aimee Minnich grew up in Kansas City, Missouri, the youngest of five kids in a big Catholic family. Her dad had an alcohol problem, so he never held much more than odd jobs. Her mom supported the family, rotating through an array of positions that at one point included a paper route. All the Minnich kids got jobs as soon as they could, and early on, Minnich learned the value of hard work. Eventually, her mom remarried and started a successful business (which she still leads today). Minnich saw her mom and stepdad give philanthropically, but she always wondered if there was a way not just to do good work through charitable giving but also to incorporate a mission into their day jobs.

Preoccupied with these and other questions, Minnich studied philosophy as an undergraduate and then went to law school. But the legal profession never quite stuck, she says:

> I went to law school, not necessarily because I wanted to, but because I got a full ride, which was really helpful. But I never quite fit in at law school. Then I got out and I started practicing. I was married in law school and got pregnant, so each day, I'd drive to work downtown, drop a baby off, and go into the office. And I remember very distinctly driving and thinking to myself, "I do not like money or power enough to make this work. I'm leaving my baby behind to do something I don't like. It has to be either money or power that would motivate me to keep doing this." And I was like, "Neither one of those are very sufficient." So, I started looking for something else to do.[26]

By that time, her parents had taken a company public and started a foundation, and as they navigated their own journey of giving, Minnich discovered the world of donor-advised funds (DAFs) and "a whole group of people who devoted their lives to making generosity a lifestyle." That idea clicked for her as central to the concept of human flourishing. She joined one of the major DAFs only to have a second revelation. There were plenty of businesses focused on impact all over the world—often doing good work that charities weren't suited to do. And holders of DAFs could invest in these impact businesses as they were waiting to distribute philanthropic capital. Minnich became so enamored of this idea that she and a colleague, Jeff Johns, split off to form a new organization, the Impact Foundation.

Minnich's concept was a DAF specifically geared for impact investing. Impact Foundation could accept money and then invest it in social-impact-oriented businesses and investment funds—infrastructure in Africa, mission-oriented movies and TV projects, and a variety of other initiatives that allowed the donor to make positive change in the world. But it would do so through investing dollars into sustainable businesses and other projects rather than simply giving the money away.

This concept is not new. Impact investing has been around for some time. But it is often only the domain of large philanthropic institutions. Impact Foundation would allow someone with a $25,000 DAF to invest the same way the Rockefeller Foundation or the Ford Foundation would. Many of these investments are oriented to generate a strong return in addition to having an impact, which allows the donor to then recycle that capital into other meaningful investments or philanthropic initiatives.

Minnich describes it this way:

> We started in 2015, and so [after] nine years, we are now over $645 million deployed. So, people grant money to us. We make investments. When those investments start paying off, either through dividends, distribution, loan repayments, sales, it comes back into the donor-advised fund and the person who recommended the investment can grant it out. And so, we've successfully seen returns of over $100 million that have been granted out to other charities. You get to use the same dollar twice, both when it's deployed and then again when it's granted.[27]

One of Minnich's favorite investments is Tahmina Tea. *Tahmina* is a Persian girl's name meaning "brave," and the company's mission is "to uplift mental wellbeing and conflict-affected communities through functional teas blended with ethically-sourced saffron."[28] The company was founded by a young woman who moved to Afghanistan upon learning of the country's devastation and that one of its only profitable export crops is poppy, which is used in heroin production. It turns out that saffron, another spice, is also quite valuable and grows incredibly well in the region. So this young woman wanted to start a company with local Afghan partners to build a sustainable and ethical agricultural business in the area.[29]

Obviously, investing in a startup agricultural and consumer company in Afghanistan is quite risky—so risky that it's not a typical investment many investors could make in a conventional portfolio. But for an impact investor who cares as much about mission as financial return and who believes sustainable change in a place like Afghanistan partly depends on building a domestic business, Tahmina is a perfect opportunity to uplift those living through conflict in poverty and to offer them meaningful, ethical work. Through the Impact Foundation, US investors were able to rally around Tahmina and give it a start, and the company has blossomed into a successful, growing enterprise.

Minnich glows about the founder (whom she knows), saying, "Even after the US government has pulled out and the country has fallen into disarray, she's still able to employ farmers. She's still able to employ her factory workers. It's not easy, but man, does she have some grit."

In addition, because Impact Foundation is a charitable institution, even those who are not typically able to invest in private markets (because of accredited-investor rules) can use their philanthropic dollars to make these kinds of one-of-a-kind missional investments.

Minnich describes what drives her to get people involved in these investments:

> I think more people need to wake up to the idea that money is very rarely neutral. It's doing something even when we think our investments are [neutral] . . . there's no such thing as a neutral investment. It's doing something for someone some- where. And so if we can begin to ask ourselves, What is my money doing, and who is it doing it with? Who is it helping and who is it hurting? . . .
>
> I'm on a quest to help people redefine what a successful in- vestment means. We've assumed that a successful investment is entirely one-sided. I, the investor, made a lot of money for the risk that I took. And we've forgotten that in order for money to [make a] round trip, there are a whole lot of people that are af- fected by that. It's a little bit like a merry-go-round on the play- ground. As an investor, you're standing on the outside of that merry-go-round and sort of pulling it with your arm, running

around on the outside. You know, spinning this around. There are people on the inside of that merry-go-round, not all of whom are strapped in. And if you remember what happens when little kids are on one of those metal merry-go-round things, they fly off. And so, I think we have to figure out how we can normalize, not sacrificing returns, but how can we normalize allowing people to consider the externalities of the way in which they make money?[30]

Minnich and others are proving there's a model of investing that is deeply aligned with a person's core values, while providing them a way to both give more through DAFs and invest dollars waiting to be deployed in worthwhile causes that can make a difference.

Vanguard and the power of proxy voting

The Vanguard Group (Vanguard) is one of the largest and most powerful asset managers in the world. Founded in 1975 by John Bogle, the firm is credited with popularizing the *index fund*, a form of passive investing by which investors hold a broad array of stocks or bonds rather than trying to actively pick winners and losers. These funds often replicate popular indexes like the S&P 500 (the five hundred largest US public companies) or the Russell 3000 (the three thousand largest US public companies), offering investors broad exposure to their preferred markets whether in the United States or internationally.

Bogle's first fund was of a Standard & Poor's index (created just before he formed Vanguard), and in the fifty years since, the passive investing approach Bogle pioneered has come to dominate the investment world.[31] At the end of 2023, in the United States, assets held in passive funds surpassed those held in active funds for the first time, topping $13.29 trillion.[32] Even perhaps the modern world's greatest investor, Warren Buffett, has advocated for the use of passive funds in investing. "In my view," he says, "for most people, the best thing to do is own the S&P 500 index fund. The trick is not to pick the right company. The trick is to essentially buy all the big companies through the S&P 500 and to do it consistently and to do it in a very, very low-cost way."[33]

Vanguard is now arguably the king of passive investing, ranking as the second-largest asset manager in the world, behind BlackRock (another firm that has expansive passive investment options). Vanguard manages more than $10 trillion, a total greater than the GDP of all but two countries in the world.[34]

Recently, however, these large firms have been plagued by controversy around their proxy voting. When an individual or institution holds shares of a publicly traded company, they are allowed to vote on important matters in that company—things like the selection of board directors, compensation for executives, or even new policies related to things like diversity, equity, and inclusion and ESG. Conventionally, when an individual holds a fund through a manager like BlackRock or Vanguard—an S&P 500 ETF, for example—the manager gets to vote on behalf of the person. The Vanguard S&P 500 ETF currently manages around $500 billion in assets on behalf of investors, and by aggregating that capital, it controls the votes of those individual investors.[35] This aggregation gives Vanguard a great deal of power. Taken collectively, the three largest asset managers in the world (BlackRock, State Street, and Vanguard) are the largest shareholder of almost 90 percent of the companies in the S&P 500. As a result, their votes matter a great deal to those companies.

This hegemony has been a source of controversy. If you've ever tried to order a pizza with two or more friends, you know that people rarely agree on anything perfectly. The practice of managers like Vanguard voting the shares of millions of individuals in accordance with its own internal firm convictions on matters of governance and corporate responsibility has led to dissatisfaction among those who view many of these fund managers as forwarding more politically progressive agendas.[36] This level of influence has led to very public battles, including congressional action, over the power of these managers.[37]

In response, Vanguard has launched something it terms *proxy voting choice*, which allows those who hold its funds to exercise some limited discretion in how Vanguard votes on their behalf—selecting from a menu of options for potential voting themes or allowing individuals to choose to not vote at all.[38] This is a partial solution, and in a world in which tens of thousands of votes happen in public companies every year, no individual has the time or resources to discern how to vote on everything without help. But it's a move toward moving the power in voting away from the large-asset managers and back into the hands of the individuals and institutions that hold their shares. With the advent of artificial intelligence and the mass customization it enables, investors might in the future be able to profile their own preferences more clearly and get much more customized voting via these platforms.

Some upstart firms, like Prospr Aligned and Vident Asset Management (with which I am affiliated), have made proxy voting and corporate engagement (the process of writing letters to companies or introducing resolutions) core to their offering to consumers, promising to better reflect the consumers' values in the votes cast on their behalf.[39] For those who aren't interested in, or wealthy enough for, alternative investing or who have no interest in active management, steps by Vident, Vanguard, and others to better reflect the interests of investors in expressing their values allow even the average person investing in index funds an opportunity to have an impact.

Accion Venture Lab, Impact Foundation, and Vanguard are just three firms among thousands globally seeking to express values through their investments. The landscape is now broad and deep enough that almost any investor can find partners that fit their values well. With those examples in mind, I will now outline a more systematic approach with practical advice on how any investor can better align their portfolio with the impact they would like to have.

Simple Principles for Aligned Investments

What are a few simple ways in which you can begin to incorporate your values into your investing? Money can be extremely complicated, so I'll advocate a few simple principles that can get you started on the road to financial flourishing in your investment portfolio (figure 6-3).

FIGURE 6-3

Seven principles for aligned investing

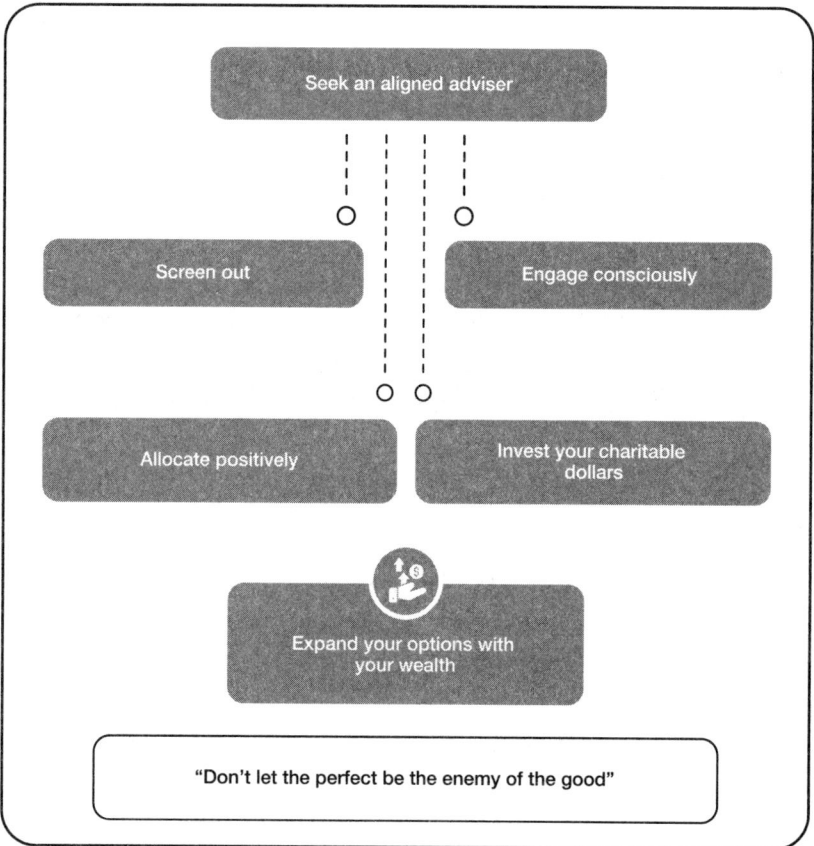

1. Seek an aligned adviser.

2. Screen out what you don't want.

3. Engage consciously.

4. Allocate positively to themes and managers you are excited about.

5. Invest your charitable dollars.

6. Expand your options with your wealth.

7. Don't let the perfect be the enemy of good.

Any one of the preceding steps is a great start—and there are probably more ways to get in the game I'm not listing here. The important concept is to understand that your investments have impact and to begin the life-long journey to embrace, enjoy, and direct that impact toward the benefit you want to see on the world.

Let's go through each principle briefly to add color to their implementation.

Seek an aligned adviser

One of the easiest first steps—and one that can enable all the others—is to find an aligned financial adviser and have a conscious discussion with them about your values so they can help seek expressions of them in your portfolio. This task might look like finding a firm that shares your values or your focus comprehensively. Or it might simply be finding an individual within a larger firm or at a solo practice with whom you resonate and who seems to understand the values you'd like to express in your portfolio.

Money is a complicated thing. If it's not your day job, trying to manage it yourself comes with a lot of risk. Even for those of us who work in financial markets, it's often wise to have an adviser for our own personal assets.

A professional financial adviser can also help you take the first steps into values-based investing. To start that conversation, you can simply sit down with your adviser and outline what matters to you. You may, for example, care deeply about the environment and want to make sure your portfolio is as environmentally friendly as possible—screening out companies with bad environmental records and including funds or companies that are making positive contributions. You may be deeply involved in combating human trafficking and want to make sure that your portfolio is aware of supply chain issues with human trafficking or supports companies focused on the issue. You may be a person of religious faith who wants to make sure your portfolio doesn't support certain industries—adult entertainment or alcohol, for example—or that you are positively focused on companies with the attributes you believe are most closely aligned with your approach to human flourishing. You may simply want to overinvest in supporting entertainment or the arts, scientific research, or biotechnology—things you believe make the world better.

Regardless of your goals, there is probably a way to begin investing with them in mind. Instruct your adviser to find ways to incorporate those goals into your portfolio. Or better yet, find a wealth management firm or adviser who is focused on the same values as you and is implementing them across multiple portfolios. Through either of these approaches, you can get the help you need to build your values into your portfolio with less confusion, time, and risk.

Screen out what you don't want

Most people's investment dollars are concentrated in cash (money markets), bonds, and stocks. Stocks are shares in publicly traded companies, such as Coca-Cola and Home Depot, held directly or through ETFs, mutual funds, or other similar vehicles. This is particularly true of retirement assets in 401(k) plans or IRAs, which are often heavily focused on stocks and bonds. For those who need liquidity—meaning they can't afford to have their assets tied up in private equity funds as they might someday need the cash—publicly traded stocks are often the best way to create long-term return. After all, the S&P 500 in the United States has averaged around a 10 percent return, meaning that, as we saw previously, investing in that index would double a person's money every seven or so years. So at least historically, stocks have been the best way for the average investor to easily access a good return.

For these public exposures, consider investment funds aligned with your values, whether these funds are sharia compliant (for Muslim investors), Christian faith aligned through a trusted manager, or oriented to your particular ideological philosophy, and avoid holding securities that might conflict with these values. There are a variety of mutual fund and ETF strategies managed to exclude securities that would conflict with the values of those who invest in them, and a professional adviser can help you navigate the options. You can also research specific mutual funds or

ETFs on your own to determine whether their screening approach matches with yours.

If you want to simply buy the index (the broad universe of stocks)—the S&P 500, Nasdaq, or Russell 3000, for example—there are several off-the-shelf offerings that screen out commonly excluded categories, such as alcohol, gambling, or other industries. There are also an increasing number of direct-indexing options like the aforementioned Vident Asset Management. These options allow you to hold the broad market directly, screening out securities you don't want. Negative screening can go too far and it is a relatively limited way in which to seek values alignment. For example, I've seen screening lists that include as many as eight hundred securities, including hotel companies with minibars and most major media companies. Such expansive screening lists may hamper returns and often capture companies that are not genuinely misaligned with a person's beliefs. But limited negative screening can offer some peace of mind that your investment dollars are not flowing to industries you'd prefer not to support. I once heard of a cancer charity, for example, that found by investing in index funds, it had more money tied up in publicly traded tobacco companies than it was granting to fight cancer each year. It made moves to make certain this would no longer be the case, specifically excluding those companies from its holdings. Today, it is often quite easy for an individual to do the same.

Engage consciously

As the shareholder of a company, you own a piece of it and are entitled to vote on the company's key initiatives periodically. This voting is often done by proxy by the mutual fund or ETF manager you invest with. For example, when you invest with BlackRock in an S&P 500 index, Black-Rock votes your shares on key initiatives in a way aligned with what it believes are the best decisions for the company. Similarly, by virtue of owning shares, BlackRock cannot just vote but can also engage. It can write letters to the CEO, introduce new resolutions, and encourage the company to take a variety of social or business positions. This is common practice now among most asset managers like Fidelity, State Street,

J.P. Morgan, and others. What are those positions? It depends on the manager. One responsibility you may have is selecting an investment manager who shares your values and advocates for them.

Finally, there is a new way of owning shares in indexes or funds. As mentioned previously, direct indexing goes even further, allowing a person to own the shares of the S&P 500 directly rather than through ETFs or mutual funds, which would give that person's vote by proxy to others. Firms like Parametric Portfolio Associates, Vident Asset Management, and others allow individuals to own shares directly and often allow people to subscribe to a proxy voting or corporate engagement offering, by which the firm will engage those shares on the user's behalf. Regardless of the approach, there are several ways to align even public stock holdings with the values of the individual.

Allocate positively to themes and managers you are excited about

Most of us desire to see some positive change in the world and believe in the power of certain industries, countries, or innovations to encourage that change. While negative screening articulates what we do not want to invest in and engagement allows us to make our voices heard, positive screening involves understanding deeply the good things we want to see in the world and the route by which we can invest in them. This can often be done while pursuing market rates of return.

My friend Finny Kuruvilla, for example, founded Eventide, a mutual fund company based in Boston, to invest in promising trends in health care. He and his colleagues screen out any technologies or companies that violate their core values, and they then select positively for products or treatments in biotechnology and related areas they believe can transform treatment of certain diseases and conditions. They are not alone. Numerous values-driven investors in the public and private markets are seeking to transform health innovation and delivery. Through his private equity firm Ascend, In Seon Hwang is trying to create scaled physician practices to serve underprivileged communities. Garheng Kong, the CEO of

HealthQuest, is investing in growth equity companies in the health space. And hundreds of other options exist globally, powering development in the health-care space. Many of these options are aspiring to market rates of return. Similarly, several ETFs and mutual funds offer passive exposure to the space for those who prefer it. By mentioning these funds, I am not endorsing them; each person must carefully evaluate their own investment opportunities. I am merely trying to demonstrate the range of approaches now available.

Some investors prefer alternative energy. Various mutual funds and ETFs across the spectrum invest in energy transition in specific sectors like electric cars, renewable energy, and climate friendliness. Similarly, some venture capital and private equity funds focus on new and alternative energy sources; others are aggressive about enforcing climate goals in the companies they support. This diversity of options exists in areas like education, food, and other categories. You can invest in funds or indexes directed at certain countries or regions and can even find newer and unique opportunities like investing in charter school bonds intended to help finance the facilities of new and existing charter schools.

The point here is not to endorse any specific investment or strategy. But if you believe strongly in seeing some positive change in the world, there may be ways to invest your financial capital in those areas out of a dual commitment to impact and the belief that solving big problems sometimes leads to positive financial return. This should all be done in collaboration with a financial adviser who understands the risks but who can turn the relatively blasé act of investing into something more deeply aligned with your values and with greater impact on the things you care about.

Invest your charitable dollars

The primary purpose of charitable dollars is, of course, charity. But many individuals and institutions choose to set aside charitable dollars now, invest them, and give them away over time. This practice is obviously true in the world of endowments and foundations. Harvard University, for example, manages approximately $50 billion, which it uses to fund student scholarships and other university initiatives through giving away the returns on its investments.[40] In Atlanta, the Robert W. Woodruff Foundation invests hundreds of millions of dollars to give to a variety of charitable causes, including education and the arts. Very often, these endowments and foundations only give away 5 to 7 percent of their assets annually, investing the remainder. This ratio allows them to grow their assets over time to give more.

We might quibble with that approach. Perhaps the world would be better if these foundations gave away their money in real time or if their wealthy donors did. There is a movement among some philanthropists to put their money in *spend-down trusts*, like the Marcus Foundation—entities intended to give all their money away over a set period rather than making it last forever. In our lives as individuals, it's important to give charitably and to help others in real time.

But there's also a rationale for being thoughtful and deliberate about charitable donations—as most foundations are—and investing in the meantime. These dollars, in particular, may be ripe for values-based investing. The Rockefeller Foundation, for example, has a detailed ethical investing policy in which its investments are intended to contribute to the same mission as its philanthropic giving (within the constraints of seeking a positive investment return).[41] The World Wildlife Fund similarly considers its investments an extension of its giving mission and positively invests in areas it wants to see grow, like regenerative agriculture and sustainable forestry.[42]

This is all well and good, you may think, for foundations with professional staffs and hundreds of millions of dollars. But how does this strategy apply to an individual? Some people are wealthy enough to have their own foundations that can act in these ways—like the Chan Zuckerberg Initiative or the Arthur M. Blank Family Foundation—but most of us aren't wealthy enough to justify a large family foundation.

That's where DAFs like the Impact Foundation, which we explored previously, can play a role. DAFs like those offered by Fidelity, Charles Schwab, the National Christian Foundation, WaterStone, or the Bradley Impact Fund can allow you to leverage institutional infrastructure to invest your personal charitable dollars. These DAFs allow a person to give money away today—to the DAF itself—while waiting to make prudent decisions to then grant that money to charity over time. Although the money, once given, technically belongs to the DAFs, these organizations hold the money in portfolios of the individual givers and take the givers' suggestions of where to ultimately grant it.

Most DAFs offer donors investment options, sometimes in ways that allow them to extend their charitable mission into their investments. This option may also be liberating for you as an investor in that you might feel comfortable taking risks or engaging in concessionary investing (investing that intentionally yields a substandard return in pursuit of a positive social mission) with charitable dollars, as those dollars are intended to help others, anyway. This might be as simple as allocating to individual stocks or ETFs that align with your values through your DAF investments. Or it could involve allocating to private investments that meet your specific goals, using groups like the Impact Foundation. As a personal example, I have used some of my DAF dollars to invest in entertainment projects I thought meaningful and have explored investing in charter school bonds, which would allow me to loan dollars to public charter schools serving disadvantaged kids.

Expand your options with your wealth

One of the great joys of being an investor is the privilege of allocating to remarkable entrepreneurs you believe in. As an investor in private equity, venture capital, and real estate, I have the option to directly support entrepreneurs designing world-changing companies. I could also purchase companies that treat their employees well and craft extraordinary cultures, and I could put money into real estate developments intended to create community and positive relationships. While publicly traded stocks, ETFs, mutual funds, and other instruments can be strong investments with high impact. There are myriad opportunities in the *private markets*—companies, real estate developments, and other entities not listed on public exchanges— that can offer expanded opportunities for return and impact.

In the United States, numerous regulations prevent people with more typical wealth from buying certain investments. Below $1.1 million in net worth (as of 2025), for example, most people are not allowed to buy private securities (those not available on public exchanges), and it takes $5 million or more in investable assets for someone to be a qualified purchaser, someone who can invest in almost anything they choose. Investment firms' general partners, like me, get special rights to make these investments because of their expertise in the areas, regardless of their financial status. But the overall regulations are intended to protect investors less familiar with these instruments from entering into vehicles they don't understand or that are illiquid, or hard to exit. In industry terms, *illiquid* describes investment dollars that you sometimes can't access for five years or more and that consequently impose more risk on someone who might need their funds to cover events in their lives.

But as you reach these financial thresholds and your wealth grows, the variety of options available to you grows as well. These include investments in startups, more mature companies, real estate in all its forms, credit to private companies, and even airline leases and litigation finance. It's a fascinating world, though complex enough that deep understanding and advice becomes even more important to accessing it. And given that private investments often have board representation in companies or control entire companies or real estate investments, they can offer an even deeper opportunity for positive impact through thematic investing or cultural formation.

Don't let the perfect be the enemy of the good

One of my favorite life principles is, "Never let perfect be the enemy of good." The quote is attributed to people as diverse as Voltaire and architect William McDonough, but its intent is to remind people that striving for perfection can often be an impediment to progress.

Running a values-based investment firm, I often hear people struggle with the idea of incorporating their values into their investment strategy. The topic can be overwhelming. They can't come up with ways to convert 100 percent of their portfolio to values-based investing, so they give up before they start. Can your public equities portfolio ever completely re-flect your values, particularly if you simply prefer to use low-cost indexes? What happens if your 401(k) plan doesn't seem to have any options for values-based investing? What about your bond portfolio or the cash you have in money markets? These are great questions. But trying to solve them all at once can be both exhausting and counterproductive.

No one's investment portfolio is perfect. Few, if any, are 100 percent values-aligned—including my own. And some holdings, like gold or US treasuries, may be critical to an investment portfolio but have no or only tenuous connections to a person's values. If you haven't been consciously thinking about the incorporation of your values into your investment portfolio and the impact that may have on the world, start by simply iden-tifying one change you'd like to make in that direction. Maybe it's adding one thematic ETF aligned with your values to your portfolio. Maybe it's making a private investment into something you are passionate about. The ways to start are nearly infinite, but by dipping a toe in the water, you will quickly get a sense of what works for you, and you can experiment with second, third, or fourth steps along the way.

A Good Money approach to investing cares about both values and returns—coupling financial responsibility with positive social good.

Chapter 7

Save for Freedom,
Not Retirement

Rick Woolworth designed quite possibly the perfect retirement. He lived his life with purpose. For more than thirty years, from 1977 to 2010, Woolworth led a successful, enviable career on Wall Street, much of that time with Morgan Stanley. He was famous for the Woolworth rule: "Do the right thing by the clients." People who worked with him remember him as joyful, encouraging, and effective, traits he would carry into his unique career pivot. When he retired from investment banking and investment management in 2010, he had enough financial resources to truly unplug, spend more time on the golf course, and devote more attention to his wife, daughters, and friends.

Woolworth did those things, certainly. He had a wife of more than thirty years, three siblings, and three daughters—to which he would add two sons-in-law and three grandkids. Slowing down his career gave him more time with them all. But he also felt called to honor what he called a shadow that had been chasing him, to do something more with the next chapter of his life. He was drawn to mentorship. Woolworth had benefited from wonderful mentors and had loved mentoring others in his job. He took a holistic approach to that practice, wanting the young people he spent time with to develop great character, to form great relationships (particularly marriages), to serve others, and to work with purpose—tenets of flourishing that echo those of Seligman and VanderWeele.

Encouraged by his wife, Jill, a marriage and family therapist, he created an organization called the Telemachus Network to foster community among older, more experienced couples and their younger counterparts. In Homer's *Odyssey*, when the hero Odysseus left home for the Trojan War, he placed his son Telemachus in the care of an older man named Mentor, whom he trusted to guide and shape him. It's from this guiding character that we get the English word *mentor*. Woolworth loved the name Telemachus because it placed the focus where he thought Mentor would have wanted it, on the young protégé, not his guide.

The Woolworths helped to fund this new enterprise (having built the means to spend more on others in retirement) and hosted an annual gathering complemented by individual coaching and speaking sessions they would host all over the country. They didn't charge for this. They just wanted to share with younger leaders what they had learned. Their goal was simple: to see a new generation lead centered and meaningful lives. The Woolworths were remarkably effective. Hundreds of people, old and young, joined Telemachus. And the network reached thousands more as they traveled the country sharing the importance of mentorship and the principles they had learned for marriage and work.

In addition, Woolworth never stopped learning and even went back to school to further his education. He participated in the Stanford Distinguished Careers Institute, where he further investigated the topic of mentorship, about which he'd become so passionate. My wife and I had the privilege of learning from the Woolworths on several occasions. He defined his lifelong mission in investments and in mentoring as "to grow fruit on other people's trees." And he grew as much fruit as any person I've met.

Woolworth was healthy, energetic, almost amazingly fit, and full of joy, which made it all the more shocking when he suddenly passed from an aortic dissection at sixty-nine years old.[1] The community he and his wife had built was heartbroken. As one mentee of Woolworth's put it, "Rick was the embodiment of love."[2]

That's a remarkable "retirement," isn't it? If Woolworth had ended his career after his time in investments, he would have still been remembered fondly. But the decade he dedicated to others afterward ended up being perhaps (after his lovely family) his most significant impact on the world—a legacy that shaped thousands of lives.

It's with Woolworth's life in mind that I want to question the culturally dominant version of retirement and encourage those seeking flourishing to reconceive of that milestone and how they save for it in radical ways.[3]

Retirement is a dream for most people globally. Work can be difficult, and the idea of being able to spend more time on leisure, to reduce stress, and to enjoy friends and family is alluring. The reality is that at some point, each of us who lives long enough will exit the workforce, whether we retire at a time of convenience or are forced to do so by poor health or other obligations. In addressing habits, mindsets, and values around financial flourishing, retirement is a critical topic. Global data is difficult to come by, but in the United States, retirement savings is often the first- or second-most-cited reason for saving money (often behind emergency funds, which indicates the dearth of financial security among many people). Data from the Organisation for Economic Co-operation and Development indicates that in most countries around the world, the effective age of retirement hovers between sixty and seventy. Saudi Arabia and Luxembourg have the lowest average retirement age at fifty-nine, and Indonesia the highest at sixty-nine. The United States sits dead in the center, with an average retirement age of sixty-five.[4]

Of course, these retirement averages conceal a host of differences among cohorts. As mentioned in an earlier chapter, the internet forum Reddit has a whole community dedicated to FIRE (financial independence, retire early). In this community, participants seek to maximize earnings and savings to reach a number that allows them to retire in their thirties and forties and continue to live frugally, or they aspire to Fat FIRE, with more savings to enable things like travel and luxuries. There's some wisdom to this number targeting; it aligns with our discussion of setting a financial finish line. On the other end of the spectrum, many people never acquire the means to retire comfortably or they end up having to live a dramatically reduced lifestyle on minimal government pensions (Social Security, for example, in the United States). Around three in ten Americans over fifty-nine, for example, have no retirement savings at all.[5] And many young people start too late.

Sometimes, people are pleasantly surprised. While only 45 percent of Americans believe they are ready to retire, 74 percent end up thinking they have enough to get by when they do.[6] But only 4 percent of Americans who are retired say they are "living the dream," while half of retirees are somewhere between "living a nightmare" and "not great, but not bad."[7]

For readers of this book, retirement is probably the number one financial goal you've discussed with your advisers—even for the reasonably wealthy. The dream of hanging it up and retiring like Danny Glover's detective in *Lethal Weapon* is a core part of most people's financial goals and life plan. It's easy to see why. As we've seen earlier in this book, only 15 percent of people globally feel engaged at work. Only 6 to 43 percent of people in countries around the world rate work as a significant source of purpose in their lives. And nearly half of professionals say they are considering leaving their jobs in any given year.[8] Those are absolutely dismal statistics, and it's easy to see how many people long to leave the problems of work behind.

As a practical matter, saving so that you have enough money to retire is probably a good thing. None of us know when a medical emergency may strike or whether we will need to offer full-time care to a loved one. But this is not a book about tactics. It's about mindsets and values. I'd like to use the concluding principle of this book to challenge one of the most deeply held beliefs by most people: that they should retire, and that retirement will be good for them.

Retiring to escape a purposeless profession—and making that escape a core financial goal—is self-defeating and has the potential to hinder our ability to live truly flourishing lives. Meaningful work, done right, is a pathway to many of the core elements of human flourishing: purpose, meaning, relationships, service. And without it, people often settle for less than they might otherwise have. In addition, people of all ages who spend time dreaming of retirement—waiting out a meaningless job or grinding through work just for the money, hoping to one day pivot to something better—often miss the opportunity to live well in the moment.

For those who are healthy, retirement is a flawed concept. While you might make the transition from full-time work at some point in your life or switch careers to something you are passionate about, most people should not retire in the conventional sense. Saving for retirement, then, is misguided. Meaningful, engaging work is a critical part of living with purpose and flourishing holistically. What we really desire—or should desire—is not to stop working but to have more freedom, autonomy, and purpose in our work. Managing our finances in such a way as to make that kind of work possible should be our real goal. What we should desire is an arc like Rick Woolworth's, where, though our pace of life may change, the work we do with what the late poet Mary Oliver calls our "one wild and precious life" stays important to the end.[9]

When we save, it should be for *freedom*, not retirement. Good Money habits can enable that.

Retirement Can Be Bad for You

One core thing we need to come to grips with, as a society, is that while retirement has a number of perceived benefits, it's not the panacea many hope it will be. Done poorly, it can have significant consequences for our mental and physical health.

On the face of it, many retirees report being happy. The insurance company MassMutual (which may, admittedly, have a bias) reported in a 2024 survey that around two-thirds of retirees said they were happier than while they were working, and one-third said they were the same or worse. That's pretty good (though around 77 percent thought they would be happier than they ended up being). Around one-third of all respondents also reported feeling "forlorn at times." Common among the happier participants was the fact that they filled their times with loved ones, exercise, hobbies, and travel.[10] This would seem to indicate that all the promise of retirement is there, right? In some ways, yes, particularly if it's done well.

But peel back people's self-reported responses, and there is mounting research that retirement has a negative side.

Johns Hopkins Medicine recently reported that leaving the workforce can increase the chance of heart disease and other serious medical conditions by 40 percent but that "older adults who volunteered at least 100 hours per year were two-thirds less likely to have poor health and a third less likely to die compared with non-volunteers."[11] The Harvard School of Public Health mirrored these findings, reporting that retirees were 40 percent more likely to experience a heart attack or stroke than those still working.[12] These results are explainable when you consider that retirement often means more social isolation, less activity, and fewer sources of purpose and direction—conditions all associated with declines in mental and physical health.

The US National Bureau of Economic Research found that "complete retirement leads to a 5–16 percent increase in difficulties associated with mobility and daily activities, a 5–6 percent increase in illness conditions, and a 6–9 percent decline in mental health."[13] Though it noted that "the adverse health effects are mitigated if the individual is married and has social support, continues to engage in physical activity post-retirement, or continues to work part-time upon retirement." Oregon State University researcher Chenkai Wu found that delaying retirement by even one year (from age sixty-five to sixty-six) lowered mortality by 9 percent: "There are a lot of social benefits related to working: You're more active, you're more engaged, you're talking with your peers, and so on. Losing those when you retire can be harsh."[14] An earlier study for the Social Security Administration found an even more pronounced result: "Retiring exactly at age 62 increases the odds of dying by 23 percent relative to men retiring at age 63 and by 24 percent relative to men retiring at age 64."[15] This also lines up with increasing research connecting engagement in challenging mental activities with better health, notably warding off dementia in older people.[16]

These US results resonate with global research. The Institute for Economic Affairs found a series of troubling results among retirees in a study of more than nine thousand participants across twelve EU countries. The findings included declines in self-assessed health, increased rates of clinical depression, and increased probability of experiencing physical health issues and of needing a drug to address those issues.[17]

The study notes that on retiring, the respondents initially felt better for about a year before their physical and mental health began to noticeably deteriorate, presumably linked to the decrease in physical activity, meaning, purpose, and positive social engagement mentioned earlier. The author of the study noted, "It may be beneficial to reconsider the kind of work and retirement balance that we've established. That might be able to circumvent some of the negative health effects associated with not working."[18] In other words, the conventional view of retirement—to stop working entirely—may be counterproductive.

This makes sense, doesn't it? If we are escaping a job we find meaningless or are able to rest and relax more, there may be an initial happiness to retirement. But we know from Seligman's and VanderWeele's work that real flourishing comes from community, relationships, service, purpose, meaning, and health and well-being. All of those can be substantially diminished by retiring the wrong way—doing so without a future direction in a way that steals our sense of purpose.

The National Library of Medicine actually did a study on purpose and retirement explicitly, and while the results were mixed, the overall trend was as we would expect, as shown in figure 7-1.[19]

The researchers found a temporary boost in purpose among one group: low-income individuals who had previously not experienced much purpose in their jobs (that impact went away over time). But for individuals in higher economic bands—like many of those reading this book—losing the sense of identity and meaning that work has offered was a net negative.[20]

You've probably experienced this. If you are younger, you've seen a parent, grandparent, or mentor physically and mentally decline after retiring or witnessed someone excited about retiring into pure leisure become bored or aimless. If you are older, you may have friends who were overjoyed at the prospect of finding unlimited free time in their lives, only to find that the time came at the cost of meaning.

FIGURE 7-1

The correlation between purpose and age in retirement

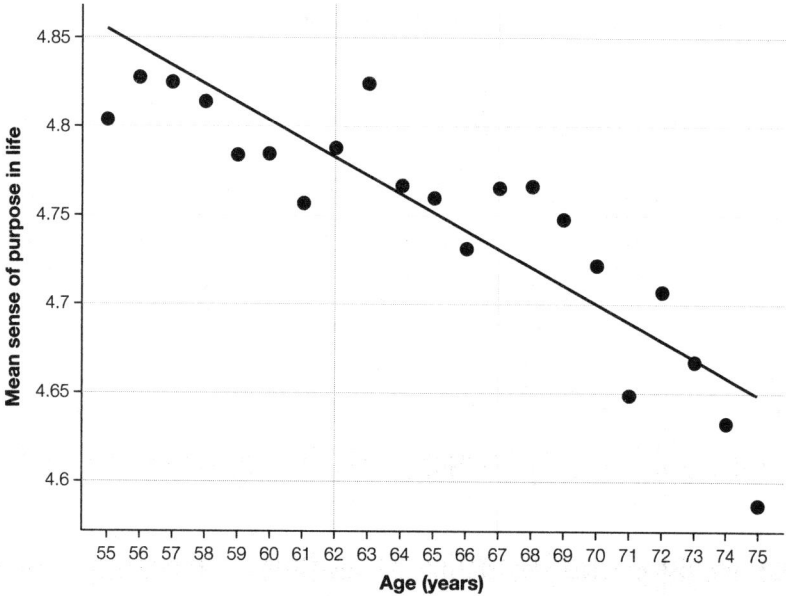

Source: Ayse Yemiscigil, Nattavudh Powdthavee, and Ashley V. Whillans, "The Effects of Retirement on Sense of Purpose in Life: Crisis or Opportunity?," *Association for Psychological Science* 32, no. 11 (October 2021): 1856–1864. Used with permission.

Beyond its negative implications for the individual, a traditional definition of retirement is bad for society. Rick and Jill Woolworth make this clear. Older people often retain an immense opportunity for contribution, their wisdom and experience a well of untapped potential that could transform families, communities, and workplaces alike. If a man in the United States makes it to seventy years old, he typically then lives to eighty-five (and half, of course, live longer). For a woman, that number is eighty-seven. Globally that number varies but is often even longer in high-longevity societies like Japan. What that means is that the average person is now living twenty to twenty-two years in retirement, with many living well into their nineties.[21] And while we don't want to live in a society that asks its eighty-year-olds to work as hard as its twenty-year-olds, losing out on the wisdom and contribution of retirees for decades is bad for the societies in which they live even as full retirement is bad for them individually. There are perennial shortages, for example, of volunteers at community organizations and in schools. Workplaces often have roles that might be best accomplished part-time by someone with experience. Although most older people do a great job leaning in with their families in retirement, there's a broader world that could use their perspective. Thinking of retirement creatively might help change its financial calculus for some individuals as well.

Does this mean you should work forever, never retire, or grind it out full-time at your current job until you die? No. But I would argue that most people should drop a conventional view of retirement from their future plans. Even if you have the finances to retire, if your goal is to flourish, you need to find a way to use those savings to support new direction, meaning, service, and relationships in life.

Save for Financial Freedom

If traditional retirement is the wrong goal, what is the right one? First, it's learning to never accept disengagement, purposelessness, or lack of meaning at work—a topic covered extensively in chapter 3. Our goal should be that we ultimately see purpose in every dollar we earn and proactively craft our workdays and careers in a way that enables that. But admittedly, one thing that makes this goal all the more possible is the financial means to buy autonomy and freedom in our work.

I saw this play out with my father-in-law, Elliot Feit. Elliot was one of the kindest, happiest, and most other-centered men I've ever met. After he met my mother-in-law, Sandy, in middle school, they rapidly became close friends before beginning to date in college. Elliot's passion for both kids and medicine led him to become a pediatrician. He excelled at the job. Parents and kids loved him, and he cared for them in a way only truly great pediatricians can. Elliot had three kids of his own and loved to spend time with them and, ultimately, their spouses and his grandkids. At one point in his career, when his hospital in Rhode Island was closing, he de-

cided to join a private practice somewhere sunnier. He moved to the sub-
urbs of Atlanta, where he quickly became a fixture in the community.
Pediatricians get to know everyone, and Elliot was an extrovert who loved
socializing and community service alike. His financial prudence (including my mother-in-law's earnings and career) made his decision to trade
out his hospital job for one with more ownership, agency, and autonomy a
low-risk move. That decision allowed him to build a life he wanted to live.

It also paid off when he decided in his late fifties to begin to gradually
reduce his workload at the practice to focus on other things. He didn't
want to entirely quit the job he loved, but he also didn't want to spend as
many weekends on call or sort through quite as much paperwork. He
wanted more time to devote to his passions—his kids and grandkids, his
model trains, his place of worship, and particularly a prison ministry in
which he'd become quite active. Every week, Elliot would spend time in a
prison nearby, leading a group intended to share love with those incarcerated. He never really slowed down as he approached retirement (maybe he
lingered in the house a bit longer on his days off), but he had the financial
means to align his life with his purpose and passion at that time.

Elliot was taken from us after a battle with pancreatic cancer. But the
approach he took to life—living every moment for others with purpose—
led to the most beautiful memorial services I've seen, with hundreds
pouring out from all walks of life to express authentic love and admiration
for him. Perhaps most impactful, we were invited to a memorial service at
the prison where he had volunteered. There, the incarcerated men in his
group celebrated his life and gifted his wife and kids with crafts they had
made in his honor. It was such a beautiful tribute to a beautiful man.

If I think about the goals most of us would have in life, it would be to
end up with a legacy like Elliot's. Part of that was his penchant for endow-
ing everything he did with purpose and his passion to see others flourish.
And part was enabled by the prudent financial management that gave him
the flexibility in his career to craft the life that worked for him at the time.
Elliot and Sandy saved aggressively throughout their careers. Both worked
for much of their lives. They never engaged in conspicuous consumption,
and although they vacationed as a family and enjoyed many experiences

together, they made sure to do so well within their means. So, when the time approached for Elliot to scale back his work, they had enough saved up for him to do so, particularly with Sandy still working a job she loved as a magazine editor. They didn't want to retire (Sandy is still working) but wanted to make sure they had time for the things they truly loved in life.

One primary characteristic that leads to human flourishing is agency. In psychology, agency refers to "the feeling of control over actions and their consequences."[22] It's the feeling that we are in the driver's seat of our own lives, and it's essential to happiness and fulfillment. One reason I like the idea that purpose is something you build, not something you find, is that it endows each of us with agency. Our lives are not something in which we are passive observers but are things that we can shape, manage, and improve. That feeling of agency, in life and at work, is central. One study in Chile, for example, found that agency was as important for psychological well-being as income.[23]

Closely related is the concept of autonomy. Put simply, autonomy is "the ability to make choices yourself rather than having them made for you by other people."[24] We are autonomous when we feel like we—and not someone else—are in control of our lives and choices. Autonomy is one of the key things we struggle with as kids and teenagers, feeling (rightly) as if our parents are in control. And while autonomy is a big determinant of happiness and life satisfaction in various areas, it's critical at work.

Earlier in this book, we looked at employee engagement and how low it is around the world. A Gallup study in 2023 put that number at 23 percent, and the same survey estimated that every year, workplaces lose $8 trillion in productivity to disengagement. This amount is equal to almost 10 percent of global GDP. Engagement is obviously good for companies, with high-engagement companies reporting high client satisfaction, higher employee retention, higher productivity, and higher profitability.[25] But more importantly it's critical for individuals. Who wants to show up every day disengaged and purposeless at work? Disengaged employees certainly long to retire.

An increasing number of studies indicate that a central tenet of better engagement is autonomy. When employees in a company feel some measure of control and self-direction in their work (autonomy) and be-lieve that the outputs of that work matter (agency), they are happier and more engaged. One study of 4,340 people in Denmark, for example, found that "job autonomy is positively associated with psychological well-being."[26] The results were quite clear even if the researchers' academic language communicating them is a bit sedate. A similar study of more than 1,100 young people in Colombia and Spain found that "almost all the dimensions on the Psychological Well-Being Scale correlate significantly and positively with the dimensions on the EDATVA scale [a scale that measures autonomy]."[27] Finally, a 20,000-person survey out of the United Kingdom found that "greater levels of control over work tasks and sched-ule have the potential to generate significant benefits for the employee, which was found to be evident in the levels of reported well-being."[28]

Again, we all know this. We work better and feel more engaged when our work matters, when it affects others positively, and when we have agency and autonomy over how to do it. If we had those things in our pro-fessional lives, most of us wouldn't want to retire in the conventional sense. We would want to contribute.

The financial goal we should all aspire to is not retirement but an ade-quate financial buffer to ensure we can always have agency and autonomy in our professional lives—with more freedom to switch jobs if needed, change schedules to part-time, travel, spend time with others, or pursue passions. We saw the impact that freedom had on Rick Woolworth and Elliot Feit, and we all sense that building the financial means to be able to take risks and make bold choices in our professional lives is a more com-pelling and rewarding goal than retirement in and of itself.

That's where some of the FIRE community on Reddit gets it right. They are focused (sometimes too intensely) on building financial flexibility early in life—avoiding debt, living within their means, investing well, earning a good living—so that they can pursue the life they want at any time. Where they often get that wrong, in my view, is among those who completely turn to a life of leisure. A better example is Anand Kesavan's freedom to enter the world of nonprofit work on schools, Davis Smith's having the resources to launch Cotopaxi, Rick Woolworth's ability to retire from Wall Street early to pioneer an organization mentoring others, and Elliot Feit's freedom to reduce his schedule for family and prison ministry. Even for those who don't switch jobs, financial freedom and autonomy may give them the confidence to truly job craft, working with an employer to shape a role more suited to their talents and the impact they can have.

The other good news in all of this is that for some, this financial goal may be easier to reach than retirement. If you are saving for retirement using the 4 percent rule that says a person can safely withdraw approximately 4 percent of their savings for living expenses each year in retirement, then you have to save quite a large sum to maintain a lifestyle. If you spend $50,000 per year on your life, for example, you need $1.25 million in savings to make sure your money doesn't run out. But if part of your intent is to have enough so that if you wanted to change jobs or reduce your schedule you could, the number might be smaller. If you're making $50,000 a year to support your $50,000-per-year lifestyle and find something that pays $35,000 and is more fulfilling, your number goes from $1.25 million to $375,000 (the amount necessary to cover the $15,000 you sacrificed in earnings using the 4 percent rule). And as long as you've built adequate emergency savings (equivalent to perhaps twelve months of expenses), you've dramatically increased the autonomy you have in your decisions. Further, this transition can come at any age. If you're saving for freedom, not retirement, that freedom can come in waves—first manifesting itself as a substantial-enough pool of savings in your twenties, thirties, or forties to pursue work you are passionate about, even if it pays less. And later in life, it allows you to make the transition to part-time work or perhaps to a life of volunteer work, travel, time with family, and cultural enrichment.

That's the story of Barbara Hillary. She battled cancer twice, in her twenties and later in her sixties, working as a nurse for fifty-five years before retiring. But Hillary had saved for freedom, not retirement. Despite losing 25 percent of her lung capacity to the cancer she eventually overcame, she went on to lead a life of adventure: at seventy-five in 2007, becoming the first Black woman to reach the North Pole and, five years later, the first Black woman to reach the South Pole. Despite her age, she pivoted to become a public speaker and an activist, even traveling to Mongolia to speak in 2019 shortly before passing away later that year. She was honored by Congress and the National Organization for Women for her exploits, ultimately earning induction into the National Women's Hall of Fame.[29]

We should all desire freedom, which appropriate savings can enable. What can this look like in practice? To borrow a concept from another author, it looks like building a fortress balance sheet and maybe a fortress life.

Build a Fortress Balance Sheet

Beyond retirement, there are many important things we save and invest for in life. When we're younger, we save for college or for a new car or phone—the essentials to get our lives off on the right foot. As we age, we build up savings for emergencies like health events or job losses, for childcare and education for our kids (through worthy tools like 529 plans), for home ownership, and for life's little luxuries like vacations and special outings. We invest that money for impact in the world and to see it grow so that our money is multiplying and compounding as we age.

At the heart of all that savings and investing is the idea that money can, if well used, provide freedom for life's most important pursuits and serve as a fortress against the many storms that may come. In a way, mastering money and saving effectively guarantee that we have freedom from money itself, that we master it instead of it mastering us.

I picked up this topic of a fortress balance sheet from Greg Brenneman, a legendary CEO and investor who writes about it in his book *Right Away and All at Once: 5 Steps to Transform Your Business and Enrich Your Life*. Brenneman led organizations as diverse as Continental Airlines, PWC Consulting, Burger King, and Quiznos before becoming a private equity investor with CCMP Capital. In his book, he lays out the principles he used to turn around and lead big companies—principles that are also relevant to leading a good life.

In one chapter, he discusses the leadership of Jamie Dimon during the great financial crisis (2007–2009) and how J.P. Morgan had built a "fortress balance sheet" that allowed it not only to survive the event but also to serve as a partner to the US government in stabilizing the broader economy. The company did so by ensuring that it always had more than enough capital to cover its obligations—well more than required by law. The move might have (in the very short term) sacrificed some shareholder returns, but it allowed the firm to withstand almost any single event. It also ultimately allowed the company to thrive when others were failing by acquiring and stabilizing peers that had not been so prudent. Brenneman used the same logic in the turnarounds he led, noting that "cash is king" and that consistently one of the first things he'd do when helping a company, nonprofit, or person would be to check their budget and balance sheet and make sure they were adequately preparing for any potential situations.

How does this translate to the individual? For retirement—or better yet, for achieving financial freedom that allows for agency and autonomy in the work we will do our whole lives—this means establishing a cash and investments position that ensures we will never be in trouble financially because of circumstances outside our control. (See the sidebar "Tips for Building a Personal Fortress Balance Sheet.") We've already covered some of those principles. The 4 percent rule, for example, guarantees that we have enough savings to live off if we need to. We should always aspire to have cash emergency savings—generally twelve months if possible—that can support us if the worst happens.

And we should never have a negative net worth. In his discussion of a fortress balance sheet, Brenneman also suggests not having any debt in life (on credit cards, cars, or other items), except, perhaps, real estate, where appropriately sized mortgages may be sensible for the average person. The overall message is that we should save in such a way that we control our money rather than being controlled by our financial obligations. If we are too insecure in our savings, we will constantly be at the whims of our jobs, the financial markets, or other circumstances outside of our control. But if we prioritize building a strong personal balance sheet, we earn the freedom to pursue our careers with purpose, to help others, and to invest with impact.

Tips for Building a Personal Fortress Balance Sheet

What does a fortress balance sheet look like? That's highly dependent on a person's age, health, spending, and other factors, but I suggest a few rules of thumb for the average person:

- Track your net worth, and never let it go negative, even early in your career. This advice is the most difficult to follow during college but can be accomplished through summer and part-time work and being clear-eyed about what education you can afford.

- Have an emergency fund in cash (or money markets) equivalent to six to twelve months of spending.

- Keep housing costs under 20 percent of your income, and if you have a mortgage, be sure to have at least 20 percent equity in your home (i.e., a down payment of 20 percent on a new home). This goal is quite difficult in markets like the United States or Australia, where housing is expensive and requires discipline.

- Have no other personal debt (business debt is a different topic), with the possible exception of a car, as discussed earlier.

- Save at least 20 percent of your income each year to put into investments (ideally 30 percent or more in your peak earning years), with a target of accruing investments adequate to cover your basic expenses by age fifty-five (whether in retirement accounts or cash brokerage accounts). For example, if you started saving $20,000 per year at twenty-two years old earning 8 percent annually, you'd have almost $3 million at fifty-five ($1.6 million adjusted for inflation)—an amount that would offer great freedom and flexibility in your career, particularly if you own your own home by that time.

- Have the appropriate disability and life insurance to guard against the most unexpected events in life and to guard the future of your loved ones.

A fortress requires discipline, realism, and sacrifice. But it also provides the foundation for a flourishing life—one that can offer you freedom, agency, and autonomy as you age.

Chapter 8

Good Money and Kids

Change how you think about money. Earn, spend, give, and invest wisely. Save for freedom, not retirement. These are concepts that are simple but rarely practiced. They are countercultural but essential to building a relationship with money that leads to human flourishing.

Once you embrace Good Money personally, it's important to look beyond yourself to the people around you, particularly your children. How can you teach your kids to manage money well? How can you give them the right financial foundation to flourish while preventing them from experiencing the destructive downsides of having too much wealth (particularly inherited wealth)? How much is enough to provide for your kids, and how much should they be expected to earn on their own?

These questions won't be immediately relevant to everyone reading this book. But as I interact with families, particularly wealthy families, Good Money's relationship to children is often the number one issue causing stress in their lives. This chapter lays out a few principles to help parents think about Good Money habits for kids.

Navigating Wealth and Kids

Almost every parent wants to offer their children a better life. In the United States, 87 percent of parents say their children are one of the most important aspects of who they are as people, and 82 percent say that having children is rewarding most or all of the time.[1] A majority of parents would give up almost anything—vacations, social media, and even best friends—to assure their children's well-being.[2] Many parents view their children's financial stability as a core concern. Some 88 percent of parents say it's extremely or very important for their kids to experience financial independence and jobs or careers they enjoy—the number one goal of parents in Pew Research Center's seminal research on the topic.[3] Parents around the world want their children to enjoy more prosperity and financial freedom than they themselves have.

That's an admirable goal, particularly for those who have experienced poverty and deprivation. As I've consistently noted in this book, it's difficult to achieve human flourishing without the financial stability to support meaningful work, health and wellness, relationships and community, and the other elements of a thriving life. But in our desire to see our kids financially successful, we sometimes unintentionally make it harder for them to flourish. Parents can fixate so much on financial security for their kids—prioritizing it as a means and not an end in their children's lives—that they teach them the wrong priorities or spend their own time in ways that are counterproductive. For example, one study found that quality time with parents was the best determinant of flourishing in kids.[4] Another noted the role parental health and well-being play in childhood flourishing—both things some parents end up sacrificing to provide financially.[5] Of course, for some families, working more hours to earn a higher paycheck is necessary. But parents often fall into the trap of thinking their kids need money accrued by working longer hours more than they need quality time with a healthy, happy parent. That's most often not the case.

As almost anyone who has interacted with wealthy people knows, an excess of money can be destructive for children. In an article based on her research in the field and titled "The Problem with Rich Kids," Suniya Luthar finds that children of the affluent "show disturbingly high rates of substance use, depression, anxiety, eating disorders, cheating, and stealing."[6] A study from the National Institutes of Health echoed these findings, stating, "Upper-class children can manifest elevated disturbance in several areas—such as substance use, anxiety, and depression—and that two sets of factors seem to be implicated, that is, excessive pressures to achieve and isolation from parents (both literal and emotional)."[7] Several studies, including one recently out of Norway, document that inherited wealth decreases labor force participation among those who inherit, perhaps not a shocking finding for those who have encountered families with multigenerational wealth.[8] But it should be a disturbing statistic for all of us who understand the importance of meaningful, mission-driven work to a flourishing life.

Being poor is more difficult than being rich—that much is true, and it's worth remembering. But being wealthy can sometimes have tragic impacts on families if that wealth is not stewarded properly.

As a result, the topic of Good Money for kids is a pressing one. For the middle-class family, this issue may involve debates about whether to pay an allowance (and when), whether to connect allowances to chores and tasks, and whether to encourage summer and after-school jobs. It can involve judgments about whether to help with a young person's first car, mobile phone, or college education and how much to let kids make purchase decisions on their own versus guiding those choices. As wealth progresses, parents decide on how nice the birthday parties, clothes, or experiences they offer their kids will be. The Good Money issue ultimately involves questions about inheritances and family giving, among other topics.

At some point, wealth becomes very complicated. Now that I work with families who have extraordinary financial means, I've seen both the good and the bad of family wealth. The bad can be quite troubling: Kids can lose focus and never find purpose in a professional career. There can be substance abuse problems. Siblings may be torn apart over money. I've seen children waiting for aging parents to die to access their inheritance and parents feeling resentful of their kids. Young people might lose touch with reality and live well beyond their means or fail to learn the value of hard work and resilience. There is a Chinese proverb that says families move "from rags to rags in three generations." For many wealthy families, that observation holds true. But more strikingly, all of those generations can find that money managed poorly is a trap that makes it more difficult to live a meaningful life.

A planned, thoughtful approach to family wealth can help people cultivate great relationships and generosity and can ensure that families have the time and opportunity to live deeply in relationship with one another. It can offer the resources to buy kids autonomy to get a good education, start a business, or take measured professional risks. I've met very few parents—particularly those who grew up without money—who don't want to make sure their kids always have the means to access proper food, shelter, and health care for themselves. My own family dreamed of this for me. Educating kids in Good Money habits from a young age, even in the absence of family wealth, can help them develop a proper relationship with money that will equip them for the future.

Many parents think that giving their children financial independence is their highest goal. But those who have accomplished that goal often realize that their true goal should have been to create a foundation for a good life, grounded in the very principles outlined so far in this book, and to teach them how money can enable that.

I've created a simple framework for parents to follow when they are thinking about guiding their kids toward good financial decisions (figure 8-1). The framework is aligned with what we've already learned about earning, spending, giving, and investing in the six steps for Good Money.

In the rest of the chapter, I'll outline takeaways on how you can ensure your children are learning about, and living, each of these ideas. First, we'll explore how families can ground Good Money principles in a family statement of mission, vision, and values. We'll then explore how financial education can be done through the prism of apprenticeship—with parents modeling appropriate behaviors, offering age-appropriate visibility and a voice on family finances, and allowing kids to learn by doing. Next, we'll walk through how this apprenticeship can connect meaningful work to money, model and moderate children's spending, share a passion for generosity, and offer an opportunity to invest together. Finally, I'll conclude

FIGURE 8-1

A simple framework for Good Money for kids

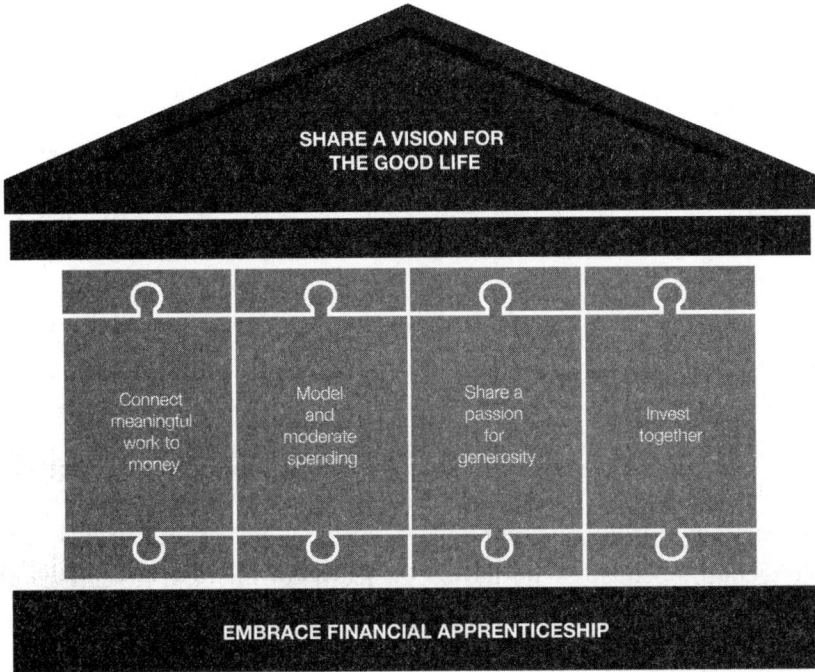

SHARE A VISION FOR
THE GOOD LIFE

Connect meaningful work to money

Model and moderate spending

Share a passion for generosity

Invest together

EMBRACE FINANCIAL APPRENTICESHIP

with a few parting thoughts on one of the most complex topics any parent faces: inheritance.

Collaborate on a Family Mission, Vision, and Values

The right way to start a discussion of Good Money and kids is, ironically, not with money. Because money is merely a means to achieving the good life, the first step in any discussion of money and kids is to outline what you and your family think about flourishing together.

Earlier in this book, we looked at frameworks for human flourishing from Tyler VanderWeele and Martin Seligman, and we touched on similar frameworks embedded in a variety of faith and philosophical traditions. Many of these elements of human flourishing are consistent across almost any person, time, and place. No one, for example, thrives without a life full of meaningful relationships, character, virtue, and service to others.

But each family is different. Every family, starting with the parents, should think consciously about what they view as a successful life and how they would like to communicate that to their children. One easy way to do this is through a family mission, vision, and values. Just as companies have mission or vision statements and embrace a set of values or virtues, families should seek to articulate the same.

My wife and I, for example, have a core mission from our faith tradition to "love God and love others" and to "live justly, love mercy, and walk humbly." We've also set a vision for maturing our kids: "To raise well-adjusted, independent, faithful adults who want to spend time with us and each other." We've communicated that mission and vision to our children and formulated our core values to be "kind, curious, and courageous"—principles we developed alongside them at a very young age. These principles are fleshed out in our life philosophy, in the rules we establish for the kids and ourselves, and in the way my wife and I model behavior in our own lives. Life is complex, and the values we embrace should be, too. But these simple statements help to anchor us when we are sorting through those more complex issues, including money.

In an article for the financial firm Ellevest, Ashley Bleckner articulates the case for a family mission statement:

> A mission statement can help give *purpose* and *direction*—which are keys to satisfaction with your life. So there's no reason to confine them to the workplace. Sitting down with your family to create your own mission statement can help you deepen your connection, resolve differences of opinion, and make more meaningful decisions.
>
> You'll use your family mission statement in all sorts of ways, but it's especially helpful when it comes to money. That's because talking about money is never just talking about money,

really. It's also talking about generational differences and gender expectations. It brings up a lot of emotion. It can be seen (especially within families) as a competition. And then there are the money taboos that make us want to avoid talking about it at all—which can definitely cause problems.[9]

Similarly, the wealth management firm Brown Advisory, which works extensively with high-net-worth families, positions the need for a family mission, vision, and values as intimately tied to how the family thinks about money—including earning, spending, giving, and investing:

> We believe a family mission statement—and a strategic plan to implement that mission—allows a family to filter out the "background noise" of day-to-day challenges and focus on long-term goals and objectives. Developing these documents provides a process for reaching agreement on the family's core values and creates a shared vision amongst all family members. . . .
>
> A family mission statement is a succinct statement of the family's purpose and core values. The three primary components are personal, financial and philanthropic. . . .
>
> A strategic plan communicates to family members the family's goals and the actions needed to achieve those goals.[10]

Money is not the goal—it's a tool to achieve our goals. As you begin the journey of considering Good Money and kids, you might start simply with a few questions that will help you shape a values-driven foundation for how you will approach financial questions.

What is our family's mission statement?

What is the core impact your family hopes to leave on the world? What does that mission indicate about your core beliefs and values? Is it pithy enough to remember but distinct enough to guide decisions?

In a *Harvard Business Review* article titled "What's Your Family's Mission Statement?," author Priscilla Claman talks about her family's mission statement growing up: "We never get seasick." That's an unusual statement to guide all of a family's decisions and actions! But as she explains it, "Yes, we never actually got seasick, but what it really meant was that no matter what others were doing around you (like throwing up), you always stepped up to the challenge. You were expected to speak up and defend your position, even with your parents. That made for loud family dinners and, later, persistent adults."[11]

Does that one statement indicate everything Claman's family believed about the world, money, relationships, meaningful work, and a host of other topics? No. But at its core, it provided a rallying cry for the family to remember: that core to their goals in life was a belief in courage, resilience, and perseverance. A series of more detailed beliefs could surround and flow from that.

In an article for the American Academy of Family Physicians, the members of the Rivo family lay out their family mission:

> During several short family meetings, the four of us talked about what was most important in our lives and what we wanted to accomplish. Each person's contribution held equal weight. For example, Jessica, who was then 9 years old, wanted to plant and tend a rose garden, become a better ice skater and do well in school. For our 6-year-old kindergartner, Julie, it was important to be a good student and make new friends. Karen and I wanted to make a positive contribution as volunteers in our community.
>
> After much discussion, we developed a short mission statement—"be thankful for what we have and what we can give to others"—and ten family priorities. . . .
>
> We've framed our family mission statement and keep it in a visible place on our kitchen counter. Each year, we review what we have accomplished, reassess our priorities and revise our mission statement.[12]

The Rivos obviously have a thoughtful and nuanced approach to life. By boiling down the essence of that mission together—one that exemplifies the core values of the family collectively—they created a framework by which the family can process all the varied challenges and opportunities life throws at them. For the Rivos, it's quite easy to see how this might connect to money. "Be thankful for what we have and can give to others" lends itself to a financial life of moderation, gratitude, and generosity. This mission is explicit in one of their ten family priorities, or what I call *values* later in this chapter: "Perform mitzvoth (good deeds) for the community." This priority further leads to another family priority: "Invest in the future financially, professionally and spiritually."

What might a family mission statement look like for you? Sit down with your family, no matter the age, and discuss what you believe about the good life and your family's distinctive approach. Don't let the perfect be the enemy of the good. Like a company, you can revise this statement as you see fit. But make it memorable, fun, distinctive, and authentic to who you are and what makes your family unique.

What is our vision, as parents, for our kids?

Vision and mission are tightly aligned concepts, sometimes used interchangeably. But in this case, a vision for parenting your children is a statement about what you hope for your children's future. This should be aligned with your mission, but it should offer more direction to you, as parents, about the choices you make in raising your kids.

As mentioned, our vision statement is to "Raise independent, well-adjusted, faithful adults who want to spend time with us and each other." Embedded in this statement are several concepts. We want the kids to gain independence in adulthood and be well adjusted to encounter all the challenges life may bring their way. This goal leads us to let them work through problems on their own, have adventures, and fail in manageable and educational ways. It also means they need to develop the financial security to live independently. We want them to be faithful to the core philosophical principles and religious faith of our family. And we want them to "want to spend time with us and each other." If that's the case in twenty years, it means we've taught them the value of family and relationships and lived in such a way as to create meaningful connections with and among them throughout their lives. It also means they will have people to accompany them in their "wild and precious" lives as long as they live.

In their book *Parenting for the Launch* and article with the same title, Dennis Trittin and Arlyn Lawrence outline a slightly more involved vision for parenting: "We will raise future leaders of excellence who will live purposefully and honorably, who will understand and passionately offer their unique assets, who will leave a legacy of significance and joyful service, who will value relationships and faith, who will exude gratitude and courage, and who will live with the confidence of knowing they are loved unconditionally and believed in emphatically."[13] Again, we see elements here of the character that Trittin and Lawrence wish for children, the generosity with which they should live, the value of the relationships they will develop, and the gratitude and courage the authors hopes the children embrace.

As a parent, what is your vision for your kids as adults, and how will that factor into how you raise them? Your vision for them should extend beyond their financial security and should embody the good life articulated in your family mission you hope they are able to lead.

What values do we embrace as a family in pursuit of that mission and vision?

A final, helpful step for many families may be fleshing out the mission you are on together and the vision you have for raising your kids into a series of values you all embrace. These values won't be comprehensive. There are almost endless virtues in the life of any flourishing person, including character, generosity, resilience, grace, love, prudence, courage, and kindness. But your values as a family should be a succinct list of the core anchor virtues you hope to exemplify together and that can help you achieve your mission together.

Author Meagan Rose Wilson, who counsels families on their mission, vision, and values, lays out her own family values in a thoughtful article on her website:

- To love one another through thick and thin

- To surround our children with what is beautiful, what is good and what is true.

- To get outside every day, to connect with and respect nature

- To plant, to grow, to get dirty, to harvest

- To be kind

- To have respect, love, compassion and empathy for others and the planet

- To share, be gracious, grateful and humble

- To teach and lead by example—to be the change we wish to see

- To be faithful, proud, honest and supportive of one another

- To be passionate about learning, expanding and growing

- To read, read and read some more

- To maintain a quiet, reflective, inward practice each day

- To surround ourselves with music, art and creativity

- To educate ourselves about different countries, languages, religions, cultures and traditions

- To find beauty in all of our differences[14]

What I like about her articulation of values is that they contain core virtues most of us would recognize—things like kindness, love, and creativity. But she presents those values in catchy, distinctive ways and mixes them with practices (e.g., "to read, read and read some more") that both embrace a core value (e.g., education) and describe a practice that enables the other values on the list.

Again, these values are often best crafted by parents in conversation with their kids, and they may evolve over time. We aligned on "kind, curious, and courageous" for our family at a point in life when the kids were young and their challenges simpler. It's also a punchy, short statement they can all remember. That may evolve as their lives grow more complex. What's important is a family discussion about who you are and developing guidance for the family as individuals and as a unit—guidance on what constitutes good and bad behavior for your family in pursuit of a flourishing life.

How does all this connect to money?

Implicit in so many of the elements of a mission, a vision, and values a family may embrace are good financial habits. Families often prize independence, a component of which is the financial freedom to live independently and pursue a thriving life. Many explicitly highlight the value of hard work—the idea that each of us has something special to offer to the world and that work is about dignity and contribution, not just money, and that money is more appreciated when it is earned. Almost every family grounded in the principles of relationship and service also highlights generosity, a core manifestation of which is financial generosity.

Regardless of the values a family embraces, those values should be most concerned with the "ends" of life, the things that are intrinsically meaningful. Values around money should emphasize financial stability as a means to achieve those ends, not a goal in itself. Anchoring in a family mission, a parenting vision, and the values a family seeks to exemplify first can direct a family's approach to money in a way that is more likely to enable kids to flourish.

Embrace Financial Apprenticeship

Once a family is anchored in a mission, a vision, and values that the kids have been a part of shaping, parents can begin quite early showing children how financial habits connect to those values. And they can begin to apprentice kids in Good Money habits.

Traditionally, those who apprenticed were attached to someone—like a carpenter—experienced in their trade and sought to learn from them firsthand until they had mastered the craft themselves. This is quite different from much of modern education, which relies on classroom instruction. A hero of the American Revolution, Paul Revere, for example, began studying as a silversmith apprentice with his father at only thirteen years old (an age more common for such a profession at the time).[15] George Washington started his own career as a surveyor's apprentice at fifteen.[16]

This is similar to many modern workplaces, where a young management consultant learns by absorbing the work of a more senior consultant and where a young electrician follows an older electrician on jobs, supporting the more experienced person until the new person too has learned the trade. Similarly, the process of training kids in good financial habits and values is best approached not by teaching them but by apprenticing them: involving them early in family financial decisions, giving them increasing responsibility, and offering them visibility into the way parents think about and manage money while simultaneously offering them ways to practice those values in their own lives.

This happens less frequently than you might think. One survey, commissioned by the firm Stockpile, found that while 64 percent of teens rely on their parents for financial education, only 20 percent of parents have regular conversations with their kids about financial matters at home.[17] Another survey showed that 45 percent of Americans of any age say they have no understanding of their parents' financial situation.[18] And while those statistics actually seem to be improving for younger generations—only 10 percent of those fifty-five and older say their parents taught them about investing, whereas 29 percent of those age eighteen to thirty-four learned investing habits from parents—there is much room to improve.[19] The truth is that kids look to their parents more than any other source for modeling and education on financial literacy. Unfortunately, many parents fail to structure meaningful conversations on these topics with their children. That lack of intentional apprenticeship and education may be one of the reasons only 33 percent of adults are financially literate worldwide.[20]

This apprenticeship on financial habits, mindsets, and values can happen after the "earn, spend, give, invest" framework. It occurs when parents model the right behaviors and values, speak openly with their children about those practices, and educate them through intentional experiences on important financial topics. Critically, it is more than teaching kids financial literacy and financial values. The apprenticeship means modeling the right behaviors for them, coaching them through their own decisions, letting them try out practices on their own, and allowing them to fail and learn from their mistakes under the careful guidance of someone who loves them and has their best interest in mind.

Connect Meaningful Work and Money

Money matters more when it is earned. Earning money devoid of meaning and purpose in your work runs counter to what we know about flourishing. So, from a very early age, parents should seek to connect the topics of meaningful work and money, offering children opportunity but not entitlement, and giving them a grounded perspective on what financial stability will require of them over time.

This approach starts with parents actively engaging their children about their own careers. Kids often ask, for example, why a parent is leaving home in the morning or dropping them at school or day care. Many parents simply say, "I have to go to work." But a step toward apprenticing a child is to extend that explanation, helping them understand that work is how a family affords food, housing, clothes, education, and other things necessary to life. As the child grows older, this practice might include beginning to let them see how much those things cost so that they have a more realistic view of what living independently entails and what a future career may need to provide to truly achieve independence. Many high school or college graduates are shocked to encounter this reality when they first become responsible for their own financial provision. Modeling the ability to earn with purpose includes age-appropriate discussions of what a parent does and why that work is meaningful for them or how they seek to make it meaningful.

This apprenticeship also involves modeling behavior. If a parent eschews the financial discipline and hard work that leading a family entails, they set an example that may damage their children over time. Conversely, if a parent with plenty of financial wealth continues to work more than is needed at the expense of quality family time, they are modeling for children that money is more important than relationship. If they never model earning with purpose—never showing their children that work is both a way to achieve financial independence and a beautiful way to direct one's talents in a meaningful and missional way—the kids may never get that there is more to a job than money. Children see far more than most parents realize, and every decision a parent makes in their professional life is a lesson their kids are absorbing, one that should be carefully modeled and just as carefully explained.

One approach I've grown to love is incorporating kids, at the right time, into a parent's work—even beyond the Take Your Child to Work Days that have become so common. I was first encouraged in this idea by a colleague in my industry. Tom spoke about how he would take his kids, when they were old enough, on business trips with him. His children would join client meetings, dress the part, and even brief and debrief with Tom on the topics being discussed. I've begun to do this with my own children, beginning with my oldest, who will sometimes go on business trips with me—traveling, meeting clients, joining lunches and dinners, and visiting the companies we invest in. This kind of direct exposure demystifies work, shows the kids why it's meaningful, and shows them how an adult can earn a living in a purposeful and intentional way.

Similarly, parents can create early opportunities for kids to earn on their own. These occasions may extend through high school as they gain independence and the opportunity to work outside the home. Almost every flourishing wealthy family I know makes their kids work from an early age—cutting grass or cleaning bathrooms when they are too young to work outside the home, waiting tables or working landscaping when they hit sixteen.

Allowances—regular allocations of cash to kids—can be a great first step. A recent survey of Americans found that more than one in three families pay allowances to children, with more than 60 percent paying less than $20 per week, and those families were more likely to thoughtfully discuss other financial decisions together.[21]

Every member of a household should bear some age-appropriate responsibility for making the household function. Some parents use a chore chart, for example, laying out tasks each child is responsible for throughout the week. A very young child of four or five may have very simple chores: getting themselves dressed after bath time, cleaning up their toys, depositing dirty clothes in a laundry hamper. As kids progress in age, the tasks may become more meaningful: walking the family dog, mowing the lawn, cleaning the dishes, setting the dinner table, doing their own laundry, or even tutoring or babysitting younger siblings. These escalating opportunities for work inside the home acclimate kids to more and more responsibility.

An allowance is a way to reward kids for the work they do and to demonstrate consequences when they fail to do so. The amount of money allotted to kids will depend on that family's approach to spending and the resources it has, but the amounts will probably increase to match the kids' obligations. Parents can pay this allowance directly in cash (with many experts advocating a three-jars method, allocating money to spending, giving, and saving).[22] They could also use an online platform designed for kids, like Greenlight, or a ledger in which deposits and withdrawals are captured by kids so that parents can help them manage what they have.

At some point, the kids' obligations will shift to work outside the home. For a twelve-year-old, this might involve pulling weeds or cutting the grass for a neighbor. Parents can make it even more fun and instructive by helping their children convert this into a business: naming it, helping them think through their strategy, and potentially getting creative with that work. They might allow their children to start Etsy craft stores or grow produce to sell at a farmers market. Obviously, parents should moderate how much time their children spend on this work, prioritizing education and the joy and wonder of childhood. But with the right balance, this approach prepares children for the age when they can work a summer or after-school job and helps them learn what full-time work might entail.

These later, formal jobs—whether they be serving as a lifeguard, working at an ice cream shop, waiting tables, or even joining a summer construction crew—are particularly important. Some of the earliest and best lessons I learned were as a sixteen-year-old Applebee's busboy and as a seventeen-year-old sales associate at an outdoor sports and fitness store during my high school summers. Those professional opportunities taught me the value of money and hard work. They also allowed me to open a bank account and begin to practice rudimentary management of my own finances before those decisions became more complex in college and beyond. Starting this work and financial management while still living at home meant I could do so while my parents still had day-to-day visibility into my decisions and could coach me.

Almost 60 percent of work-eligible teens had summer jobs in 1979, but that number had declined to 38 percent in 2024. Surprisingly, however, the highest rates of teens working summer jobs were among wealthier families, with kids from households that earned more than $100,000 working summer jobs at a rate of 44 to 46 percent and those with family incomes under $30,000 working only 27 percent of the time (figure 8-2).[23] There may be many social factors at play (including access to jobs), but one is that families with positive money mindsets are often the most prone to encourage these same attitudes in their kids, building solid habits, mindsets, and values around work that will last them well into the future.

Beyond connecting money to hard work—that is, learning the value of a dollar—children's work outside the home can also offer parents and children structured opportunities to have conversations about crafting greater purpose at work: serving others, learning and growing a craft, building positive relationships, and tailoring their work to their unique talents and capabilities. Any job, whether it's walking the dog or waiting a table at a restaurant, has purpose. The earlier children learn this, the more likely they will be to flourish in their future careers.

Grit, resilience, self-reliance, and endurance are essential life skills beyond the financial world. When you have to make it professionally and

FIGURE 8-2

Youth summer employment by family income: Children of the wealthy are more likely to work summer jobs

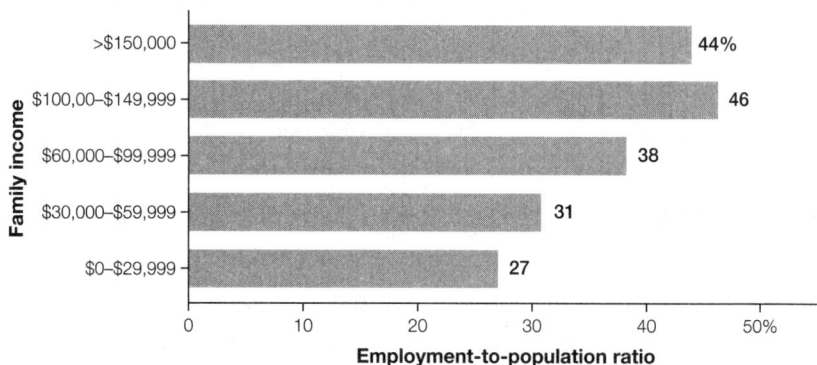

Source: US Department of Labor, "Youth Summer Employment," *Trendlines* 10 (July 2024) (analysis of Current Population Survey basic monthly samples [June–August 2023] accessed via IPUMS), www.dol.gov /sites/dolgov/files/ETA/opder/DASP/Trendlines/posts/2024_07/Trendlines_July_2024.html#youth-summer -employment-by-family-income.

financially on your own, you have to develop these skills. The best time for children to start developing them is as early as possible, under the careful apprenticeship of a loving parent or guardian who can coach them as they explore the world of work.

Model and Moderate Spending

What is a child to do with all that money that they earn through a household chore chart, their neighborhood landscaping business, or a summer job? They should learn to spend, give, and invest that money alongside their parents. The learning starts with spending.

Previously I talked with admiration about Steve Jobs's minimalism, and one of my favorite stories from the Walter Isaacson biography *Steve Jobs* recounted the Jobs family buying a washer and dryer:

> A few years later, Jobs described to *Wired* the process that went into getting a new washing machine: "It turns out that the

Americans make washers and dryers all wrong. The Europeans make them much better—but they take twice as long to do clothes! It turns out that they wash them with about a quarter as much water and your clothes end up with a lot less detergent on them. Most important, they don't trash your clothes. They use a lot less soap, a lot less water, but they come out much cleaner, much softer, and they last a lot longer. We spent some time in our family talking about what's the trade-off we want to make. We ended up talking a lot about design, but also about the values of our family. Did we care most about getting our wash done in an hour versus an hour and a half? Or did we care most about our clothes feeling really soft and lasting longer? Did we care about using a quarter of the water? We spent about two weeks talking about this every night at the dinner table." They ended up getting a Miele washer and dryer, made in Germany. "I got more thrill out of them than I have out of any piece of high tech in years," Jobs said.[24]

At that point in life, the Jobs family was extraordinarily wealthy. They could have hired a service to take the laundry off their hands. They could have simply opted for the most expensive washer and dryer. But that wasn't the way Jobs was wired. He cared deeply about design, functionality, and details. For a person of his wealth, he generally lived with surprising moderation. So, he turned the purchase of a washer and dryer, a minuscule financial decision for his family's means, into a teachable moment for the whole family. The lesson illuminated for the family members the value of money, the careful consideration of purchases, and the thoughtfulness about the goals of purchasing even mundane things.

That's apprenticeship—involving everyone in a family in financial decisions in a way that models healthy ways to make those decisions, and communicating the consideration that should go into acquiring material possessions.

In this book, we've reviewed extensively those positive outlets for spending: experiences, health, relationships, and time. We've also seen how lavish consumer spending is not fulfilling or responsible, regardless of income. But many parents either don't explain what or how they are spending or, worse, model behaviors that may ultimately hurt their kids. For parents following Good Money habits, giving kids insights into what they are spending on and why—family vacations, travel, household help targeted toward allowing for more quality time, a gym membership for health, and restrained spending on luxury goods—can help kids understand how their parents see the world and how their habits connect to that philosophy.

Good Money habits must be modeled well. If a parent preaches the idea of experiences, not stuff, to their kids but eschews the spending on a family vacation in favor of acquiring a sports car or a watch for themselves, a child is likely to internalize the lesson they see modeled, not the one they hear preached. Modeling provides an extra layer of accountability to parents, who, knowing their children are watching, may be more inclined to hold fast to Good Money principles themselves. Each purchase provides the opportunity, as it did for the Jobs family, to discuss things as a family and to highlight important concepts about proper spending.

Beyond the Good Money habits already described, parents should also think deliberately about whether the money their kids spend—or the money the parents spend on kids—creates entitlement or opportunity. Entitlement is one of the key fears of wealthy families. Entitled people often do not learn the value of hard work. When they are given too much, they naturally lose motivation or, worse, begin to expect the world to give things to them, an attitude that breeds dependency and arrogance. That's why work is important. Hard work done to earn money is the opposite of entitlement. But your spending priorities also risk cultivating attitudes of entitlement in kids. When spending on big-ticket items, parents should focus on purchases that create opportunity for advancement and growth.

Categories of spending that creates opportunity are broad. In general, our family will spend without many questions (as long as we have the means) on instructional materials and experiences: books, educational games, museums, classes or camps, and other similar items. We also try to help our children be successful in the various activities they take up as long as they work at them: a decent guitar for music practice, quality basketball shoes, and sturdy, fun book bags to take to school. Similarly, we like spending that builds relationships: birthday parties, bringing friends to the zoo, or going to a basketball game with Mom and Dad. As long as the spending is done modestly rather than extravagantly, we think the relationships these purchases build are important. We just monitor to make sure they are not leading to entitlement.

One of the biggest errors I've seen wealthy families make is giving their kids too solid a safety net or, worse, preventing them from ever struggling. Our friends Greg and Ronda Brenneman (mentioned earlier) and Britt and Julia Harris sponsor a marriage retreat that my wife and I have attended. Greg is a private equity executive and CEO. Britt is a renowned investor. Both men have more financial means than they need to survive. One of the sessions of the retreat they hosted was on navigating wealth and kids, and Britt's advice was simple: "Keep 'em poor." Basically, no matter how much money Britt and his wife had, they never let their wealth raise the standard of living for their kids or allow them to think they wouldn't have to build their own wealth and careers. I know several friends who, though they are building trusts for their children, aren't telling their kids about them until later in life, when those children have developed the right habits, mindsets, and values toward work and spending to manage that influx of wealth well.

Some families go even further. One of the wealthiest families I know owns a business, but no one in the family will ever be able to cash it in. Half its profits go to reinvestment in the company, and half to charity. The kids and grandkids are allowed to work in the business, but they must interview to get the jobs, and they are paid market rate for their work and nothing more. The parents in another wealthy family have decided that they will match their kids' earnings up to a certain amount in adulthood, effectively allowing their kids to live comfortably in professions like teaching or ministry but never creating unearned wealth.

This doesn't mean a family can't provide for the children. All parents want better lives for their kids. But certain categories of spending are naturally more likely to lead to opportunity—dollars spent on summer camps or college educations, family travel, or seed capital for small business. Providing children and young adults with the resources gained from the family's success and then forcing the kids themselves to build the financial foundation to expand their opportunities for consumer spending is a sound approach. It reinforces important lessons about taking responsibility for one's own life and earning financial agency and autonomy over time.

Share a Passion for Generosity

Previously we explored the example of David Robinson, who learned a passion for helping others from his legendary father, Jackie. Time and again, we see that when parents are generous and involve their children in that generosity, sharing a zeal for it with them, those kids become more generous themselves.

Recent research from Fidelity Charitable found that among the 69 percent of parents who give, 81 percent had children who had engaged in generosity over the prior year, with 51 percent giving financially alongside their time spent in community service. Further, that survey found that 54 percent of parents said having kids increased the priority of giving in their own lives.[25] Another study by Fidelity Charitable found that families with "strong giving traditions" reported greater financial giving, greater rates of volunteering, and closer family bonds within both their immediate and extended families.[26] This finding should come as no surprise. As we've explored previously in this book, service to others (including giving) is a key way in which people achieve greater meaning and happiness in their lives. Those who adopt attitudes of generosity enjoy better relationships and better well-being, alongside the inestimable good they do for others along the way. It makes sense that families who give and serve together would be closer and happier.

The Korn family is an example of this. Parents Usa and Tommy regularly volunteer with their teenaged children Iris and Lucas at Feeding San Diego, a nonprofit in Southern California dedicated to fighting hunger in the area. In this case, the kids got their parents involved after serving at the nonprofit as part of a school requirement, and a family tradition was created. Recounting their experience, Iris says, "We really love spending our Friday evenings here at Feeding San Diego because it's a nice way to connect with the family. It's kind of a refresh at the end of the week." Usa notes, "It's great bonding together. We don't really have any parent-teenager problems." Community service brings them closer, improves their family dynamics, and allows them to feel purpose and joy in helping others.[27]

It's the same thing my family has learned sponsoring economically disadvantaged kids overseas through Compassion International, and it's a lesson that can grow in sophistication and scale as a family's resources grow. One family I've worked with on investments, for example, has enormous wealth. They now work together across four generations. They spend sparingly. But they are conscientious about how they give and invest. And they try to do both with all family members involved. Their giving is run by a committee of family members empowered with decisions about where to allocate their philanthropic assets, and all family members are invited to participate both to learn how to carefully approach giving and to see generosity modeled by their elder members. For both giving and investing, the opinions of family members are considered even when the decisions are made by the more experienced subset of the group. My friend Katherine Dunlevie, a veteran multifamily office leader, calls this practice distinguishing between a "voice and a vote."[28] Kids may have the opportunity to broadly contribute to a conversation without needing ultimate decision-making authority. And that may grow into a vote over time.

On a smaller scale, another family I know meets each Thanksgiving to allocate giving from their family DAF each year. Thinking of it as the perfect time to give and remember how much they have to be thankful for, this small immediate family allows everyone to bring ideas. They talk them through, make allocations, and then celebrate together the gratitude they feel at having the resources to help others.

This kind of committed, multigenerational family giving is self-perpetuating, allowing new generations to learn the benefits to flourishing for them and for their communities of generosity and to grow closer together as a result. It also helps kids and parents alike develop a healthier relationship with money, learning that those who have resources and talents have some obligation to pay these forward to others.

As mentioned, many parents encourage their children—whether with cash jars, ledgers, or online financial platforms—to allocate the money they earn from allowances and outside jobs to spending, giving, and investing. Many of the families I work with encourage their kids to give first—before they allocate to spending or investing—so that they develop the habit of giving consistently, freely, and with increasing scale over time. Many families couple this with community service and direct involvement in the organizations they help.

If you need further evidence of the benefits of apprenticing kids in this behavior, a study published in *Psychological Science* found that, mirroring research in adults, "when children help others at a cost to themselves, they could be playing an active role in promoting their own well-being as well as the well-being of others."[29] Sara Loftin, a clinical therapist at Children's Health in Dallas, notes that giving helps kids exhibit greater gratitude, which is foundational to optimism and joy in day-to-day life. She further explains that it fosters greater empathy, kindness, and perspective-taking, essential elements that allow those children to develop more meaningful personal relationships.[30] According to Charitable Advisors, a nonprofit news network, "a study from UTHealth Houston found that children who volunteer are 18–35% less likely to experience anxiety or depression," and "research from the National Institute on Out-of-School Time shows that 76% of children who volunteer feel happier and more connected than their peers."[31]

Our lives are better when we give to others—of our time, talents, and treasure. The impacts of such generosity can be particularly high for children and can bring families closer together and build lifelong habits for flourishing. Good Money families should bake the habits of generosity into their family mission and values and engage in giving and serving together. Such apprenticeship across generations can be impactful for both our children and the world in which they live.

Invest Together over Time

Proper investing habits can be transformative. If you had a new baby to-morrow and deposited $10,000 into an investment account for that child in the S&P 500, their account would be worth $1.2 million in nominal terms (more than $200,000 adjusting for inflation) when they turned fifty, even if they never deposited another dollar into the account.[32] Similarly, if a fifteen-year-old opened an account with $10,000 today and deposited $10,000 more each year until they turned fifty, they would have nearly $1.3 million dollars (inflation adjusted) at maturity—more than 4 times the net worth of the median American today and 144 times the median wealth of a person globally.[33] We saw the power of compounding in chapter 6, but it's particularly powerful for kids who can start so early under the careful apprenticeship of their parents.

Families highly prize financial stability for their kids, as we've seen. It's important to keep that priority in context, always secondary to the higher vision of a flourishing life. But if parents want wealth for their kids, the best way to provide it is by teaching them the basic principles of investing early and apprenticing them in managing their money. If parents follow this pathway, by the time their children are adults, they have the habits, mindsets, and values in place to invest successfully.

One simple step is to start an investment account for your children as early as possible, even on the day they are born. The initial amount could be as little as $500. The investment can be done as a formal vehicle that belongs to them like a trust (a concept we will discuss more in a later section). It could also be done through a custodial account (an account that is the child's but is managed by a parent until they reach the age of maturity). Or you could simply create a subaccount in your brokerage account that you can track over time (noting that you might have to pay a gift tax in the future if you transfer this to them). The account will start them early on compounding returns and give you a starting point for working with them as they invest. A parent may similarly choose to start a 529 education savings plan (or whatever vehicles are available in your region) that invests regularly to pay for a child's future education—with the dual apprenticeship opportunity of guiding a child to value and plan for education while teaching them the complexities of investing.

As your children become aware, you can pursue simple strategies to help them understand the concept of investment returns very simply. My friend Christian Hempell, for example, once told me how he and his wife, Brooke, use the concept of the "bank of Mom and Dad" with their kids. The kids receive an allowance. They allocate money to giving, saving, and spending (one-third in each bucket). Christian and Brooke then double any money in their giving bucket, pay a 50 percent return on money in their savings bucket (adjusting down over time as their savings grow), and pay nothing on spending. This practice keeps things simple for the kids but introduces the idea that money not spent is money that can earn extra money—the central tenet of investing.

As a child matures, advancing this concept to investments in markets—money market funds, public equity ETFs, or individual securities—can make the lessons more real for a child. As they monitor their own accounts, the experience is naturally turned into a game where they get to see how their decisions influence the money they have. They also begin to learn more-challenging lessons. They learn that markets can always go down and money can be lost; they learn when it's right to persevere through a downturn and when it's right to cut losses; and they learn about the risks and rewards of investing in riskier or safer things. A child exposed to such lessons at twelve or thirteen will be much better equipped to handle their own money when they leave home, and they will be much more likely to have absorbed the lessons—both the principled and the practical ones—that can offer them financial freedom in the future.

Finally, there may come a time in each child's life when it is appropriate to include them in the family's broader investment decisions. This step should be approached with caution. A parent, for example, may have $100,000 or even $1 million invested—an amount that might be hard to fathom for a child. Seeing those totals may teach kids the wrong lessons: They might end up comparing their own family's wealth with others', violating the privacy of the family unintentionally. Or they might misperceive that the money is theirs—and develop feelings of entitlement as a result. Some kids may be ready for this responsibility earlier than others. Some parents may choose to never make their finances fully transparent to their kids. But there are some benefits to including children at the right point. The financial firm Newport Capital Group discusses some considerations: "Age isn't the only factor. Maturity often matters more than chronology. Some kids show early curiosity and accountability. Others take longer to grasp abstract or long-term concepts. The complexity of your financial situation and your long-term goals for your children—whether that means business succession, philanthropy or personal financial independence—should also influence your timing and approach."[34]

Getting visibility into a parent's portfolio can introduce a child to more complex investments that only adults have access to. In a world in which only half of people understand their parents' financial situation, knowledge of family finances may give children perspective and peace of mind. It may also prepare them for the eventual opportunity and responsibility of taking that money on when parents pass.

This is a step quite common for the adult children of wealthy families. Most of those families I work with eventually introduce one or more of their children to their *family offices*, the vehicles they use to steward their investments. In particular, families with multigenerational wealth may need newer generations of family members to take responsibility for the family's investments over time. I have several friends who now lead the investment portfolios for their parents, siblings, and sometimes even cousins. They often do so with the advice of professional advisers and with family "investment committees"— groups of educated family members who vote to approve new investments and help the person leading the family office think through the right way to allocate. Some children of wealthy families neither want nor are equipped to handle this responsibility, relying instead on a professional financial adviser or the family office run by others. But highly successful families who learn to work together for decades (or even centuries, as in the case of a few families I know) often have a thoughtful process for bringing new generations of family members into the portfolio and allowing them to take it over when the times is appropriate to do so.

In the midst of all of this apprenticeship, you can teach kids the basics of financial literacy—mortgages, student loans, retirement plans, emergency savings accounts, proper use of credit cards, credit scores, and other tools essential to life as a modern adult. These lessons will stick more thoroughly if they are both taught and guided through real-world management than if they are only learned in the classroom or from a book.

Central to these lessons is the family's mission, vision, and values and the fundamental opportunity to invest for impact. My children are aware, for example, that we have investments in a few private companies, funds, and even movie productions, and they have had the opportunity to visit some of these investments in person. This exposure makes the process of investing more real than simply looking at numbers on a page. It shows them the values our family seeks to express through our investments, emphasizing the importance of both creating a solid financial foundation and making a positive impact on the world. A family that holds stock in a company may want to visit that company together and talk about the corporate practices they admire and how they seek to make their employees' and customers' lives better. Investment dollars are enablers of almost every real estate development and company in the world. They have influence over the way those things are run—for good or bad. Seeing the work of those investment dollars can help bring that lesson home more than any spreadsheet could.

Approach Inheritance with Care

Before leaving the topic of Good Money and kids, I will touch on one final matter that's often the most complicated for families with significant financial means: inheritance. The question of how to transfer long-term wealth is a difficult one. Each family has to make its own decision about how much to leave to children, how to do it, who is responsible for overseeing the transfer, what rules (if any) to put in place for heirs to receive the funds, and what structure makes the most sense. This is not a book on tax avoidance or legal structure, and I won't endeavor to offer a solution here. An estate attorney or a wealth adviser is better suited to do that. Instead, I'll propose a series of values and tools you should consider.

In general, unearned wealth is bad for people. It hurts a person's sense of self-worth, their resilience, and their drive. It can cause wandering and purposelessness or feed entitlement and addiction. Sudden wealth is even worse, as studies of lottery winners and professional athletes show, and can lead to calamitous results for unprepared individuals who encounter it. In addition, older, more settled people tend to have already established careers and are at a point in life to make more prudent financial decisions. Younger people are often rash.

So, any transfer of wealth should be limited. This is one reason I love the idea of income matching, which I've seen some wealthy families employ, allowing kids or grandkids to pursue professions they love but softening the financial trade-offs they must make. If a child takes a job earning $35,000 per year, under this framework, their parents will match that $35,000—providing the child with a total income of $70,000 (and many families cap the amount they will match so that these numbers don't get out of hand over time). I also like the idea of parents limiting what they give to children and developing a logic around how much they want to pass down—establishing an *inheritance finish line* in the same way they have set their own financial finish line. There is also some logic to paying for opportunity-creating expenses—education, small-business startups, or other similar activities for kids or grandkids alike—while still empowering and tasking those future generations with creating their own path in life. That said, I also know peers who have inherited vast sums of money and led fulfilling, well-adjusted, hardworking lives in spite of their inherited wealth. Again, each family is different. Each person is different. Just think carefully about the impact wealth can have on a person and what you truly want for your kids.

As wealth grows, so does the complexity of some issues that families deal with. The next few questions are primarily for families that have accumulated enough money that others might consider them wealthy. And sometimes even things that are good at the right time—a family foundation or a vacation home—can be bad if managed improperly in the long run. The possibilities here are endless, but I'll highlight a few areas I've seen families grapple with.

What do we do about vacation homes and properties?

It can be a dream come true for parents to buy a home, particularly in a fun location that their kids want to come back to and spend time with them at, even in adulthood. For those with means, a family place at the beach, in the mountains, or in a distant country can create memorable experiences. But those places often create friction when the parents have passed. Kids get in arguments over the right use of the property. They similarly have to debate how to pay for maintenance and upkeep. The costs often outweigh the benefits.

One elegant solution I've seen a few families employ is to specify that on their passing, the properties are immediately sold by the trustee of their will and the money either donated to charity or shared among the children. Alternatively, the aforementioned Katherine Dunlevie suggests bringing kids into the decision ahead of time so that they own the process moving forward and have discussed how to manage it well in advance of needing to do so.

Should we pursue a family foundation?

Similarly, family foundations can be a joy. Giving is an extraordinarily enriching experience in life, and doing so as a family is rewarding. But perpetual family foundations often end up being a burden and source of division rather than a blessing. Kids argue over causes to support. Some are more or less involved. They often have developed very different passions and values.

Again, one elegant solution is a sunset provision to any foundation (described in chapter 5 with the example of Bernie Marcus). The other is to simply split such a foundation on death into individual foundations or DAFs for each surviving child to use as they see fit with their own families.

What about setting up a trust?

Trusts can be complicated. Many families create trusts and face crucial questions. Does each kid get an equal share or the share they need? Do they each manage their own investments or do it separately? What happens if one of the kids abuses their resources and runs out of money?

As noted earlier, many wealthy families are ambivalent about leaving anything to their kids, fearing the entitlement and lack of purpose that can come with unearned wealth. But families that do establish trusts have more often than not split them into individual trusts of equal amounts overseen by a trusted friend or family members who can hit the brakes if a child develops an addiction or otherwise misuses the funds. Here, family office or corporate trustees may also play a role whenever the organizations or families in play are complex and where timeless representation is needed.

How can we prevent our children's misuse of money as they get older?

Implicit in each of these decisions is one of the most challenging matters any family can deal with: enabling bad habits or, worse, some kind of abuse for their loved ones. This issue can be more complicated than it seems. At a young age, avoiding bad habits may look like refusing to buy kids iPads to use as proxy babysitters or video games that distract them from developing valuable life skills. But the issue becomes more complicated as children age.

One family I know, for example, has above-average means and has an adult child who has struggled with addiction and professional purpose, sometimes living on the verge of homelessness or hunger because of poor life decisions. For a while, the parents would contribute cash to their child when the child became desperate, but they eventually realized that doing so was enabling the poor decisions the child was making. Ultimately, they made the very hard decision to cut that child off, promising support only for a rehabilitation program or a house and food if the child moved home (and obeyed house rules). It was a hard decision and led to a great deal of angst and friction but ended up being the wake-up call this adult child needed to begin to reverse course.

At the beginning of this book, we discussed extensively the perils of sudden, unearned wealth. Lottery winners, professional athletes, and entertainers who come into money without the right process of apprenticing to manage it well are often overwhelmed by it and end up making tragic decisions. Similarly, money can be a good thing if directed to flourishing but can be a terrible enabler if someone is already prone to self-destructive behaviors. Money can enable apathy, drug and alcohol abuse, and even the mistreatment of others who are less fortunate.

Some of these dangers can be countered preemptively by the right, gradual apprenticeship discussed thus far. The downsides of wealth can be mitigated by forcing kids to earn their resources gradually and through hard effort—as with allowances and summer jobs. But even with those precautions, people can make missteps, and money can make those missteps bigger and less controllable. Some children may suffer with psychiatric, intellectual, or psychological issues that make them less able even as adults to grapple with the potential excess that wealth can create.

That's one reason many people who leave their kids inheritances do so through the aforementioned trusts. These trusts can wait to release funds to a person until they are old enough to manage them well. They often include provisions allowing the trustee (the person appointed to oversee the distribution of the money to the recipient) to fund only certain valid expenses (education, housing, etc.) or to withhold distributions if the intended recipient is in a vulnerable place. Examples include struggling with addiction or engaging in unethical activity—situations that might be worsened by the sudden influx of financial wealth. Like anything else, these provisions controlling children's financial resources can be abused, and some parents use wealth to control their children in unhealthy ways. But it has its purposes. The average twenty-year-old, for example, is probably ill equipped to receive $1 million, which they might end up spending unwisely (most of us would have made bad decisions with that much money at twenty!). But the average thirty-year-old is typically settled enough in life and experienced enough with money that they may have learned to manage this wealth more appropriately. And there are certain behaviors—like drug abuse—that shouldn't be enabled at any age.

Sometimes it's easy to overlook the bad habits money develops if it makes life easy. Often, it's excruciatingly difficult to watch a child making bad decisions struggle and suffer. While every situation is different and requires careful thought, in general "helping" a child in a way that enables their worst impulses is rarely truly helping at all.

There are no perfect answers here, but whenever a family makes a financial decision, it should think long and hard about the consequences of that decision over time. And the family should prioritize frequent and open communication to prevent surprises that can cause friction among loved ones.

Conclusion

Good Money for the Good Life

D o you really just want to be rich? Or do you want the true riches of a life filled with purpose and meaning?

There is great alignment among ancient tradition and modern social science about what works and what doesn't work with regard to money. And both the data and the anecdotes—from lottery winners, pro athletes, high earners, wealthy heirs, and others—offer ample proof that money can be both good and bad. That's why in a culture that often sends us one message about money—"make as much as you can, because your worth, happiness, and social standing depend on it"—we need to approach the topic more thoughtfully. Whether we are poor or rich, our mindsets and values around money will shape our relationship with it and with ourselves. Our habits around financial accumulation and wealth will determine whether the economic stability we all seek will give us greater freedom or entrap us in a cycle of negative mindsets and behaviors.

As I have maintained throughout this book, money is a means, not an end. It's a tool, not a totem. And while approaching money thoughtfully is essential to a prudent, free, and fruitful life, developing bad mindsets and values about money can be uniquely ruinous. My hope is that the simple

FIGURE C-1

Good Money: A six-part framework for financial flourishing

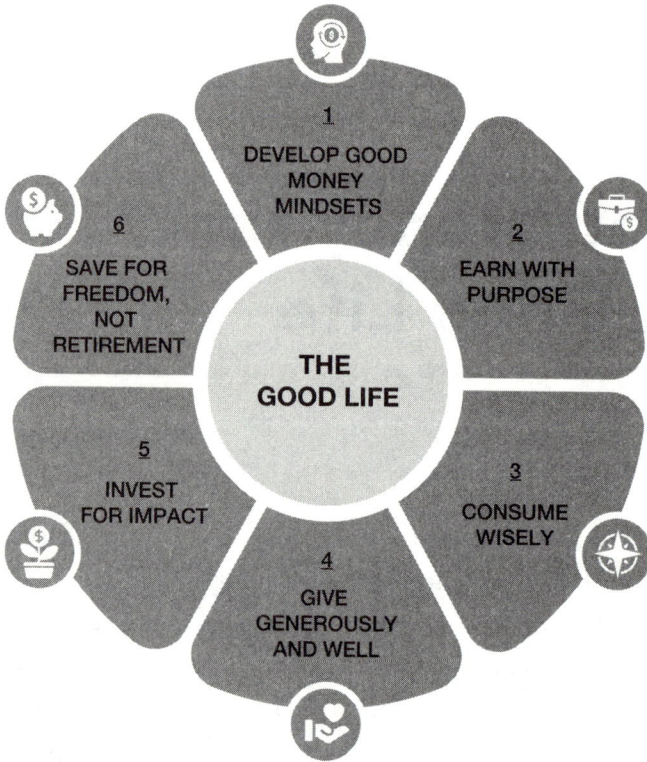

framework presented in this book and summarized in figure C-1 has given you and your family the ammunition you need to look at your unique circumstances and begin to approach the topic of money and flourishing more consciously than you have before.

We live in a privileged moment in history. The average person globally is richer than at any point in history. Many people are now grappling with the problems of excess, not deprivation. If you are reading this book, you probably have, or will have, more money than you will need to survive. That's a situation our ancestors would envy.

But our goal as people is not to survive but to thrive. And money can stand in the way of that. Richer countries right now are not more flourishing. Wealthier people have often warped their mindsets so much that even in the midst of prosperity, they struggle to achieve the more meaningful things in life: relationships, character, meaning, purpose, service to others, and joy. Like Ebenezer Scrooge, they too often end up bitter, hollow, and alone. We are tempted to make money our scoreboard but don't even know what game we are trying to win—or when that game will end. And we conclude our lives with money in the bank and regrets that we didn't make more of this "wild and precious life" we lead.

Your life is wild and precious. It's one of a kind. It can be happy and fulfilled. It can make the world a better place. You can flourish personally and be part of building a culture where your family, community, nation, and world can thrive as well. But the wrong habits, mindsets, and values around your financial life can stand in the way.

Don't let that happen. Whether you are a college graduate approaching the choice of a first real job after school or a retiree looking to rewire your life for significance, it's never too early or late to begin thinking about money differently and to craft a life of deep meaning, purpose, joy, and flourishing.

Start today. Use the principles in this book. Challenge them and add your own. But don't sleepwalk into a false obsession with your finances that allows their accumulation to become a hollow and self-destructive force in your life. Earn with purpose. Consume wisely. Give generously and well. Invest for impact. Live purposefully your whole life—and ensure that focus on purpose lives on for future generations.

The choice is yours. Will money be a good thing in your life or something destructive and distracting? Will it be a means to flourishing or a misplaced end? We all want the good life. Sometimes money can stand in the way. Good Money can help you thrive.

Notes

Chapter 1

1. Martin E. P. Seligman, "Learned Helplessness," *Annual Review of Medicine* 23 (1972): 407–412, https://ppc.sas.upenn.edu/sites/default/files/learnedhelplessness .pdf.

2. Pursuit of Happiness, "Martin Seligman," https://www.pursuit-of-happiness .org/history-of-happiness/martin-seligman-psychology/.

3. Martin E. P. Seligman, *Flourish: A Visionary New Understanding of Happiness and Well-Being* (New York: Simon Element, 2012); and Melissa Madeson, "Seligman's PERMA+ Model Explained: A Theory of Wellbeing," *Positive Psychology*, February 24, 2017, https://positivepsychology.com/perma-model/.

4. Courtney E. Ackerman, "What Is Flourishing in Positive Psychology?," PositivePsychology.com, May 9, 2018, https://positivepsychology.com /flourishing/.

5. Tyler J. VanderWeele, interview with author, September 24, 2024.

6. Tyler J. VanderWeele et al., "Flourishing in Critical Dialogue," *SSM - Mental Health* 3 (2023): https://doi.org/10.1016/j.ssmmh.2022.100172.

7. Tyler J. VanderWeele, interview with author, September 24, 2024.

8. Jack Caporal, "American Households' Average Monthly Expenses: $6,440," *Motley Fool Money*, February 14, 2025, https://www.fool.com/the-ascent/research /average-monthly-expenses/.

9. Marium Zaidi, "27 Most Charitable Countries in the World," *Yahoo Finance*, March 13, 2024, https://finance.yahoo.com/news/27-most-charitable-countries -world-045115517.html.

10. Marium Zaidi, "5 Most Charitable Countries in the World," *Insider Monkey*, March 13, 2024, https://www.insidermonkey.com/blog/5-most-charitable-countries -in-the-world-1273254/5/.

11. Wikipedia, "List of Countries by Charitable Donation as Percentage of GDP," https://en.wikipedia.org/wiki/List_of_countries_by_charitable_donation_as _percentage_of_GDP.

12. Ashleigh Jackson, "Here's the Average Net Worth of Americans by Age," *The Hill*, November 5, 2023, https://thehill.com/homenews/4290971-heres-the-average -net-worth-of-americans-by-age-how-do-you-stack-up/.

13. Lara B. Aknin et al., "Prosocial Spending and Well-Being: Cross-Cultural Evidence for a Psychological Universal," *Journal of Personality and Social Psychology* 104, no. 4 (2013): 635–652.

14. Morgan Stanley, "Sustainable Signals," August 7, 2017, https://www
.morganstanley.com/pub/content/dam/msdotcom/ideas/sustainable-signals/pdf
/Sustainable_Signals_Whitepaper.pdf.

Chapter 2

1. Carol S. Dweck and David S. Yeager, "Mindsets: A View from Two Eras,"
Association for Psychological Science 14, no. 3 (2019), https://doi.org/10.1177
/1745691618804166.
2. Mayo Clinic, "Positive Thinking: Stop Negative Self-Talk to Reduce Stress,"
November 21, 2023, https://www.mayoclinic.org/healthy-lifestyle/stress
-management/in-depth/positive-thinking/art-20043950.
3. Wikipedia, "Learned Optimism," https://en.wikipedia.org/wiki/Learned
_optimism.
4. Cece Li, "What Is a Growth Mindset?," Decision Lab, https://thedecisionlab
.com/reference-guide/neuroscience/growth-mindset.
5. Wei Zhao et al., "The Impact of a Growth Mindset on High School Students'
Learning Subjective Well-Being: The Serial Mediation Role of Achievement
Motivation and Grit," *Frontiers in Psychology* 15 (2024), https://doi.org/10.3389
/fpsyg.2024.1399343.
6. Neha John-Henderson, "Health Mindsets as a Predictor of Physical Activity
and Body Mass Index in American Indian College Students," *Journal of Health
Psychology* 26, no. 12 (2020), https://doi.org/10.1177/1359105319901284.
7. Stanford Report, "Your Powerful, Changeable Mindset," September 15, 2021,
https://news.stanford.edu/stories/2021/09/mindsets-clearing-lens-life.
8. Wikipedia, "Ebenezer Scrooge," https://en.wikipedia.org/wiki/Ebenezer
_Scrooge.
9. Jackie Robinson Foundation, "David Robinson," https://jackierobinson.org
/people/david-robinson/.
10. CSQ, "Jackie Robinson: How to Build a Legacy That Matters," April 15,
2022, https://csq.com/2022/04/jackie-robinson-how-to-build-a-legacy-that
-matters.
11. Jackie Robinson Foundation, "David Robinson," https://jackierobinson.org
/people/david-robinson/.
12. Sweet Unity Farms, "Our Mission," https://www.sweetunitycoffee.com
/pages/our-story.
13. CSQ, "Jackie Robinson."
14. Wikipedia, "Daniel Kahneman," https://en.wikipedia.org/wiki/Daniel
_Kahneman.
15. Wikipedia, "Angus Deaton," https://en.wikipedia.org/wiki/Angus_Deaton.
16. Daniel Kahneman and Angus Deaton, "High Income Improves Evaluation of Life but Not Emotional Well-Being," Center for Health and Well-Being,
Princeton University, August 4, 2010, https://www.princeton.edu/~deaton
/downloads/deaton_kahneman_high_income_improves_evaluation
_August2010.pdf.

17. John Jennings, "Does Money Buy Happiness? Actually, Yes," *Forbes*, February 12, 2024, https://www.forbes.com/sites/johnjennings/2024/02/12/money-buys-happiness-after-all/.

18. Tyler J. VanderWeele, interview with author, September 12, 2024.

19. Nitasha Tiku, "Y Combinator Learns Basic Income Is Not So Basic After All," *Wired*, August 27, 2010, https://www.wired.com/story/y-combinator-learns-basic-income-is-not-so-basic-after-all/.

20. OpenResearch, "Cash Increases Possibility," https://www.openresearchlab.org/studies/unconditional-cash-study/study.

21. Eva Vivalt et al., "The Employment Effects of a Guaranteed Income: Experimental Evidence from Two U.S. States," working paper 32719, National Bureau of Economic Research, Cambridge, MA, July 2024, https://www.nber.org/papers/w32719?utm_campaign=ntwh&utm_medium=email&utm_source=ntwg3.

22. Matthew T. Lee et al., "Complete Well-Being Throughout the World: Lessons from the First Wave of the Global Flourishing Study," 2025, p. 20, https://humanflourishing.web.baylor.edu/sites/g/files/ecbvkj2151/files/2025-08/gfsreport_final.pdf.

23. Arthur C. Brooks, "Abundance without Attachment," *New York Times*, December 12, 2014, https://www.nytimes.com/2014/12/14/opinion/sunday/arthur-c-brooks-abundance-without-attachment.html.

24. VanderWeele, interview with author.

25. Jordan Weissman, "There Are No Rich People in America," *Slate*, March 3, 2025, https://slate.com/business/2015/03/how-americans-define-rich-somebody-who-has-more-money-than-they-do.html.

26. Dylan Croll, "Here's Why Americans with $1 Million Don't Think They're Wealthy," *Yahoo Finance*, November 18, 2023, https://finance.yahoo.com/news/heres-why-americans-with-1-million-dont-think-theyre-wealthy-124012895.html.

27. Abigail Tierney, "Millionaires in the U.S.—Statistics and Facts," Statista, July 3, 2024, https://www.statista.com/topics/3467/millionaires-in-the-united-states/#topicOverview.

28. Ali Hassan, "15 Countries with the Highest Percentage of Millionaires in the World," *Yahoo Finance*, April 2, 2024, https://finance.yahoo.com/news/15-countries-highest-percentage-millionaires-231031176.html; and Macrotrends, "World GDP per Capita," https://www.macrotrends.net/global-metrics/countries/WLD/world/gdp-per-capita.

29. Rebecca Webber, "The Comparison Trap," *Psychology Today*, November 2017, https://www.psychologytoday.com/us/articles/201711/the-comparison-trap.

30. Michael W. Kraus and Jacinth Tan, "A Key Factor in Well-Being: Others' Apparent Wealth," *Yale Insights*, January 26, 2021, https://insights.som.yale.edu/insights/key-factor-in-well-being-others-apparent-wealth.

31. Sheila Dolinger, "Casey Crawford: Generosity on the Move," *TwoTen Magazine* 13 (first quarter 2016), https://twotenmag.com/magazine/issue-13/articles/casey-crawford-generosity-on-the-move/.

32. Finish Line Pledge, "How Does It Work?," https://www.finishlinepledge.com/how-does-it-work/.

33. Alexandra Kerr, "Financial Independence, Retire Early (FIRE): How It Works," *Investopedia*, October 25, 2024, https://www.investopedia.com/terms/f/financial-independence-retire-early-fire.asp.

34. Jessica Dickler, "Who Wants to Be a Billionaire? 6 in 10 Americans Strive to Be Mega-Wealthy, Report Finds," *CNBC*, August 31, 2022, https://www.cnbc.com/2022/08/31/44percent-of-americans-think-they-can-achieve-billionaire-status.html.

35. Steve Randall, "Higher Income Households More Likely to Have Long-Term Credit Card Debt," *Investment News*, August 8, 2023, https://www.investmentnews.com/industry-news/news/higher-income-households-more-likely-to-have-long-term-credit-card-debt-240820.

36. History, "Mother Teresa," https://www.history.com/topics/religion/mother-theresa.

37. Nobel Prize, "Mother Teresa, Biographical," https://www.nobelprize.org/prizes/peace/1979/teresa/biographical/.

38. Aaron O'Neill, "Population of India from 1800 to 2020," Statista, August 9, 2024, https://www.statista.com/statistics/1066922/population-india-historical/.

39. United States Census Bureau, "Historical Estimates of World Population," https://www.census.gov/data/tables/time-series/demo/international-programs/historical-est-worldpop.html.

40. Aaron O'Neill, "Child Mortality Rate (under Five Years Old) in India from 1880 to 2020," Statista, August 9, 2024, https://www.statista.com/statistics/1041861/india-all-time-child-mortality-rate/; and ET Now Digital, "1947: India in Numbers—What Was the Country's GDP, Population, per Capita Income?," *Times Now News*, August 14, 2020, https://www.timesnownews.com/business-economy/economy/article/1947-india-in-numbers-what-was-the-country-s-gdp-population-per-capita-income/636908.

41. Mongabay, "1950 Population Estimate for Calcutta, India," https://books.mongabay.com/population_estimates/1950/Calcutta-India.html; and Aaron O'Neill, "Population of the Republic of Ireland from 1821 to 2011," Statista, August 9, 2024, https://www.statista.com/statistics/1015403/total-population-republic-ireland-1821-2011/.

42. History, "Mother Teresa."

43. History, "Mother Teresa."

Chapter 3

1. At the time of this writing, my firm, Sovereign's Capital, is a significant investor in the Southeast Lineman Training Center.

2. Southeast Line Man Training Center, "Programs," accessed December 29, 2024, https://www.lineworker.com/programs.

3. Jacqueline DeMarco, "Average US Salary by State," SoFi, January 28, 2025, https://www.sofi.com/learn/content/average-salary-in-us/.

4. Lydia Berglar, "'Lineman Country' Podcast Shares Stories of SLTC Students and Instructors," *Dade County Sentinel*, October 5, 2023, https://www.dadecountysentinel.com/2023/10/05/lineman-country-podcast-shares-stories-of-sltc-students-and-instructors/.

5. Birdeye Reviews, "Southeast Lineman Training Center," https://birdeye.com/southeast-lineman-training-center-168122409270994?page=2#reviews.

6. Sean O'Connor, quoted on Southeast Lineman Training Center home page, https://www.lineworker.com/.

7. Southeast Lineman Training Center, "Testimonials of Instructors, Justin Marro's Story," YouTube, November 19, 2024, https://www.youtube.com/watch?v=ILsF3udW0AQ.

8. Modhurima Moitra et al., "Global Mental Health: Where We Are and Where We Are Going," *Current Psychiatry Reports* 25, no. 7 (June 27, 2023): 313, doi: 10.1007/s11920-023-01426-8.

9. For people willing to trade money for more meaning in their work, see Shawn Achor et al., "9 Out of 10 People Are Willing to Earn Less Money to Do More-Meaningful Work," hbr.org, November 6, 2018, https://hbr.org/2018/11/9-out-of-10-people-are-willing-to-earn-less-money-to-do-more-meaningful-work. For employee engagement, see Ryan Pendell, "Employee Experience vs. Engagement: What's the Difference?," Gallup, October 12, 2018, https://www.gallup.com/workplace/243578/employee-experience-engagement-difference.aspx.

10. Chris Johnson, "According to a New Survey, Only 20% of Americans Still Carry One of These Around. And Most Who Do Are 65 or Older. What Is It?," Kool 98.3, April 17, 2020, https://kool98.com/chris-johnson/according-to-a-new-survey-only-20-of-americans-still-carry-one-of-these-around-and-most-who-do-are-65-or-older-what-is-it/.

11. Pew Research Center, "Where Americans Find Meaning in Life," November 20, 2018, https://www.pewresearch.org/religion/2018/11/20/where-americans-find-meaning-in-life/.

12. Wikipedia, "Grant Study," https://en.wikipedia.org/wiki/Grant_Study.

13. George E. Valliant, *Triumphs of Experience: The Men of the Harvard Grant Study* (Cambridge, MA: Belknap Press, 2015).

14. Wikipedia, "Rajat Gupta," https://en.wikipedia.org/wiki/Rajat_Gupta.

15. Mission statement found at https://www.thewonderproject.com/home. I am currently a board member of, and a financial investor in, the Wonder Project.

16. Kelly Merryman Hoogstraten, email to author, January 13, 2025.

17. Bob P. Buford, *Halftime: Moving from Success to Significance*, 20th anniv. ed. (Grand Rapids, MI: Zondervan, 2015).

18. Bonnie Ware, "No Regrets," https://bronnieware.com/regrets-of-the-dying/; and Daniel Kahneman and Angus Deaton, "High Income Improves Evaluation of Life but Not Emotional Well-Being," *Psychological and Cognitive Sciences* 107, no. 38 (2010): 16489–16493, https://doi.org/10.1073/pnas.1011492107.

19. Elise, email to author, May 27, 2005.

20. Elise, email to author.

21. Elise, email to author.

22. Science History Institute, "Oral History Interview with Kazuo Inamori," by Thomas R. Tritton and Richard Ulrych, April 19, 2010, and November 13, 2010, https://digital.sciencehistory.org/works/ij4h44r.

23. Wikipedia, "Kyocera," https://en.wikipedia.org/wiki/Kyocera.

24. Science History Institute, "Oral History Interview with Kazuo Inamori."

25. Science History Institute, "Oral History Interview with Kazuo Inamori."

26. "Inamori Kazuo's 20 Classic Quotations, the Sentence Makes People Slap!," *Sinowester*, June 21, 2019, http://www.sinowester.com/blog/inamori-kazuo-s-20 -classic-quotations-the-sentence-makes-people-slap.

27. Kazuo Inamori, *A Compass to Fulfillment: Passion and Spirituality in Life and Business* (New York: McGraw-Hill Education, 2010), 77.

28. Official Site of Kazuo Inamori, "Profile," https://global.kyocera.com/inamori /about/profile.html.

Chapter 4

1. Harbor Freight, "Alabama High School Students Make Prosthetic Legs for Amputees in Central America," September 28, 2022, https://hftforschools.org /newsroom/alabama-high-school-students-make-prosthetic-legs-for-amputees-in -central-america/.

2. Jenny Percival, "Baker Who Won £9M on Lottery Dies Penniless, Five Years On," *Guardian*, April 2, 2010, https://www.theguardian.com/uk/2010/apr/03/baker -won-lottery-dies-penniless.

3. "'I Was Much Happier When I Was Broke,'" *Daily Mail*, May 13, 2023, https://www.dailymail.co.uk/femail/article-12077821/Tragic-tale-16M-lottery -winner-1M-debt-year.html.

4. Eric Lagatta, "Lotto Regret: Pitfalls of Powerball, Lottery Winners Serve as Cautionary Tales as Jackpots Swell," *USA Today*, July 20, 2023, https://www .usatoday.com/story/news/nation/2023/07/19/powerball-mega-millions-winners -instant-billionaire-regrets/70430571007/.

5. Wikipedia, "Personal Finances of Professional American Athletes," https://en .wikipedia.org/wiki/Personal_finances_of_professional_American_athletes.

6. Jenifer Kuadli, "9 Mind-Blowing Bankruptcy Statistics for 2023," Legaljobs, May 20, 2023, https://legaljobs.io/blog/bankruptcy-statistics.

7. Jay Stone, "Carry's Been Busted," *Ottawa Citizen*, December 16, 2005.

8. Daniel Kahneman and Edward Diener, eds., *Well-Being: The Foundations of Hedonic Psychology* (New York: Russell Sage Foundation, 1999), 302.

9. Shehryar Nabi, "Thirteen Million US Households Have Negative Worth. Will They Ever Move from Debt to Wealth?," Aspen Institute, May 25, 2022, https://www.aspeninstitute.org/blog-posts/thirteen-million-us-households-have -negative-net-worth-will-they-ever-move-from-debt-to-wealth/.

10. Serah Louis, "Nearly One-Third of Americans Have a Net Worth of $0 or Less—Here's How to Calculate Yours and Give It a Boost," *Yahoo Finance*, May 22,

2023, https://finance.yahoo.com/news/nearly-one-third-americans-net-153000682.html.

11. Rakesh Kochhar and Mohamad Moslimani, "The Assets Households Own and the Debts They Carry," Pew Research Center, December 4, 2023, https://www.pewresearch.org/2023/12/04/the-assets-households-own-and-the-debts-they-carry/.

12. Federal Reserve Bank of New York, "Center for Microeconomic Data," https://www.newyorkfed.org/microeconomics/hhdc.

13. Melanie Hanson, "Student Loan Debt Statistics," Education Data Initiative, March 16, 2025, https://educationdata.org/student-loan-debt-statistics.

14. IMF, "Household Debt, Loans, and Debt Securities," https://www.imf.org/external/datamapper/HH_LS@GDD/CAN/GBR/USA/DEU/ITA/FRA/JPN/VNM.

15. U.S. Courts, "Bankruptcy Filings Rise 16.8 Percent," January 26, 2024, https://www.uscourts.gov/news/2024/01/26/bankruptcy-filings-rise-168-percent.

16. Dan Martinez and Margaret Seikel, "Credit Card Interest Rate Margins at All-Time High," Consumer Financial Protection Bureau, February 22, 2024, https://www.consumerfinance.gov/about-us/blog/credit-card-interest-rate-margins-at-all-time-high/.

17. Hanson, "Student Loan Debt Statistics"; and Abigail Tierney, "Median Annual Earnings of U.S. College Graduates from 1990 to 2022," Statista, June 27, 2025, https://www.statista.com/statistics/642041/average-wages-of-us-college-graduates/.

18. Emily Guy Birken, "Average Student Loan Debt for Law School," Credible, January 10, 2025, https://www.credible.com/statistics/average-law-school-debt; and NALP, "Employment Market for Class of 2022 Law Graduates Reaches a 35-Year High," September 2023, https://www.nalp.org/0923research.

19. Melanie Hanson, "Average Graduate Student Loan Debt," Education Data Initiative, September 1, 2024, https://educationdata.org/average-graduate-student-loan-debt.

20. Maddy Scheckel, "Average Cost of College Tuition," *Business Insider*, November 12, 2024, https://www.businessinsider.com/personal-finance/student-loans/average-college-tuition.

21. Tyler York, "Trade School vs. College: Making the Right Choice for Your Future," *Achievable* (blog), July 18, 2023, https://blog.achievable.me/college-admissions/trade-school-vs-college-making-the-right-choice-for-your-future/.

22. Dianne Apen-Sadler, "Couple Sold Their Belongings to Fund a $100K Trip Exploring Their Roots with Their Three Children," *Daily Mail*, November 7, 2018, https://www.dailymail.co.uk/femail/article-6362153/Florida-family-five-set-world-trip-closer-roots-taking-DNA-test.html.

23. Exploring Legacy, "We Are the Anderson Family," https://exploringlegacy.com/.

24. Adila Matra, "Family of Five That Travels in Search of Their Ancestral Lineage," *Travel and Leisure*, April 14, 2022, https://www.travelandleisureasia.com/in/people/interview-with-natalee-anderson-of-exploring-legacy-traveller-who-searches-for-ancestral-lineage/.

25. Exploring Legacy, "The African Birthright and Rite of Passage Program," https://exploringlegacy.com/rite-of-passage/.

26. Apen-Sadler, "Couple Sold Their Belongings."

27. Elizabeth Dunn and Michael Norton, *Happy Money: The Science of Happier Spending* (New York: Simon & Schuster, 2013), 3–5.

28. Dunn and Norton, *Happy Money*, 5.

29. World Health Organization, "Mental Disorders," https://www.who.int/news-room/fact-sheets/detail/mental-disorders.

30. Queensland Brain Institute, "Half of World's Population Will Experience a Mental Health Disorder," Harvard Medical School, July 31, 2023, https://hms.harvard.edu/news/half-worlds-population-will-experience-mental-health-disorder.

31. Children's HopeChest, "Global Mental Health Statistics," September 19, 2022, https://www.hopechest.org/global-mental-health-statistics/.

32. Julie Ray, "Tracking the World's Emotional Health," Gallup, October 12, 2025, https://news.gallup.com/poll/695963/tracking-world-emotional-health.aspx.

33. Pew Research Center, "Key Findings from the Global Religious Futures Project," December 21, 2022, https://www.pewresearch.org/religion/2022/12/21/key-findings-from-the-global-religious-futures-project/.

34. World Health Organization, "Global Status Report on Physical Activity 2022," https://www.who.int/teams/health-promotion/physical-activity/global-status-report-on-physical-activity-2022.

35. Priyanjana Pramanik, "Global Physical Inactivity Rises, Challenging 2030 Reduction Targets," *News-Medical*, June 27, 2024, https://www.news-medical.net/news/20240627/Global-physical-inactivity-rises-challenging-2030-reduction-targets.aspx.

36. World Health Organization, "Obesity and Overweight," https://www.who.int/news-room/fact-sheets/detail/obesity-and-overweight.

37. Patrick Webb et al., "Hunger and Malnutrition in the 21st Century," *BMJ* 361 (2018): 361:k2238.

38. Hannah Ritchie and Max Roser, "Obesity," Our World in Data, August 2017, https://ourworldindata.org/obesity.

39. National Center for Health Statistics, "Obesity and Overweight," https://www.cdc.gov/nchs/fastats/obesity-overweight.htm.

40. Armin Garmany and Andre Terzic, "Global Healthspan-Lifespan Gaps Among 183 World Health Organization Member States," *JAMA Network Open* 7, no. 12 (2024): e2450241.

41. Ashley Whillans et al., "Buying Time Promotes Happiness," *PNAS* 114, no. 32 (2017): 8523–8527.

42. Ashley Whillans and Michael Norton, "If You Want to Feel Better, Spend Money on Saving Time," *Wall Street Journal*, December 7, 2018, https://www.wsj.com/articles/if-you-want-to-feel-better-spend-money-on-saving-time-1505095980.

43. Dan Boedigheimer, "Business Jet: The Modern-Day Time Machine," *Forbes*, July 15, 2010, https://www.forbes.com/sites/wheelsup/2010/07/15/business-jet-the-modern-day-time-machine/.

44. Tanza Loudenback, "Study: Adding 20 Minutes to Your Commute Makes You as Miserable as Getting a 19 Percent Pay Cut," *Inc.*, October 23, 2017, https://www.inc.com/business-insider/study-reveals-commute-time-impacts-job-satisfaction.html.

45. George Vaillant, "Yes, I Stand by My Words, 'Happiness Equals Love—Full Stop,'" *Positive Psychology News*, July 16, 2019, https://positivepsychologynews.com/news/george-vaillant/200907163163.

46. Carly Smith, "How Social Connection Supports Longevity," *Stanford Lifestyle Medicine*, December 18, 2023, https://longevity.stanford.edu/lifestyle/2023/12/18/how-social-connection-supports-longevity; and Dan Buettner, *The Blue Zones: Lessons for Living Longer from the People Who've Lived the Longest* (Washington, DC: National Geographic, 2010).

47. Clayton M. Christensen, "How Will You Measure Your Life?," *Harvard Business Review*, July–August, 2010, https://hbr.org/2010/07/how-will-you-measure-your-life.

48. "Ulysses and the Sirens," *History Today*, 71 (July 7, 2021), https://www.historytoday.com/archive/foundations/ulysses-and-sirens.

49. Brent Schlender and Rick Tetzeli, "How Steve Jobs Found Buddhism," Lion's Roar, November 3, 2015, https://www.lionsroar.com/how-steve-jobs-found-buddhism/.

50. Brown Living, "Buddhism and Minimalism: The Four Noble Truths," January 5, 2022, https://brownliving.in/blogs/sustainable-living-journal/buddhism-minimalism-the-four-noble-truths.

51. Josh Sanburn, "America's Clutter Problem," *Time*, March 12, 2015, https://time.com/3741849/americas-clutter-problem/.

52. James Tozer, "Would Shoe Believe It? One in Eight Women Own a Staggering 100 Pairs of Footwear . . . with up to Four Million Passing the Century Mark," *Daily Mail*, August 10, 2021, https://www.dailymail.co.uk/femail/article-9881835/Would-shoe-believe-One-eight-women-staggering-100-pairs-footwear.html.

53. Cory Stieg, "Millennials Who Buy Less and Save More Are Happier," *Make It*, October 10, 2019, https://www.cnbc.com/2019/10/10/study-millennials-who-buy-less-and-save-more-are-happier.html.

54. Harvard Health Publishing, "Having Fewer Choices Can Promote Happiness," January 16, 2024, https://www.health.harvard.edu/healthbeat/having-fewer-choices-can-promote-happiness.

55. Madeleine Vollebregt et al., "Reducing without Losing: Reduced Consumption and Its Implications for Well-Being," *Sustainable Production and Consumption* 45 (March 2024): 91–103.

56. Wikipedia, "The Minimalists," https://en.wikipedia.org/wiki/The_Minimalists.

57. Joshua Fields Millburn, "Minimalism," *Bullet Journal* (blog), September 5, 2017, https://bulletjournal.com/blogs/bulletjournalist/minimalism.

Chapter 5

1. Patagonia, "Company History," https://www.patagonia.com/company-history/.

2. Wikipedia, "Yvon Chouinard," https://en.wikipedia.org/wiki/Yvon_Chouinard.

3. Patagonia, "Company History."

4. Wes Woods II, "'Heart of the Business': Patagonia's Humble Blacksmith Shop Named Ventura Landmark," *Ventura County Star*, February 25, 2024, https://www.vcstar.com/story/news/2024/02/25/patagonias-humble-blacksmith -shop-named-ventura-landmark/72512640007/.

5. Patagonia, "Company History."

6. For employee numbers, see Wikipedia, "Patagonia, Inc.," https://en .wikipedia.org/wiki/Patagonia,_Inc. For other data, see Trevor Laurence Jockims, "Is Patagonia the End Game for Profits in a World of Climate Change?," CNBC, November 20, 2022, https://www.cnbc.com/2022/11/20/is-patagonia-the-end-game -for-profits-in-a-world-of-climate-change.html.

7. Lora Kolodny, "Patagonia Founder Just Donated the Entire Company, Worth $3 Billion, to Fight Climate Change," CNBC, September 14, 2022, https:// www.cnbc.com/2022/09/14/patagonia-founder-donates-entire-company-to-fight -climate-change.html.

8. Revolution Foods, "Our Story," https://www.revolutionfoods.com/about.

9. CEW, "Beatrice Dixon," https://cew.org/people/beatrice-dixon/.

10. Union University, "Barnhart: Generosity Breaks Power of Greed," press release, March 13, 2024, https://www.uu.edu/news/release.cfm?ID=2927.

11. Wikipedia, "Ronald Read (Philanthropist)," https://en.wikipedia.org/wiki /Ronald_Read_(philanthropist).

12. Alliance, "Traditions of Giving in Hinduism," https://www.alliancemagazine .org/feature/traditions-of-giving-in-hinduism/.

13. Thich Nhat Hanh Foundation, "Practice of Generosity," https:// thichnhathanhfoundation.org/practice-of-generosity.

14. Aisha Stacey, "Generosity," Religion of Islam, October 4, 2009, https://www .islamreligion.com/articles/1668/generosity.

15. Utilitarianism, "Action on Utilitarianism," https://utilitarianism.net/acting -on-utilitarianism.

16. Effective Altruism, "Find the Best Ways to Help Others," https://www .effectivealtruism.org/.

17. Stephen Hicks, "Kant and 'Giving Back,'" *Stephen Hicks Ph.D.* (blog), March 7, 2016, https://www.stephenhicks.org/2016/03/07/kant-and-giving-back/.

18. Thomas Hobbes, *Leviathan* (London: 1651), part 1, ch. 13.

19. Summer Allen, "The Science of Generosity," working paper, Greater Good Science Center at UC Berkeley, Berkeley, CA, May 2018, https://ggsc.berkeley.edu /images/uploads/GGSC-JTF_White_Paper-Generosity-FINAL.pdf.

20. Allen, "Science of Generosity," 19–20.

21. Allen, "Science of Generosity," 23–24.

22. Allen, "Science of Generosity," 27–28.

23. Jenny Santi, "The Secret to Happiness Is Helping Others," *Time*, n.d., https://time.com/collection/guide-to-happiness/4070299/secret-to-happiness/.

24. Charities Aid Foundation, "Gross Domestic Philanthropy: An International Analysis of GDP, Tax and Giving," January 2016, https://www.cafonline.org/docs /default-source/about-us-policy-and-campaigns/gross-domestic-philanthropy-feb -2016.pdf.

25. PNC Insights, "Philanthropic Giving: Headwinds and Tailwinds Analysis 2024," October 3, 2024, https://www.pnc.com/insights/corporate-institutional /manage-nonprofit-enterprises/philanthropic-giving-headwinds-and-tailwinds. html.

26. Charities Aid Foundation, "World Giving Index 2023: Global Trends in Generosity," https://www.cafonline.org/docs/default-source/updated-pdfs-for-the -new-website/world-giving-index-2023.pdf.

27. Dan Pilat and Sekoul Krastev, "Precommitment," Decision Lab, https:// thedecisionlab.com/reference-guide/psychology/precommitment.

28. Wikipedia, "Donor-Advised Fund," https://en.wikipedia.org/wiki/Donor -advised_fund.

29. Kat Boogaard, "Decision Fatigue: What to Do When Endless Choices Are Sapping Your Energy," *Work Life* (Atlassian), December 8, 2023, https://www .atlassian.com/blog/productivity/decision-fatigue.

30. Philanthropic Initiative, "Passion: Discovering the Meaning in Your Philanthropy," 2014, https://www.ncfp.org/wp-content/uploads/2018/09/Passion -Discovering-meaning-in-your-philanthropy-TPI-2014-passion-discovering -meaning-in-your-philanthropy.pdf.

31. CFK Africa, "Our Impact," https://cfkafrica.org/impact/, accessed October 27, 2025.

32. Rye Barcott, email to author, January 5, 2025.

33. Ben Guarino, "University to Buy $1 Million Football Scoreboard with Thrifty Librarian's Money, Outraging Critics," *Washington Post*, September 16, 2016, https://www.washingtonpost.com/news/morning-mix/wp/2016/09/16 /university-to-buy-1-million-football-scoreboard-with-thrifty-librarians-money -outraging-critics/.

34. University of New Hampshire (UNH), "The Librarian's Gift," *UNH Today*, August 30, 2016, https://www.unh.edu/unhtoday/2016/08/librarians-gift.

35. UNH, "The Librarian's Gift."

36. Michael Hobbes, "Stop Trying to Save the World," *New Republic*, November 17, 2014, https://newrepublic.com/article/120178/problem-international -development-and-plan-fix-it.

37. Peter Lipsett, "Philanthropy Horror Stories: Donor Intent Gone Wrong," DonorsTrust, October 30, 2017, https://www.donorstrust.org/donor-intent-horror -stories/.

38. Lipsett, "Philanthropy Horror Stories."

39. Jeff Joireman et al., "You Did What with My Donation?! Betrayal of Moral Mandates Increases Negative Responses to Redirected Donations to Donor-to-Recipient Charities," *Journal of the Association for Consumer Research* 5, no. 1 (2020): 83–94.

40. Eden Stiffman, "Charity Navigator Founder Hands Control to Tech-Savvy Successor," *Chronicle of Philanthropy*, June 23, 2016, https://www.philanthropy.com /article/charity-navigator-founder-hands-control-to-tech-savvy-successor/.

41. Jonathan Goodman and Erin Wuertz, "Charity Navigator," Learning to Give, https://www.learningtogive.org/resources/charity-navigator.

42. Ann Goggins Gregory and Don Howard, "The Nonprofit Starvation Cycle," Bridgespan Group, August 24, 2009, https://www.bridgespan.org/insights/the-nonprofit-starvation-cycle.

43. Eun Kyung Kim, "'Three Cups' Author Greg Mortensen: 'I Let a Lot of People Down,'" *Today*, January 21, 2014, https://www.today.com/books/three-cups-author-greg-mortenson-i-let-lot-people-down-2D11961320.

44. Hope Hodge Seck, "After Public Crisis and Fall from Grace, Wounded Warrior Project Quietly Regains Ground," Military.com, August 9, 2019, https://www.military.com/daily-news/2019/08/09/after-public-crisis-and-fall-grace-wounded-warrior-project-quietly-regains-ground.html.

45. Marcus Ruzek, email to author, December 30, 2024.

46. Marcus Foundation, https://marcusfoundation.org/.

47. Bridgespan Group, "Not in Perpetuity: Bernie Marcus to Sunset His Foundation," November 27, 2013, https://www.bridgespan.org/insights/bernie-marcus/not-in-perpetuity-bernie-marcus-explains-his-deci.

48. Philanthropy Roundtable, "Seven Stories of Donor Intent Violations in Higher Education Giving," December 23, 2021, https://www.philanthropyroundtable.org/resource/seven-stories-of-donor-intent-violations-in-higher-education-giving/.

49. GEO, "What Does It Take to Spend Down Successfully?," https://www.geofunders.org/resource/what-does-it-take-to-spend-down-successfully/.

50. Angelique Serrano, "How a News Segment Moved a Woman to Donate Her Kidney to a Stranger," *Health Matters*, December 21, 2022, https://healthmatters.nyp.org/how-a-news-segment-moved-a-woman-to-donate-her-kidney-to-a-stranger/.

51. ThermoFisher Scientific, "Vadrien's Story," https://corporate.thermofisher.com/us/en/index/newsroom/Our-stories/counting-on-you/vadriens-story.html.

52. Capital Ideas, "Soaring with Capital Group Vice Chair Jody Jonsson," *Capital Ideas* podcast, December 26, 2024, https://capitalideas.libsyn.com/soaring-with-capital-group-vice-chair-jody-jonsson.

53. Wikipedia, "Angel Flight," https://en.wikipedia.org/wiki/Angel_Flight.

54. Steve Bates, "The Story Behind the Brand: Cotopaxi," Quest Outdoors, March 9, 2023, https://www.questoutdoors.com/blogs/news/the-story-behind-the-brand-cotopaxi/.

55. Marissa Lundeen, "Cotopaxi Founder Davis Smith Steps Down as CEO to Serve as Mission President," *Daily Universe*, January 13, 2023, https://universe.byu.edu/2023/01/13/cotopaxi-founder-davis-smith-steps-down-as-ceo-to-serve-as-mission-president/.

Chapter 6

1. David Nadelle, "At What Age Did Warren Buffett Become a Millionaire?," *Yahoo Finance*, April 4, 2024, https://finance.yahoo.com/news/age-did-warren-buffett-become-182332572.html.

2. Vishaal Sanjay, "The Buss Family Is Set to Sell the Los Angeles Lakers for $10 Billion, After Buying It for Just $68 Million—Here's Why the 15,284% Return Is Far from a Slam Dunk," *Benzinga*, June 19, 2025, https://www.benzinga.com/news

/sports/25/06/46013150/the-buss-family-is-set-to-sell-the-los-angeles-lakers-for-10 -billion-after-buying-it-for-just-68-million-heres-why-the-15284-return-is-far-from -a-slam-dunk.

3. James Tieng, email to author, February 28, 2025.

4. For median household income, see Gloria Guzman and Melissa Kollar, "Income in the United States: 2022," United States Census Bureau, September 12, 2023, https://www.census.gov/library/publications/2023/demo/p60-279.html. For expenditures, see Chase, "A Look at the Average American's Monthly Expenses," https://www.chase.com/personal/banking/education/budgeting-saving/average -american-monthly-expenses-and-bills.

5. Philanthropy Roundtable, "Statistics on U.S. Generosity," https://www .philanthropyroundtable.org/almanac/statistics-on-u-s-generosity/.

6. Liz Knueven and Sophia Acevedo, "Understanding the Average American Net Worth: Insights and Analysis," *Business Insider*, July 23, 2024, https://www .businessinsider.com/personal-finance/average-american-net-worth.

7. Jack Caporal, "How Many Americans Own Stock? About 162 Million—But the Wealthiest 1% Own More Than Half," *Motley Fool*, June 23, 2025, https://www .fool.com/research/how-many-americans-own-stock/.

8. Neale Godfrey, "Are You Rich? U.S. Net Worth Percentiles Can Provide Answers," *Kiplinger*, August 21, 2024, https://www.kiplinger.com/personal-finance /605075/are-you-rich.

9. Douglas Robinson, "Episcopal Church Urges G.M. to Close Plants in South Africa," *New York Times*, February 2, 1971, https://www.nytimes.com/1971/02/02 /archives/episcopal-church-urges-gm-to-closed-plants-in-south-africa.html.

10. Morton Mintz, "Activist Minister Took Bold Step at GM Annual Meeting in 1971," *Washington Post*, June 2, 1987, https://www.washingtonpost.com/archive /business/1987/06/03/activist-minister-took-bold-step-at-gm-annual-meeting-in -1971/2d987195-c457-4a44-8bb6-1e4d17502428/.

11. BCG Global Asset Management Annual Reports (2017–2024); the latest report is titled "AI and the Next Wave of Transformation."

12. Erin El Issa, "Survey: Just 23% of Investors Align Most Investments to Their Values," *Nerd Wallet*, February 8, 2022, https://www.nerdwallet.com/article /investing/survey-just-23-of-investors-align-most-investments-to-their-values.

13. Lydia DePillis, "Private Equity Is Starting to Share with Workers, with-out Taking a Financial Hit," *New York Times*, January 28, 2024, https://www .nytimes.com/2024/01/28/business/economy/kkr-private-equity-employee -ownership.html.

14. Principles for Responsible Investment (PRI), "What Are the Principles for Responsible Investment?," https://www.unpri.org/about-us/what-are-the-principles -for-responsible-investment.

15. Bloomberg, "Global ESG Assets Predicted to Hit $40 Trillion by 2030, Despite Challenging Environment, Forecasts Bloomberg Intelligence," Bloomberg, February 8, 2024, https://www.bloomberg.com/company/press/global-esg-assets -predicted-to-hit-40-trillion-by-2030-despite-challenging-environment-forecasts -bloomberg-intelligence/.

16. Wikipedia, "Islamic Banking and Finance," https://en.wikipedia.org/wiki/Islamic_banking_and_finance.

17. Wikipedia, "Islamic Banking and Finance,"

18. Shaima Hasan and Shereen Mohamed, "Global Islamic Finance Assets Expected to Exceed $6.7 Trillion by 2027," LSEG, February 26, 2024, https://www.lseg.com/en/insights/data-analytics/navigating-uncertainty-global-islamic-finance-assets-expected-to-exceed-67-trillion-by-2027.

19. Brightlight, "Research Paper: Faith-Based Options in Public Markets," October 2024, https://www.brightlightimpact.us/s/Listed-Markets-Research-Paper-2024.pdf.

20. Committee on Budget and Finance, United States Conference of Catholic Bishops, "Socially Responsible Investment Guidelines for the United States Conference of Catholic Bishops," US Conference of Catholic Bishops, Washington, DC, 2021; and American Baptist Churches USA, "(Draft) Investment Policy," June 28, 2027, https://abc-usa.org/wp-content/uploads/2019/02/BGM-Item-5B-Investment-Policy-1.pdf.

21. Amee Parbhoo, video interview conducted by author, October 31, 2024.

22. Parbhoo, video interview.

23. Parbhoo, video interview.

24. Apollo Agriculture, "We're Apollo Agriculture," https://www.apolloagriculture.com/about.

25. Parbhoo, video interview.

26. Amee Parbhoo, video interview conducted by author, September 25, 2024.

27. Parbhoo, video interview, September 25, 2024.

28. Tahmina, "Vision," https://www.tahminatea.com/pages/vision.

29. For security reasons, I am declining to use the names of the people involved. While the company has a website and is transparent regarding its operations, my understanding is that the names of the leadership and staff are not publicized, because of concerns for their safety.

30. Parbhoo, video interview, September 25, 2024.

31. Wikipedia, "John C. Bogle," https://en.wikipedia.org/wiki/John_C._Bogle.

32. Jeff Cox, "Passive Investing Rules Wall Street Now, Topping Actively Managed Assets in Stock, Bond, and Other Funds," CNBC, January 18, 2024, https://www.cnbc.com/2024/01/18/passive-investing-rules-wall-street-now-topping-actively-managed-assets-in-stock-bond-and-other-funds.html.

33. Aditi Ganguly, "Warren Buffett Believes in S&P 500 Index Funds—But Are They Really Worth It?," Yahoo Finance, May 14, 2024, https://finance.yahoo.com/news/warren-buffett-believes-p-500-170220804.html.

34. Statista, "Assets Under Management (AUM) of Vanguard in Selected Years from 1975 to April 30, 2025," August 19, 2025, https://www.statista.com/statistics/1260855/vanguard-aum/.

35. VettaFi, "Largest ETFs: Top 100 ETFs by Assets," https://etfdb.com/compare/market-cap/.

36. Lindsey Stewart, "Proxy Voting: Expect More Divergence on ESG Among Investors," Morningstar, March 5, 2024, https://www.morningstar.com/sustainable-investing/proxy-voting-expect-more-divergence-esg-among-investors.

37. Daniel F. C. Crowley et al., "GOP ESG Bills Await US House Floor Consideration," K&L Gates, September 5, 2023, https://www.klgates.com/GOP-ESG-Bills -Await-US-House-Floor-Consideration-9-5-2023.

38. Lindsey Stewart, "New Proxy-Voting Options for IVV and Other Index Funds from BlackRock, State Street, and Vanguard," Morningstar, December 13, 2023, https://www.morningstar.com/funds/new-proxy-voting-options-ivv-other -index-funds-blackrock-state-street-vanguard.

39. Morningstar Manager Research, "Vident Financial," Morningstar, July 28, 2025, https://www.morningstar.com/asset-management-companies/vident-financial -BN00000FTN.

40. Wikipedia, "Harvard Endowment," https://en.wikipedia.org/wiki/Harvard _University_endowment.

41. Rockefeller Foundation, "Ethical Investing Policy" (adopted November 2020), https://www.rockefellerfoundation.org/wp-content/uploads/2021/04/The -Rockefeller-Foundation-Ethical-Investing-Policy-Framework.pdf.

42. World Wildlife Fund, "Impact Investing Strategy," https://www .worldwildlife.org/pages/impact-investing-strategy.

Chapter 7

1. "Obituary: Rick Woolworth," *Greenwich (CT) Sentinel*, June 12, 2022, https://www.greenwichsentinel.com/2022/06/12/obituary-rick-woolworth/.

2. Trevor Hightower, "This Is Good: Your Memorial," *This Is Good* (LinkedIn series), December 6, 2023, https://www.linkedin.com/pulse/good-your-memorial -trevor-hightower-bk81c/.

3. Source for this passage are my experiences with Rick; they were confirmed and approved by his wife, Jill Woolworth, on December 30, 2024.

4. Rida Khan, "Charted: Retirement Age by Country," Visual Capitalist, October 2, 2023, https://www.visualcapitalist.com/retirement-age-by-country/.

5. Aimee Picchi, "Many Americans Want to Stop Working and Live to 100. Can They Afford It?," CBS News, April 18, 2024, https://www.cbsnews.com/news /retirement-income-how-to-fund-40-years-of-retirement/.

6. Frank Newport and Jeffrey M. Jones, "Why Americans Are Pleasantly Surprised in Retirement," Gallup, August 22, 2024, https://news.gallup.com/poll /648773/why-americans-pleasantly-surprised-retirement.aspx.

7. Lorie Konish, "Just 4% of Current Retirees Say They Are 'Living the Dream,' Survey Finds. Here's Why," CNBC, May 9, 2024, https://www.cnbc.com /2024/05/09/4percent-of-current-retirees-say-they-are-living-the-dream-survey -finds.html.

8. Morgan Smith, "Nearly 50% of People Are Considering Leaving Their Jobs in 2024—More Than During the 'Great Resignation,'" CNBC, May 8, 2024, https://www.cnbc.com/2024/05/08/nearly-50percent-of-people-are-considering -leaving-their-jobs-in-2024.html.

9. The phrase "wild and precious life" comes from "The Summer Day," a poem by the late Mary Oliver, https://www.loc.gov/programs/poetry-and-literature/poet

-laureate/poet-laureate-projects/poetry-180/all-poems/item/poetry-180-133/the
-summer-day/.

10. MassMutual, "MassMutual Research: Most Retirees Are Happier in Retirement vs. Working Thanks to Financial Preparation, but More Than One Third
Report Feeling Lonely," March 13, 2024, https://www.massmutual.com/about-us
/news-and-press-releases/press-releases/2024/03/massmutual-research-most
-retirees-are-happier-in-retirement.

11. Johns Hopkins Medicine, "Protect Against a Retirement Risk," https://www
.hopkinsmedicine.org/health/wellness-and-prevention/protect-against-a-retirement
-risk.

12. Patrick J. Skerrett, "Is Retirement Good for Health or Bad for It?," *Harvard
Health Publishing*, December 10, 2012, https://www.health.harvard.edu/blog/is
-retirement-good-for-health-or-bad-for-it-201212105625.

13. Dhaval Dave, Inas Rashad, and Jasmina Spasojevic, "The Effects of Retirement on Physical and Mental Health Outcomes," working paper 12123, National
Bureau of Economic Research, Cambridge, MA, March 2006.

14. Nicole Torres, "You're Likely to Live Longer If You Retire After 65," *Harvard
Business Review*, October 2016, https://hbr.org/2016/10/youre-likely-to-live-longer-if
-you-retire-after-65.

15. Hilary Waldron, "Links between Early Retirement and Mortality," Social
Security Administration, August 2001, https://www.ssa.gov/policy/docs
/workingpapers/wp93.html.

16. Scott Gottlieb, "Mental Activity May Help Prevent Dementia," *BMJ* 326,
no. 7404 (June 2003): 1418.

17. Institute of Economic Affairs (IEA), "Work Longer, Live Healthier," IEA
discussion paper, May 2013, https://www.iea.org.uk/wp-content/uploads/2016/07
/Work%20Longer,%20Live_Healthier.pdf.

18. Bryan Borzykowski, "Can Retirement Kill You?," BBC, August 13, 2013,
https://www.bbc.com/worklife/article/20130813-the-dark-side-of-the-golden
-years.

19. Ayse Yemiscigil, Nattavudh Powdthavee, and Ashley V. Whillans, "The
Effects of Retirement on Sense of Purpose in Life: Crisis or Opportunity?," *Association for Psychological Science* 32, no. 11 (October 2021): 1856–1864.

20. Yemiscigil, Powdthavee, and Whillans, "Effects of Retirement on Sense of
Purpose."

21. Daniel de Visé, "How Long Does Retirement Last? Most American Men
Don't Seem to Know," *USA Today*, October 12, 2023, https://www.usatoday.com
/story/money/2023/10/12/how-long-does-retirement-last/71074947007/.

22. James W. Moore, "What Is the Sense of Agency and Why Does It Matter?,"
Frontiers in Psychology 7 (2016), https://doi.org/10.3389/fpsyg.2016.01272.

23. Daniel A. Hojman and Álvaro Miranda, "Agency, Human Dignity, and
Subject Well-Being," *World Development* 101 (January 2018): 1–15.

24. John Johnson, "What Is Autonomy and Why Is It So Difficult to Achieve?,"
Psychology Today, June 9, 2020, https://www.psychologytoday.com/us/blog/cui
-bono/202006/what-is-autonomy-and-why-is-it-so-difficult-to-achieve.

25. Ryan Pendell, "Employee Engagement Strategies: Fixing the World's $8.8 Trillion Problem," Gallup, June 14, 2022, https://www.gallup.com/workplace/393497 /world-trillion-workplace-problem.aspx.

26. Thomas Clausen et al., "Job Autonomy and Psychological Well-Being: A Linear or a Non-Linear Association?," *European Journal of Work and Organizational Psychology* 31, no. 3 (2021): 395–405.

27. Ángel De-Juanas, Teresita Bernal Romero, and Rosa Goig, "The Relationship between Psychological Well-Being and Autonomy in Young People According to Age," *Frontiers in Psychology* 11 (December 2020), https://doi.org/10.3389/fpsyg .2020.559976.

28. University of Birmingham, "Autonomy in the Workplace Has Positive Effects on Well-Being and Job Satisfaction, Study Finds," *Science Daily*, April 24, 2017, https://www.sciencedaily.com/releases/2017/04/170424215501.htm#google_vignette.

29. Wikipedia, "Barbara Hillary," https://en.wikipedia.org/wiki/Barbara_Hillary.

Chapter 8

1. Rachel Minkin and Juliana Menasce Horowitz, "Income and Parenting," in *Parenting in America Today*, Pew Research Center, January 24, 2023, https://www .pewresearch.org/social-trends/2023/01/24/income-and-parenting/.

2. SWNS, "American Parents Willing to Give Up 'Pretty Much Anything' If It Means Protecting Their Children from This: Survey," *New York Post*, September 13, 2024, https://nypost.com/2024/09/13/lifestyle/what-would-parents-give-up-for-a -healthy-child/.

3. Rachel Minkin and Juliana Menasce Horowitz, *Parenting in America Today*, Pew Research Center, January 24, 2023, https://www.pewresearch.org/social-trends /2023/01/24/parenting-in-america-today/.

4. Karah A. Waters, Abraham Salinas-Miranda, and Russell S. Kirby, "The Association between Parent-Child Quality Time and Children's Flourishing Level," *Journal of Pediatric Nursing* 73: e187–e196, https://pubmed.ncbi.nlm.nih.gov /37775429/.

5. Brown University School of Public Health, "How Does Parental Health Impact a Child's Ability to Flourish?," November 20, 2024, https://sph.brown.edu /news/2024-11-20/parents-health-children-flourishing.

6. Suniya S. Luthar, "The Problem with Rich Kids," *Psychology Today*, November 5, 2013, https://www.psychologytoday.com/us/articles/201311/the-problem-rich-kids.

7. Suniya S. Luthar and Shawn J. Latendresse, "Children of the Affluent: Challenges to Well-Being," *Current Directions in Psychological Science* 14, no. 1 (2005): 49–53, https://pmc.ncbi.nlm.nih.gov/articles/PMC1948879/.

8. Xiaoguang Ling, "Heterogeneous Earning Responses to Inheritance: New Event-Study Evidence from Norway," September 21, 2022, https://doi.org/10.48550/ arXiv.2209.10256.

9. Ashley Bleckner, "How (and Why) to Make a Family Mission Statement," *Ellevest Insights*, December 18, 2020, https://www.ellevest.com/magazine/family -mission-statement. Emphasis in original.

10. Stuart Dorsett, "The Family Mission Statement and Strategic Plan," Brown Advisory, February 8, 2023, https://www.brownadvisory.com/intl/insights/family -mission-statement-and-strategic-plan.

11. Priscilla Claman, "What's Your Family's Mission Statement?," hbr.org, August 4, 2020, https://hbr.org/2020/08/whats-your-familys-mission-statement.

12. Marc Rivo, Karen Rivo, Jessica Rivo, and Julie Rivo, "Family Mission Statements," *Family Practice Management* 6, no. 4 (1999): 60, https://www.aafp.org /pubs/fpm/issues/1999/0400/p60.html.

13. Dennis Trittin and Arlyn Lawrence, "Parenting for the Launch: Developing a Parenting Mission Statement," https://www.dennistrittin.com/resources /Developing%20a%20Parenting%20Mission%20Statement.pdf; and Dennis Trittin and Arlyn Lawrence, *Parenting for the Launch: Raising Teens to Succeed in the Real World* (Gig Harbor, WA: LifeSmart Publishing, 2013).

14. Meagan Rose Wilson, "Creating a List of Family Values," Meagan Rose Wilson, May 2016, https://meaganrosewilson.com/2016/05/list-family-values/.

15. Wikipedia, "Paul Revere," https://en.wikipedia.org/wiki/Paul_Revere.

16. Neely Tucker, "George Washington: Land Surveyor," *Timeless Stories from the Library of Congress* (blog), January 10, 2025, https://blogs.loc.gov/loc/2025/01 /george-washington-land-surveyor/.

17. Stockpile, "Parents Are Biggest Influence on the Way Teens Think about Money," PRWeb, September 22, 2022, https://www.prweb.com/releases/parents-are -biggest-influence-on-the-way-teens-think-about-money-832667145.html.

18. US Bank, "Survey: Nearly 1 in 4 of All Parents and Half of Gen X Parents Worry Their Kids Will Be Financially Dependent on Them in Adulthood," press release, September 26, 2024, https://ir.usbank.com/news-events/news/news -details/2024/Survey-Nearly-1-in-4-of-All-Parents-and-Half-of-Gen-X-Parents -Worry-Their-Kids-Will-Be-Financially-Dependent-on-Them-in-Adulthood /default.aspx.

19. RBC Wealth Management, "87% of Americans Say Financial Literacy Should Be Taught in Schools: RBC Wealth Management & City National Bank Poll," PR Newswire, April 5, 2016, https://www.prnewswire.com/news-releases/87-of -americans-say-financial-literacy-should-be-taught-in-schools-rbc-wealth -management--city-national-bank-poll-574600611.html.

20. "Financial Literacy Statistics for 2025: 28 Facts Revealed," April 19, 2025, https://signalskills.com/financial-literacy-statistics/?utm_source.

21. Jeanine Skowronski, "Survey: 63% of Parents Have Talked Money with Their Kids," *Policygenius*, June 11, 2019, https://www.policygenius.com/personal-finance /news/survey-parents-talk-money-kids/.

22. Skowronski, "Survey: 63% of Parents."

23. Vanessa Wong, "Teens from Upper-Income Families Are Far More Likely to Work Summer Jobs Than Poor Teens. What's Going On?," MarketWatch, June 28, 2025, https://www.marketwatch.com/story/teens-from-upper-income -families-are-far-more-likely-to-work-summer-jobs-than-poor-teens-whats-going -on-e695fca2.

24. Walter Isaacson, *Steve Jobs* (New York: Simon & Schuster, 2011), 276.

25. Fidelity Charitable, "Study Shows That More Than 80% of Parents Find Success in Modeling Philanthropic Behavior for Their Children—Growing the Next Generation of Givers," press release, November 14, 2023, https://www.fidelitycharitable.org/about-us/news/study-shows-that-more-than-80-percent-of-parents-find-success-in-modeling-philanthropic-behavior.html.

26. Fidelity Charitable, "Family Giving Traditions Study," https://www.fidelitycharitable.org/articles/family-giving-traditions-study.html?.

27. Christina Gunning, "3 Benefits to Volunteering as a Family," Feeding San Diego, April 11, 2023, https://feedingsandiego.org/3-benefits-to-volunteering-as-a-family/.

28. Katherine Dunlevie, email to author, February 12, 2025.

29. Jonas G. Miller, Sarah Kahle, and Paul D. Hastings, "Roots and Benefits of Costly Giving: Children Who Are More Altruistic Have Greater Autonomic Flexibility and Less Family Wealth," *Psychological Science* 26, no. 7 (2015): 1038–1045, https://journals.sagepub.com/doi/10.1177/0956797615578476.

30. "How to Inspire a Spirit of Generosity in Your Child," Children's Health, https://www.childrens.com/health-wellness/how-to-inspire-a-spirit-of-generosity-in-your-child.

31. Charitable Advisors, "Empathy in Action: Why Volunteering with Kids Today Shapes a Better Tomorrow," June 9, 2025, https://charitableadvisors.com/empathy-in-action-why-volunteering-with-kids-today-shapes-a-better-tomorrow/.

32. This simple calculation assumes a 10 percent average return in the S&P 500 (close to the fifty-year rate of historical returns) and a 3.5 percent rate of inflation.

33. For US figures, see Paul Deer, "The Average Net Worth by Age in America," *Currency*, July 17, 2025, https://www.empower.com/the-currency/life/average-net-worth-by-age. For worldwide figures, see Wikipedia, "List of Countries by Wealth per Adult," https://en.wikipedia.org/wiki/List_of_countries_by_wealth_per_adult.

34. Michelle Bennett, "What's the Right Age to Bring Kids into the Family Wealth Conversation?," Newport Capital Group, June 25, 2025, https://newportcapitalgroup.com/whats-the-right-age-to-bring-kids-into-the-family-wealth-conversation/.

Index

Acknowledgments

First and foremost, I am deeply grateful to my wife, Jackie, for her stead-fast support, thoughtful insights, and tireless work as my earliest editor. Her fingerprints are on every page, and her belief in me and in this project made it all possible. She is my best friend and an indispensable partner in my life, faith, work, and writing. She keeps me grounded, and together we've raised four children who give us more inspiration and purpose than anything else in the world.

I want to thank my longtime editor, Courtney Cashman, with whom I've had the privilege of working for nearly fifteen years. Her expertise, patience, and encouragement have shaped this work in countless mean-ingful ways.

The outstanding team at Harvard Business Review Press—including Melinda Merino, Jen Waring, Felicia Sinusas, Stephani Finks, Julie Devoll, and many others—deserve heartfelt thanks. Your partnership, creativity, and commitment brought this book to life. I'm also grateful to *Harvard Business Review* for providing me a platform to test and refine many of these ideas through my early writing.

I'm indebted to Martin Seligman for his pioneering work in positive psychology, and to the research teams at Harvard University, Baylor University, and Gallup for their contributions to the Global Flourishing Study—especially Tyler VanderWeele and his leadership of the Human Flourishing Program at Harvard's Institute for Quantitative Social Science.

My thanks go to Greg Brenneman, Barry Rowan, Ross Roggensack, Katherine Dunlevie, and others who provided thoughtful editorial feed-back on early drafts. I'm also thankful to the many who generously shared their perspectives and experiences, including Amee Prabhoo, Aimee

Minnich, James Tieng, Kelly Merryman Hoogstraten, P. J. Nardy, Davis Smith, Henry Kaestner, Casey Crawford, Elise Piehl, and Rye Barcott.

I am similarly indebted to the mentors and friends who have helped me navigate a life and career with purpose, including Peter Lawler, Frank Stephenson, Steve Briggs, Rick Gilbert, Price Harding, Ben Johnson, Rick Woolworth, Tom Barkin, Luke Roush, Rob Yanker, Duncan Miller, Bill George, David Gergen, Nick Burns, Jon Doochin, Alex Taussig, Mina Nguyen, Evan Baehr, Bridgett Wagner, David Ridley, and many others whose names could fill another page. You have each shaped my life in ways I can never fully repay.

And of course I'm grateful to my parents, John and Shea Coleman, and to my father- and mother-in-law, Elliot and Sandy Feit. I've been blessed to have you as family.

Finally, I want to thank my clients, the leaders of our portfolio companies, and my colleagues at Sovereign's Capital. Your work, stories, and personal examples have inspired this book and made the space to write it possible.

About the Author

JOHN COLEMAN is an executive, an investor, a writer, and a husband and father focused on encouraging human flourishing and purpose at work. He is co-CEO of Sovereign's Capital, a diversified, values-driven investment firm. He previously held leadership roles at Invesco and McKinsey & Company and has worked with thousands of families and institutions on their investments. He serves on a range of corporate and nonprofit boards.

Coleman is the author of five books, including the *HBR Guide to Crafting Your Purpose*. His work has been published or featured in *Harvard Business Review*, the *New York Times*, the *Financial Times*, *Forbes*, the *Washington Post*, Fox News, and other major outlets. He has spoken to hundreds of audiences, including major corporations, universities, and nonprofit organizations.

A summa cum laude graduate of Berry College and chosen to be its student commencement speaker, Coleman holds an MPA from the Harvard Kennedy School, where he was both a Zuckerman Fellow and a George Fellow, and an MBA with High Distinction from Harvard Business School, where he was a Dean's Award winner and Class Day speaker.

You can reach him at johnwilliamcoleman.com and subscribe to his newsletter, *On Purpose,* via the QR code below.